▶ A Primer for Stuttering Therapy

Howard D. Schwartz
Northern Illinois University

Allyn and Bacon

Boston • London • Toronto • Sydney • Tokyo • Singapore

Executive Editor: Stephen D. Dragin
Editorial Assistant: Elizabeth McGuire
Editorial-Production Administrator: Joe Sweeney
Editorial-Production Service: Walsh & Associates, Inc.
Composition Buyer: Linda Cox
Manufacturing Buyer: Megan Cochran
Cover Administrator: Jennifer Hart

Library of Congress Cataloging-in-Publication Data

Schwartz, Howard D.
    A primer for stuttering therapy / Howard D. Schwartz
      p.   cm.
    Includes bibliographical references and index.
    ISBN 0-205-27556-7
    1. Stuttering—Treatment. I. Title.
    [DNLM: 1. Stuttering—therapy. 2. Speech Therapy—methods. WM
475 S398p 1998]
    RC424.S36   1998
      616.85'5406—dc21
    DNLM/DLC
    for Library of Congress   98-23833
                                        CIP

Printed in the United States of America
10 9 8 7 6 5 4 3 2 1   02 01 00 99 98

This book is dedicated to
Reggie
and
The Big Kahuna

Contents

Preface

During the past few years I have become increasingly concerned that fewer and fewer practicing speech-language pathologists believe that they have the necessary training to work with children and adults who stutter. As a result, I focused my attention on methods for teaching clinicians the practice of stuttering therapy. At the university level, I have developed two courses that enable me to work directly with graduate students to provide stuttering therapy for adult clients. I not only supervise these clients and provide suggestions for improving their clinical skills but I also work directly with clients in the therapy room with the students present. The students are able to directly observe my interactions with clients and then move into the clinician role and continue working with clients. When I have concerns about the interaction between graduate student and client, I might stop the therapy session and model a better method of interacting with the client. When the client needs some encouragement or counseling, I may stop the client and make suggestions for improvement. I have found that this method of teaching has worked very well with my graduate students.

When interacting with practicing clinicians at seminars and convention presentations, I continue to find clinicians who believe that they lack the skills for stuttering therapy. Because of my concerns for graduate student training and concerns for practicing professionals, I wrote this book and developed the accompanying video. I know that there are a number of good books that are available to teach clinicians to do therapy. However, while observing those clinicians who are observing me in therapy, I came to realize that clinicians not only want descriptions of therapy, they also want to be shown how therapy is accomplished. I hope that this book is able to complete both tasks.

Acknowledgments

I often view myself as the professional great-grandson of two distinct families in stuttering treatment. My earliest influences began with the Gene Brutten–Marty Adams–John Hutchinson line. Throughout my career, Gene Brutten has been extremely influential despite the fact that I never attended Southern Illinois University. At a time in my career when I was isolated from the professional stuttering community, Gene and I maintained an active correspondence that helped to keep me in tune with stuttering and helped to shape my ideas for therapy. Marty Adam's research continues to be an important part of my teaching, and working directly with John Hutchinson while attending Michigan State convinced me that therapy with persons who stutter was the way to go.

On the other side of my family are Wendell Johnson, Dean Williams, and Ed Conture (the big Kahuna). I was not fortunate enough to know Johnson or Williams, although I explored their philosophies and thinking during my doctoral training and subsequent development as a practicing clinician. The influences of Johnson and Williams are clear in the teachings of Ed Conture, although Ed has taken these perspective and grown and developed beyond his mentors. Ed was my mentor at Syracuse University and, as I noted in my dissertation, he never asked more of his students than he was willing to give of himself. I believe that Ed Conture sets the standard for professionals working in the area of stuttering, and we would be a significantly better profession if we all produced at Conture's level.

Having acknowledged my stuttering family, I believe that I have grown and developed beyond these influences. I have developed my own approach to therapy that has borrowed from the family members that I have mentioned as well as many other persons along the way.

In addition to those in the aforementioned thanks, I would like to thank three individuals who were responsible at various points in my career for helping to shape the person and clinician that I am today. These individuals exhibited personality characteristics that were often 180 degrees out-of-phase with my own impulsive, aggressive style of interaction. These persons—Marion Mills at the Child Guidance Clinic of Greater Winnipeg; John Saxman, former chair at Syracuse University and present chair at Columbia University; and Jim Andrews, former chair and present clinic director at Northern Illinois University—have all been extremely influential in helping me to modify my interpersonal interactions and influence the manner in which I conduct therapy.

I would like to thank my wife Reggie who has been with me since the beginning when I had no letters after my name, no reputation but a "lot of potential." Reggie has been the foundation of my professional and personal life and the glue that has kept us together. And thanks also to Jenn and Jeff who continue to remind me that life is ever changing and you shouldn't be locked into one belief because your kids have a funny way of surprising you.

Thanks go also to my past and present students who have helped shape my thinking about teaching and providing therapy. In recent years we had "The Stuttering Police" and "The Dream Team" as major contributors toward ideas in this book. Special thanks is offered to Pat Blasen, Deb Strum, and John Atchley who helped out with the video proposal for this book. Thanks to Sandy Nicholson and Kim Hoffer who were willing to take time away from other activities to provide feedback regarding various chapters in the book. Tricia Sabathne and Marianne Kieffer, two ace graduate assistants, were instrumental in helping me to edit the manuscript and complete the project on time. Thank you all.

I would also like to recognize my colleagues within the Department of Communicative Disorders, Northern Illinois University. Many of us came to Northern with the idea that we would be moving on when a better position became available. We quickly came to realize that there aren't better positions available or colleagues more supportive. Thanks to everyone.

Thanks to Doug Cross (Ithaca College), Ellen Kelly (Purdue University), and Tricia Zebrowski (University of Iowa) for reviewing the proposal for this book. Thanks to Dorothy Olsen (University of Wisconsin, Steven's Point) and Ellen Kelly for their helpful comments when reviewing the entire manuscript. Additional thanks to Steve Dragin and Liz McGuire at Allyn and Bacon who made sure that I met my deadlines without threatening to break any arms or legs.

Special thanks to friends who provided emotional support and encouragement along the way: Bubba, Kelly, Bob, Doogie, Jean-Paul, Laurie, Sandy, Tom, Kevin, Michelle, Robin, and John.

In conclusion, I would like to thank all of my former and present clients. My interactions with my clients have enabled me to not only see clinical success and failure but also to become part of their family. I know when Bobby's sister is having her tonsils out and when Bob and his wife are having problems. I get invited to weddings and hopefully not many funerals. My clients let me into their lives and they become part of my clinical family. I learn as much from my clients as they learn from me. I thank each and every one.

▶ 1

Requisite Background

Primer: any book of elementary principles
(Random House Webster's College Dictionary, p. 1072)

The *Primer for Stuttering Therapy* will serve as the foundation for the development of a comprehensive stuttering treatment program. This treatment program focuses on both the client's speech skills and the client's emotional awareness and reactions associated with his or her stuttering. However, this book is not a cookbook filled with recipes for successful fluency therapy. We believe that every client who stutters is different. Certainly, we see similar behaviors among some clients, but we recognize that the population of stutterers is heterogeneous and thus, our therapy techniques need to be modified to meet the individual needs of our clients. Our goal is to help develop clinicians who face the diverse nature of the stuttering problem and not technicians who can only follow one recipe for fluency. It is our intention to explore the multidimensional nature of stuttering and describe a number of skills that lead to the development of a more fluently speaking client who is pleased with the changes associated with this fluency.

WHY DO WE NEED ANOTHER BOOK DESCRIBING STUTTERING THERAPY?

Stuttering therapy involves the active participation of both the client and clinician. Learning the requisite skills necessary to provide stuttering therapy

1

cannot be learned from books alone. As a result, graduate training programs and projected mentoring programs (e.g., ASHA Special Interest Division—Fluency) require both an academic component and a clinical training component to develop well rounded, competent clinicians. The focus of this book is to provide a description of the fundamental procedures and skills necessary to provide stuttering therapy for children and adults. Throughout the text, the reader will note *TECHNIQUE* sections that are separated from the main text. These descriptions focus on the necessary clinical vocabulary for describing the cause of stuttering, explaining how speech is produced, and teaching fluency skills. These *TECHNIQUE* sections are provided to assist readers toward developing their own therapy vocabulary. It is anticipated that in order for readers to implement the described skills, they can observe the accompanying videotape and observe these skills being used. The video can provide an audio/visual reference for both the clinician and the client.

USING THE VIDEOTAPE TO AUGMENT THE TEXT

Throughout the text you will note a video time code that will be associated with the specific information being presented. The video time code (VTC) in the book is presented in **hours:minutes:seconds:video frames.** When readers encounter a video time code reference in the text, they can identify that same time code on the upper left hand portion of the videotape. As a result, readers can not only view the entire videotape to help improve their diagnostic and treatment skills, but also can repeatedly return to those specific areas for which more intensive and frequent viewing is desired.

VTC: 00:00:19:21

WHAT IS STUTTERING?

Although a definition of stuttering is a prerequisite toward both the evaluation and treatment of stuttering, we recognize that "a definition is an invitation to all corners to" (Van Riper, 1971). As a result we can observe that the literature is filled with definitions for stuttering. These definitions range from the psychoanalytical, "Stuttering is a psychoneurosis caused by the persistence into later life of early pregenital oral nursing, oral sadistic, and anal sadistic components (Coriat, 1943 as cited in Van Riper, 1971), to a four factor definition, "Stuttering is (1) a developmental communication disorder beginning in childhood of (2) unknown origin that (3) results in a person viewing the communication process differently from a normal speaker (4) due to experiences with overt or covert factors that disrupt normal communication" (Culatta & Goldberg, 1995, p. 7). Even though the Culatta and Goldberg definition is an excellent attempt to account for stuttering, we believe that for the purposes of this book, a working definition that describes the behavioral characteristics of stuttering is most appropriate. First, we recognize that stuttering is a perceptual event. While we live in a technological society and computers are ever present, we do not have a machine, computer program, or device that will consistently identify stuttered speech. As a result we must rely upon our ability to identify stuttering in the spontaneous speech of the individual speaker. As Young (1984) reported: "The ultimate detection and measurement instrument for stuttering and stutterers is a human observer, as it should be, since 'stuttering' and 'stutterers' represent human judgments. All other tools of measurement, both acoustical and physiological, eventually must be validated against the judgments of human observers " (p. 28). Although some investigators (e.g., Cordes & Ingham, 1994) have questioned the methods available to reliably identify stuttering, we believe that it is possible to provide a behavioral description of stuttering that when applied in a consistent manner will yield information valuable to the diagnosis and treatment of the problem. We view stuttering as a temporal disruption in the forward flow of speech characterized by sound and syllable repetitions and sound prolongations (audible and inaudible). In our case we are suggesting as many others have suggested (e.g., Van Riper, 1971) that stuttering is a disorder of the timing of speech and when this speech timing is disrupted, the client will produce a unique type of disfluency called stuttering. In order to best understand the aforementioned definition, it is necessary to provide a perspective on the nature of speech disfluency.

DISFLUENCY AND STUTTERING

We would like to suggest that the term *disfluency* be used to describe any behavior that interrupts the forward flow of speech. In other words, disfluency is a generic umbrella term that encompasses many different types of behaviors.

TABLE 1–1   **Categorizing Disfluency**

D				i			s
f			l			u	e
		n		c		y	
	(					A	
		n				y	
D		i		s		r	u
p				t			i
o							n
		i				n	
t				h			e
F	o		r		w	a	r
		d	l				
F			l		o		w

To further differentiate these terms we will divide disfluency into two unique categories. The first category will be described as between-word disfluencies (Conture, 1982) or those disfluencies that occur across word boundaries.

Between-Word Disfluencies

Between-word disfluencies are often viewed to be "normal" disfluency and in the young child are typically seen as part of normal language development. Within this category we generally find four types of disfluencies: (1) phrase repetitions; (2) revisions; (3) interjections; and (4) multisyllabic whole-word repetitions. Phrase repetitions, "I want, I want, I want to go," involve the repetition of two- or three-word phrases. Revisions, as part of normal language development involve a change in thought or topic. A young child talking to his mother might say, "Mommy, can we go. . . . I want to go to the park." This child has begun to produce a phrase and in the middle of the thought the child stops, reformulates, and produces another phrase. The second phrase may or may not be related to the original thought. An interjection involves the introduction of various words and sounds to fill the pauses prior to, during, or following a word. For example, an adolescent might say "I was uh, uh, going to the uh store, you know, the 7-11 to get um um, a coke." While these interjections clearly result in a perceived decrease in fluency, it is unlikely that the average listener would judge this person to have a speech problem. The final category of between-word disfluency is multisyllablic whole-word repetitions. For example, a preschooler might ask,

"Mommy, mommy, mommy, I want to go." Once again, these multisyllabic whole-word repetitions are more likely to be judged to be normal disfluencies by the average listener.

Between-Word Disfluencies and Stuttering

While between-word disfluencies have been described as a component of normal language development and are present in everyone's speech, there are occasions where persons who stutter use these disfluencies as a method of adapting or reacting to their stuttering. This might best be illustrated by the following example. The mother of an adolescent client reported that her son was repeating all of the time and that his stuttering interfered with his daily communication. During the evaluation, we spoke at length with this client and observed that he would frequently repeat a phrase "My name, my name, my name, my name, my name, my name, my name . . . .is Tony." It appeared that in anticipation of the word "is" and the expected difficulty on this word, Tony would repeat a phrase until he believed that he was able to fluently move through the subsequent sounds. Because these repetitions occurred during most sentences, Tony's short-duration sound prolongations were easily masked by this repetitive behavior. Obviously, the average listener will focus on the repetitions and will probably be oblivious to the stuttering in Tony's speech. As speech-language pathologists, we focus on the client's stuttering and note that the client is also reacting to his or her stuttering by producing frequent phrase repetitions.

Within-Word Disfluencies

Within-word disfluencies (Conture, 1982) are those disfluencies that tend to break up a word. These disfluencies are often perceived as abnormal and have been called stuttering. Within-word disfluencies include sound and syllable repetitions, mono-syllabic whole-word repetitions, and sound prolongations (audible sound prolongations, inaudible sound prolongations and broken words). Sound repetitions can be described as the repetition of a consonant or vowel that is usually in the initial position of a word. A child might say "I want t-t-t-t to go outside." A syllable repetition includes the repetition of a syllable or part of a syllable usually in the initial sound position. An adult might ask "Are we go-go-go going to the movies?" A second type of within-word disfluency is the monosyllabic whole word repetition. This type of stuttering often occurs at the beginning of a sentence or phrase and may be characterized by "I, I, I, want to go," or "My, my window is broken." The next category of within-word disfluency includes audible and inaudible sound prolongations and broken words. Audible sound prolongations can be described as a voiced sound that might be prolonged as in the word "Aaaaaaaple, Apple" or "goooing." In addition, it is possible to have a sound prolongation on a voiceless sound. In this case a client will prolong a fricative sound (e.g., /s/ or /sh/) as in "Ssssssssoup, soup." The second type of sound prolongation can be called a block or inaudible sound prolongation (Conture, 1982). This type of stuttering typically occurs in the inital position of a word where the client attempts to produce the sound and no sound is emitted. The client attempts to say "I want to go," and a silent interval precedes the intended word. The third type of sound prolongation, a broken word, occurs when the client produces an inaudible sound prolongation in the middle of a word. The word sounds as if it was broken in two when the client says "I was go. . . ing." Our clinical experience suggests that broken words are produced by a relatively small number of persons who stutter. We speculate that when these stutterings are observed in a client's speech, they occur with some degree of frequency. It appears to us that the client uses these inaudible prolongations to inappropriately break up a word.

VTC: 00:01:41:07

THE ONSET AND DEVELOPMENT OF STUTTERING

It is our belief that many clinicians have the opinion that a discussion of stuttering onset and development is an academic exercise without direct, clinical applicability. We would like to suggest that if clinicians do not have a clear, up-to-date understanding of our present knowledge of stuttering onset and development, they will have a great deal of difficulty establishing credibility with parents and these clinicians will lack the basic, fundamental information that is vital to decisions on when to enroll a preschooler in therapy.

When questioned by a parent about the cause of stuttering, the average speech-language pathologist is reduced to the typical graduate school response, "We don't really know the cause of stuttering, although a number of theories have been suggested regarding stuttering onset and development." Though this safe response may appease some parents, we believe that most parents and clients want to know your opinion regarding the onset of stuttering. If you can provide a clear rationale that is substantiated with research information, we believe that you can furnish a well-thought-out response to the question.

Our discussion of stuttering onset and development is based upon the work of a number of investigators (Conture, 1990; Schwartz & Conture, 1988; Schwartz, Zebrowski & Conture, 1990; Yairi, 1983, 1997a, 1997b; Yairi & Ambrose, 1992a, 1992b; Yairi, Ambrose, Paden, & Throneburg, 1996; Yairi & Lewis, 1984).

A *Summary of Stuttering Onset and Development*

1. The population of persons who stutter is heterogeneous.
2. The speech of children who stutter appears to be different from the speech of normally fluent speakers, right from the onset of stuttering.
3. Stuttering runs in families, although the exact method for genetic transmission remains unknown.
4. Stuttering onset may be gradual or sudden.
5. Stuttering is a disorder of children with the largest onset occurring prior to age 5.
6. Stuttering often begins as sound/syllable repetitions although some children clearly produce (in)audible sound prolongations at stuttering onset.
7. Nonspeech Associated Behaviors are often present from stuttering onset.
8. A large percentage of children (between 70%–80%) spontaneously recover from the problem.
9. The greatest amount of recovery occurs within 1 year post stuttering onset.
10. Early stuttering is often characterized by higher frequencies of stuttering that decline within the first 2 years post onset.
11. Lack of positive change (decrease in frequency) in stuttering by 7 months post stuttering onset suggests the need for evaluation and possible treatment.
12. While spontaneous recovery can occur for some children beyond 1 year post onset, intervention is encouraged by 1 year post onset.
13. The development of stuttering occurs as a result of the clients' speech skills, the communicative environment, and the clients' awareness of, and reactions to, stuttering and the environment.

OUR PHILOSOPHY TOWARD THE
DEVELOPMENT OF STUTTERING

"The reasons for the onset of stuttering, then, are not to be sought most significantly within the child or even in the way he speaks, but primarily 'inside his parent's head,' or, rather, in the parent's attitudes and reactions to the child and especially to the way the child speaks (Johnson & Associates, 1956, p. 242). Johnson explains the development of stuttering by stating that "stuttering is what a speaker does when (1) he expects stuttering to occur, (2) dreads it, and (3) becomes tense in anticipation of it and in (4) trying to avoid doing it" (217). In essence, Johnson describes stuttering as a multidimensional problem, with all children considered to have equal potential to develop stuttering and parents responsible for the onset of the problem.

As times changed, we gained more insights into the relationship between the child and the environment as well as objective information that suggested that the child may bring a unique set of speech skills to a situation, and it is the interaction between the child's speech skills and the environment that accounts for the development of stuttering. We can thank Johnson for his suggestion that stuttering is a multidimensional problem. However, we believe that we must minimize Johnson's suggestion to focus primarily on this environment while ignoring potential speech differences between fluent children and children who stutter. More recently, Conture (1982) stated, "Stuttering most likely results from a complex *interaction* between the stutterer's environment (for example, parental standards for child behavior) *and* the skills/abilities the stutterer brings to that environment (e.g., gross and fine motor coordination)" (p. 33). Unlike Johnson, Conture suggested that we adjust our thinking to give equal weight to the child's speech abilities and the communicative environment. The manner in which the characteristics of the child interact with the characteristics of the environment will provide a more clear picture regarding the development of stuttering. To examine this interaction in more depth, we are led to a discussion of Capacities and Demands that is provided by Peters and Guitar (1991). These authors refer to the work of Neilson and Neilson (1987) and the report of Andrews, and colleagues by describing the development of stuttering as a function of the child's capacities for fluent speech production that interacts with demands for speech performance. It is important to note the Starkweather (1987), Starkweather, Gottwald, and Halfond (1990), and Starkweather (1997) have expanded upon this model to describe capacities and demands that focus on speech motor control, language development, social and emotional functioning, and cognitive development. In the section that follows, we continue a discussion of the development of stuttering as it relates to the child's speech, the environment, and the child's emotional development.

A MULTIDIMENSIONAL PERSPECTIVE

Speech Skills

We believe that only a small group of children are born with speech abilities that place them at risk for stuttering. We view these speech abilities to be biologically predetermined. Specifically, we are suggesting that all children do not possess equal potential to develop stuttering. Given our current knowledge of the genetics of stuttering (Yairi, Ambrose, & Cox, 1996) and recent research reports on the nature of disfluencies at stuttering onset (e.g., Yairi, 1997a), we are suggesting that a group of children between the ages of 2 and 5 are born with a biological predisposition to stutter. Unlike Johnson and Associates (1956), who believed that stuttering emerges from normal disfluency, we believe that children who stutter are more likely to produce stuttered disfluencies right from the onset of their problem. Van Riper (1992) described a study that he conducted examining the onset and development of stuttering. Van Riper reported that he argued frequently with Johnson that stuttering does not emerge from normal disfluency. Van Riper wrote, "I did not find any evidence to support this belief although I tried. Some of these stuttering children had far fewer normal disfluencies than nonstutterers and the parents never seemed to be concerned about them. Often they would 'correct' the child when he stuttered but never when he merely repeated a phrase or had word-finding difficulty. When I told Jack (Wendell) what I was discovering he doubted me and said he would have to do his own investigation" (p. 27).

The biological predisposition to stutter might be viewed as an increased sensitivity to communicative demands that are generated externally by the communicative environment or internally by the child's emotional system. When a young child confronts an external or internal demand, the child responds by using the speech production system in a manner that exceeds the child's ability to remain fluent. As a result, the child is more likely to stutter at these times. The characteristics of early stuttering have been identified by Yairi (1997a) who suggested that the speech of young stutterers includes more total disfluencies, more stuttered-like disfluencies and greater proportions of stuttering to total disfluencies, when compared to normally fluent children.

Communicative Environment

A child born with a predisposition to stutter will encounter both external demands (e.g., environmental time demands) or internal demands (e.g., the child's need to match adult speaking rates) that will impact the child's speech abilities. We believe that the onset and development of stuttering is related to the interaction between the child's speech abilities and these demands.

Examination of the literature, frequent discussion with students, and interactions with colleagues often results in discussions that focus on identifying some negative characteristics within the child's communicative environment that contribute to stuttering development. We would like to believe that we can identify a typical home environment or typical parent that would characterize all parents of children who stutter. However, this is clearly not the case. After reviewing the available literature on communicative environments and children who stutter, Yairi (1997b) reported "I also concur with Adams' (1993) view that children who stutter do not grow up in a home environment that is clearly pathologic" (p.42). Yairi (1997b) stated: "It is clearly time to declare that the belief that parents' personalities or attitudes are causally related to stuttering is null and void for purposes of counseling and treatment. For many years, too many parents have been, either directly or indirectly, wrongly faulted for their child's stuttering" (p. 44).

What is the role of the communicative environment in the development of stuttering? How can we explain the interaction between the environment and the child. It may be possible that normal routine adult activities require the predisposed child to exceed his or her ability. As a result, this predisposed child attempts to maintain a speaking rate consistent with normally fluent adults. Additionally, the predisposed child may be exposed to normal adult turn switching pauses during conversational interactions. As the child attempts to "keep up" with these adults, the child exceeds personal ability to remain fluent. It is our belief that normal daily occurrences may contribute to the development of stuttering in children more than the presence of a pathological environment. We also should point out that positive experiences can also contribute to the development of stuttered speech. It is when a child is excited during play activities, birthday parties, and holidays (e.g. Halloween, Thanksgiving, and Christmas) that he or she is more likely to move beyond personal fluency capabilities, which increases the likelihood of stuttering. However, it is our belief that stuttering will only continue to develop when the child is aware of his or her environment or stuttering and reacts in some way to make the problem worse (e.g., increase physical tension in larynx, avoiding specific situations). We believe that the child's reactions more than the environment account for continued stuttering development. As a result, we also need to focus on the child's awareness and reactions to stuttering and the environment.

Awareness and Reactions to Stuttering and the Environment

Do very young children react to their stuttering and communicative environment? We believe that all young children place emotional and behavioral demands upon themselves to varying degrees. These demands may range from "I have to keep my toys in order" to "I have to get my speech out in a hurry." We don't believe that many young children could express to their parents these emotional demands and yet they can be observed during daily activities. When a child is biologically predisposed to stutter and makes demands upon himself, we believe that this increases the child's likelihood of stuttering. From a purely clinical perspective we have encountered a number of 3-year-olds and 4-year-olds who have stated to their parents, "Mommy I don't talk so good" or "I can't say that word." On some occasions, parents have reported that their child has attempted to say a word, stuttered, gave up, and walked away without trying to complete a thought. Schwartz, Zebrowski, and Conture (1990) examined nonspeech behaviors that were produced in association with stuttering. The authors stated that nonspeech behaviors were viewed as a child's behavioral attempt to adapt or cope with stuttering. The children in this investigation were 3 to 5 years of age and all within 1 year of stuttering onset. The results of this investigation revealed that all children, regardless of time from stuttering onset, were producing behaviors in association with their stuttering. More recently, Yairi, Ambrose, and Nierman (1993) reported that children within 3 months of stuttering onset produced associated head and neck movements. These findings suggest that children close to stuttering onset appear to be reacting to their stuttering, and these reactions need to be considered when evaluating a child's potential for continued stuttering development.

Having described the research detailing the onset and development of stuttering and our philosophy regarding stuttering as a multidimensional problem, we would like to provide a typical explanation that we provide to parents on our perceptions about the cause of stuttering:

Technique—Explaining the Cause of Stuttering

You've asked what causes the problem of stuttering. Let me explain my philosophy to you. I believe that a select group of children are born with a predisposition to stutter. Yes, your child is different from your other children and his or her fluent peers. How is he or she different? Your child is not intellectually, academically, or socially different from fluent children. The differences lie with your child's ability to produce smooth fluent speech. A number of investigators believe that your child's predisposition is actually an inherited trait that is transmitted through families. Your child's speech-coordinating skills appear to be sensitive to internal and external demands. You ask, "What are these internal and external demands?" A demand will be any behavior or situation that requires your child to exceed his or her speech coordinating skills. You might consider your child's speech coordination skills as a window of fluent speech. As long as your child remains within that window of acceptability, his or her speech remains fluent. When these coordinating skills are exceeded, your child's speech fluency will break down in a unique manner. For the child who is predisposed to stutter, he or she is more likely to break up a word in a unique way when he or she exceeds his or her skills and abilities. When faced with a time or emotional demand, your child responds by breaking up a word, repeating the syllables or prolonging the syllables and at times, holding the syllable for too long a period of time. Does your child consciously respond in this manner? We don't think so. These unique speech behaviors are the responses to the demands and appear to be the core features of stuttering. Recent investigations have suggested that 70 percent to 80 percent of children who exhibit stuttering grow out of the problem within two years following stuttering onset. However, when the problem continues to develop, we believe that your child remains sensitive to the demands he or she faces and often begins to react to the problem. These reactions can result in either changes in the type of stuttering, changes in the behaviors associated with the problem, or changes in attitudes and emotions related to the stuttering. It is the role of the speech language pathologist to identify the problem and determine the speech and emotional characteristics associated with your child's stuttering.

SUMMARY

Within the previous section we described the onset of stuttering from a multidimensional perspective. We have focused on the child who stutters because stuttering is a disorder of childhood (Conture, 1990), and the complex nature of stuttering onset sets the stage for the evaluation and treatment of the problem. By the time an adult arrives at our clinic, we know that if the client is stuttering, a number of factors have contributed to the development of that stuttering. These same factors—speech abilities, communicative environment, and awareness and reactions to stuttering, and the environment—also need to be examined to plan an effective treatment program.

WHAT TO EXPECT IN THE CHAPTERS
TO FOLLOW

We continue our discussion of stuttering as a multidimensional problem by describing the evaluation process in Chapter 2 as it relates to the client's speech abilities, communicative environment and the client's awareness and reactions to stuttering and the environment. We believe that our treatment program begins with the diagnostic evaluation. In Chapter 3, we focus on teaching the client a new set of speech skills, and in Chapter 4 we discuss counseling as it applies to all clients. From our perspective, we wanted to address basic speech modification strategies and counseling as separate chapters, while issues related to the client's communicative environment were best addressed within the context of each chapter that addressed therapy. Chapter 5 focuses on young children who have not completed kindergarten. Within this chapter, a variety of therapy options are discussed because of the diverse nature of this group. Chapter 6 focuses on the older child and adolescent. This chapter contains the fundamental information for structuring a therapy program progressing from simple to complex activities. A lot of information presented in this chapter can be adapted for use with adults who stutter. Chapter 7 is a description of methods for providing an intensive fluency therapy program. This program is designed for a selected group of adults who stutter. Within this chapter the reader will note that the basic fluency skills presented in Chapter 3 are taught using a conversational therapy approach. This approach will have applications for the long term therapy program described in Chapter 8. Chapter 8 also contains descriptions of our group therapy program and additional suggestions for counseling adults who stutter. Chapter 9 contains a letter from me to you. Bon Voyage!

▶ 2

Evaluating the Person Who Stutters

In our opinion, the first day of any treatment program begins with an evaluation of the clients' speech, his or her communicative environment, and the client's awareness and reactions to his or her speech and the environment. We believe that the problem of stuttering is multidimensional with a breakdown in fluency as the core of the problem. However, a single-minded focus on the client's speech will provide the clinician with a very narrow view of the client's problem.

We believe that the population of persons who stutter is heterogeneous. Every individual who stutters brings a unique set of speech and emotional characteristics to the evaluation. It is our job to examine the constellation of behaviors that the client brings to the situation and determine whether a problem exists. When a problem exists, can we provide some form of treatment that will assist clients toward improving their speech and modifying the behaviors and emotions associated with their stuttering?

Prior to beginning our discussion of the component parts of the evaluation, we believe that it necessary to discuss the setting for the evaluation and provide an overview of the intended activities.

SETTING

The ideal setting for any evaluation begins with a therapy room in a quiet environment and the ability to observe the client through a one-way mirror. Most of us do not work within this type of environment and must adjust accordingly. Clinicians working within a university clinical environment have the opportunity to view parent–child interactions from an observation room while the client and parent interact in an adjacent room. Many others work under stair wells, in nurse's offices, and in individual therapy rooms that lack observation rooms. Within our private practice setting, we work in an individual office where observations have to occur directly within the therapy room. There is no one correct setting for evaluating a client. We learn as speech language pathologists to be flexible and to adjust to our environments. For a list of suggestions for maximizing the setting for the evaluation, we refer the reader to Table 2–1.

To conclude our discussion of setting, we would like to make one final point. The clinician has set aside a period of time in which to complete the evaluation. Whether this period of time is 60 minutes, 90 minutes, or 120 minutes, the client is functioning according to an internal clock. This is especially true with the young child below the age of 6. Our experience suggests that the clinician is playing the old television game entitled *Beat the Clock*, where the client is given a fixed amount of time to accomplish a task. During the evaluation, the clock starts to tick for young children as soon as they enter the clinic waiting room. When we delay the beginning of our evaluation, the client's clock has begun to count down. The longer we delay, the less time we have available to work before the child become restless and uncooperative. Our experience indicates that young children are often able to work for about 60 minutes when waiting time has been kept to a minimum. Bearing this in mind, we may need to adjust our evaluation to ensure that enough time is allowed to work with the child. When the client begins to reach their time threshold, he or she lets us know by moving around in his or her chair, losing his or her focus on the activity at hand, and requesting one

TABLE 2–1. **Maximizing the Setting for the Evaluation**

1. Conduct the evaluation in a quiet environment that provides the opportunity for observation if possible.
2. Audio tape record or video tape record the session for future data analysis and report writing.
3. Maximize the lighting (natural or artificial) to insure quality video recordings.
4. Remember to turn on the microphone.
5. Make sure that your equipment not only lights up but also records.
6. Chairs and tables need to be appropriate to the age of the client.
7. Room temperatures will affect your client's ability to continue working.
8. Toilet breaks are essential for younger clients (and some adults as well).

or both parents. We often try to push the child a bit further to gain as much information as possible. However, we do not want to push the child to the point where he or she is hysterical and screaming for a parent. With some experience, a clinician will learn just how far he or she can go with the child before it's too late. At this point we recognize that our time is up and we're probably not going to gain any additional information. Typically when we work with adults, we know that our time is not limited to 1 hour. Occasionally, a client arriving for an evaluation doesn't realize that the evaluation will last from 90 minutes to 120 minutes. On these occasions we instruct the client that they can return at a time when they are able to remain for the full length of time or only complete a portion of the evaluation. Experience suggests that during the initial contact with the client, we inform them about the nature and length of the evaluation to preclude any potential time problems. It is only in the rarest of cases that an adult becomes impatient to the point that we need to discuss our rationale for the length of time that we spend during the evaluation.

AN OVERVIEW OF EVALUATION ACTIVITIES

Depending upon the setting in which a clinician works, the sequence of activities to complete the evaluation may need to be modified. Our evaluation experiences typically occur within a university setting and a clinical private practice. We recognize that clinicians work in a variety of settings and encourage the readers to make necessary modifications to meet the needs of work environments. The sequence of activities for children (Table 2–2) and adults (Table 2–3) can be examined as a prelude to our discussion of evaluating the multidimensional nature of stuttering.

PRE-EVALUATION PAPERWORK

In preparing for the evaluation of both children and adults, we use a case history form to obtain objective and subjective information from a parent of a child who stutters or from an adult client. The case history form is divided into a number of subsections, which generally focus on the client's basic information (e.g., name, address, family members), history of the speech problem, speech and language development, developmental history, medical history, and daily behavior.

TABLE 2–2. **Overview of Evaluation Sequence of Activities for Children**

1. Parents and child are greeted in waiting area by the clinician.
2. Parents are informed about the sequence of activities that will comprise the evaluation.
3. University Clinic–Parent and child are escorted to clinic room where parent-child interaction is observed behind a one-way mirror by diagnostic team.

    Private Practice—Parent-Child interaction takes place within treatment room while the clinician sits in the room and observes. Age-appropriate materials are provided to encourage conversational interaction.
4. Parent-Child interactions are observed and videotape-recorded. Attempts are made to determine frequency, duration, and type of stuttering. Speaking rates, turn switching pauses, parental reactions to the child, and the child's reactions to the parents can be observed and noted.
5. University Clinic—After approximately 15 minutes, parents are escorted to a second clinic room where they will be interviewed by a clinician. The child is introduced to a second clinician who will begin evaluating the child.

    Private clinic—the parents are interviewed while the child remains in the waiting area. When the parental interview is completed, the child is brought into the room for the evaluation.
6. Evaluating the child may include a short interview, obtaining a conversational speech sample, and additional standardized and nonstandardized testing.
7. University clinic—Following the evaluation and parent interview, the parent and child are escorted to the waiting room while the diagnostic team discusses results and formulates a management plan.

    Private clinic—Clinician makes necessary calculations, summarizes results, and prepares summary for parents.
8. Parents return to evaluation room where clinician interprets the evaluation results and makes recommendations regarding the child's problem. Parents are provided with the opportunity to ask questions about the evaluation process and the nature of stuttering.

In an ideal world, we are able to schedule our clients so that they have time to fill out the forms before the evaluation and mail the forms back to our clinic. In this manner, the clinician is able to read through the case history form and prepare a set of interview questions that are directed toward the specifics of the client's problem. For example, if a parent reports a normal history of labor and delivery on the case history form, we do not reiterate all of the questions pertaining to labor and delivery. On the other hand, if a parent reports a child's history of chronic otitis media, we may want to develop additional questions to determine the potential impact of the child's hearing problems on their speech and language development. When we have

TABLE 2–3.   **Overview of Evaluation Sequence of Activities for Adults**

1. Adult client is greeted in the waiting room by the clinician. The sequence of evaluation activities is explained to the client. If the client has not returned the case history form and additional questionnaires, these materials are returned at this time.
2. University clinic—Client is escorted to clinic room and introduced to clinician who will conduct interview. Diagnostic team members remain behind a one-way mirror and observe.

   Private practice—The clinician escorts the client to the evaluation room and conducts the interview.
3. University clinic—Diagnostic team members obtain information on frequency and duration of stuttering, speech disfluency types, rate of speech, and articulatory abilities. The clinicians also observe the client's interactions with the clinician.

   Private practice—The clinician is responsible for conducting the client interview while at the same time recording information relative to the characteristics of the client's stuttering and behavioral/emotional characteristics.
4. University clinic—Following the interview, a second clinician replaces the interviewing clinician and converses with the client. During this time, observing clinicians are able to examine the characteristics of the client's stuttering when conversing with a new listener. At this same time, observing clinicians can note any changes in the behavioral/emotional characteristics of the client. Evaluation procedures are now completed.

   Private Practice—Upon completion of the client interview, the clinician will complete a variety of evaluation activities.
5. University clinic—When the client evaluation is completed, the client is asked to sit in the waiting area while the diagnostic team discusses results and formulates a management plan.

   Private Practice—The client is asked to return to the waiting room while the examining clinician summarizes the results.
6. Client returns to the evaluation room where the clinician discusses the results of the evaluation with the client. The client is given the opportunity to ask questions on the evaluation process, the results of the evaluation, and stuttering.

the case history in hand before the evaluation, we can often expedite the interview of parent or client.

For many clinicians, including this author, obtaining the case history form prior to the evaluation is impossible. At times, we are unable to get the case history form to the parent or client with enough time to have it returned before the evaluation. Sometimes, the client fails to return the form or fails to bring the form to the evaluation. As stated previously, speech-language pathologists must learn to be flexible to unforeseen situations. Whether we have the case history 2 weeks before the evaluation or are handed the form immediately before the evaluation, we can use this information to expedite the interview with the parent or client.

THE EVALUATION—A MULTIDIMENSIONAL PERSPECTIVE

Introduction

Given our previous discussions on the multidimensional nature of stuttering, we continue to promote this idea as it relates to the evaluation process. Because we believe that a variety of factors need to be considered before we classify a child or adult as a person who stutters, we will discuss the evaluation of stuttering relative to the client's speech abilities, their communicative environment, and their awareness and reactions to speech and the environment.

As we obtain results throughout the evaluation, we often invoke a mental image of a scale or balance (Figure 2–1), which can help us decide whether a stuttering problem exists and, if therapy is needed. As clinical results are obtained, they are either added to one side of the balance, suggesting the presence of stuttering, or to the other side, indicating that there is no stuttering problem or a different problem. As we continue throughout our evaluation, we are adding weights to one side of the balance or the other. At the end of the evaluation, our decision on the presence of a problem and potential enrollment in therapy will be determined by the number of weights and the direction in which our balance is leaning.

The discussion that follows describes the components of a stuttering evaluation and our attempts to classify these components as speech abilities, communicative environment, and awareness and reactions of stuttering and the environment. To assist the reader, we provided a method of classifying the components of the evaluation prior to each discussion so that the reader will better understand our perception of stuttering as a multidimensional disorder. As noted in Table 2–4, the clinician can classify the various aspects of the evaluation according to the three headings provided. In this manner, when the evaluation is completed, the results are analyzed by looking at the relative contributions of the client's speech, the environment, and the client's emotional reactions.

Clinical Decision Regarding Stuttering

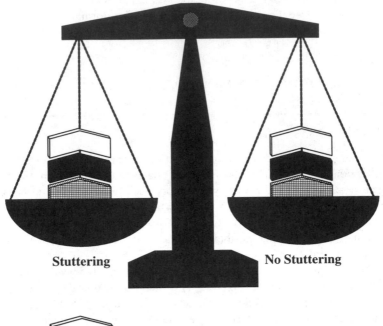

Stuttering   No Stuttering

Speech Abilities

Communicative Environment

Awareness and Reaction

FIGURE 2–1   **Clinical Decisions Regarding Stuttering**

Speech Abilities

Our focus on speech abilities begins with a description of the characteristics of stuttering and a rationale for their examination. Included in this discussion will be frequency of occurrence, types of stuttering, most frequently occurring stuttering type, and duration of stuttering. Additional components of the evaluation include speaking rates, consistency and loci of stuttering, diadochokinetic speech rates, articulatory skills, and language skills. The discussion to follow is generally applicable for young children who stutter, older children, adolescents, and adults.

TABLE 2-4. A Multidimensional Evaluation of Stuttering

Speech Abilities	Communicative Environment	Awareness and Reactions to Speech and the Environment
1. Frequency of occurence of stuttering	1. Parent interview	1. Avoiding words and situations
2. Speech disfluency types	2. Client interview	2. Number and variety of associated behaviors
3. Sound prolongation index	3. Observe parent-child interaction	3. Cognitive awareness of stuttering
4. Duration of stuttering	4. Observe clint-clinician interaction	
5. Speaking rate		
6. Consistency and loci of stuttering		
7. Diadochokinetic speaking rates		
8. Articulation skills		
9. Language skills		

Frequency of Occurrence of Stuttering

$$\frac{\# \text{ Stutterings}}{\# \text{ Syllables or words}} = \text{Frequency of Stuttering}$$

Frequency of occurrence of stuttering is calculated as the number of stutterings observed during a sample of speech that is counted in terms of syllables or words. We use the number of stutterings divided by the number of syllables because we believe that syllables provide a more accurate measure of the speech produced by the client. When a client is using multisyllabic words, we are able to get a more accurate measure of stuttering relative to the total syllables produced when compared with the number of words produced. When we report a client's frequency of stuttering, we report the mean number of stutterings per 100 syllables of conversational speech and include the range of stuttering to reflect the potential variation in frequency from sampling situation to another.

In order to obtain a representative sample of the client's speech, it is advisable to obtain at least 300 syllables of conversational speech. When obtaining samples of the client's conversation, we are always concerned with the question, "Are we obtaining a representative sample of the client's speech?" With children, we attempt to calculate the child's frequency of occurrence by obtaining conversational samples during parent–child interactions and clinician–child interactions. In this manner, we can examine potential differences in frequency during different situations and discuss with the parents whether they believe we have obtained a representative sample of the child's speech. With adults, we can calculate frequency of occurrence from speech samples that are taken during different tasks throughout the evaluation. We often ask the client or parent if the speech sample we obtained sounds the same as the parent's speech or the child's speech outside of the therapy room. When the client or parent indicates that speech is different outside of therapy, we spend some time trying to determine these perceived differences. On some occasions, we also may ask a parent to provide a tape recording of their child's speech at home when the parent believes that the samples of conversation that we have obtained are not consistent with their child's speech at home.

When working with children, the question arises as to how much stuttering is too much? As discussed previously, we know that fluent children and children who stutter both produce within-word disfluencies. Studies comparing children who stutter made close to stuttering onset, compared with normally fluent children, differ in terms of the number of within-word disfluencies produced (e.g., Johnson & Associates, 1959, Yairi & Lewis, 1984). In addition we know that normally fluent children typically produce less than 3 within-word disfluencies per 100 words of conversational speech (Davis, 1939, Yairi, 1997a). As a result, we follow the suggestions of Zebrowski (1994b) and Conture (1997) who indicated that three or more within-word (stuttered) disfluencies exhibited by a young child suggest that this child is at risk for continued stuttering. Importantly, this red flag or negative sign is recognized as only one piece of a much larger puzzle. We never make our clinical decision based upon one piece of diagnostic information.

VTC: 01:24:49:25

Speech Disfluency Type
When attempting to characterize the client's speech, we analyze the client's conversational sample by determining the frequency of occurrence of all speech disfluency types (see Chapter 1). Our goal is to describe the disfluent characteristics of the client's speech and to determine the types of disfluencies that are present. During our analysis, we separate the within-word disfluencies (stuttering) from the between-word disfluencies. To calculate the frequency of occurrence, we total all of the stutterings and divide the number of sound/syllable repetitions by the total stutterings and the number of sound prolongations by the total stutterings. In a similar fashion, we divide the number of interjections, revisions, phrase repetitions, and multisyllabic whole-word repetitions by the total number of between-word disfluencies. In this manner, we can make some determination regarding types of disfluencies produced. We attempt to view these results relative to developmental characteristics of stuttering (e.g., sound prolongations being more developed than sound/syllable repetitions and the client's attempts to cope/adapt to stuttering using between-word disfluencies.)

Sound Prolongation Index

$$\frac{\text{\# Sound Prolongations}}{\text{\# Stutterings}} \times 100 = \text{SPI}$$

Schwartz and Conture (1988) suggested that the percentage of sound prolongations exhibited by children was one of three variables that help clinicians to differentiate among young children who stutter. The sound prolongation

index (spi) is calculated by dividing the total number of sound prolongations by the total number of stutterings. Schwartz and Conture (1988) stated
that a spi greater than 25% for young children could be viewed as one indication for continued stuttering development. Additionally, Conture (1996)
has suggested that sound prolongations may be viewed as reflecting a more
advanced stage of stuttering. When evaluating children or adults, we attempt
to determine the percentage of sound prolongations as an indicator of stuttering development. As a result, determining the frequency of occurrence of
sound prolongations will provide the clinician with another important piece
to the diagnostic puzzle.

Duration of Stuttering

When calculating the duration of stuttering, it is best to analyze at least ten
stutterings taken from two or three conversational samples throughout the
evaluation. In this manner, the clinician will be gaining a representative sample of the client's stuttering. One word of caution is in order. When identifying those stutterings to be measured, the clinician should select a random
sampling of the client's stuttering. In this way, the clinician can avoid the
tendency to select only those stutterings that are most perceptible. These
stutterings are perceptually more obvious because they are longer in duration and contain voicing. The clinician needs to measure the short-duration
sound prolongations in addition to the longer-duration sound/syllable repetitions.

Conture (1996) has suggested that measurements made during the stuttering evaluation may provide both quantitative information (e.g., frequency of stuttering) or qualitative information (e.g., severity of stuttering).
Historically, the duration of stuttering has been viewed as an indicator of
stuttering severity (e.g., Johnson, Darley, & Spriestersbach, 1978). Clinicians are encouraged to measure the duration of stuttering and to assign a
severity rating based upon the measured duration. Recent attempts to relate
the measured duration of stuttering to a child's chronological age, time from
the onset of stuttering, or stuttering frequency (Schwartz & Conture, 1988;
Schwartz, Zebrowski & Conture, 1990; Zebrowski, 1994a) have failed to
reveal any clear relationship. As a result, the duration of stuttering might be
used in a manner similar to that described in the *Stuttering Severity Instrument* (Riley, 1980) in which the duration of the three longest stutterings are
used in a severity formula. This severity judgement provides us with a qualitative description of the client's stuttering.

Speaking Rate

$$\frac{\text{Syllables}}{\text{Time (sec)}} \times 60 = \text{Rate (spm)}$$

We calculate speaking rate by dividing the number of syllables produced by the client during a period of time (measured in seconds) and multiplying by 60 to arrive at a speaking rate in syllables per minute. When calculating a client's speaking rate, we recognize that both the frequency and duration of the client's stuttering will affect the client's speaking rate. As the number of stutterings increase during a conversational sample, they occupy more time, which results in a slower speaking rate. Additionally, as the duration of stutterings increase, this too takes more time and slows down the client's speaking rate. Calculations of speaking rate can be completed from randomly selected samples of conversation that include stuttering or from the fluent segments of a client's conversation. Neilson and Andrews (1993) suggested a target speaking rate of 200 spm for adult clients within their therapy program. This rate is reported to be "well within documented ranges for fluent speakers (Andrews & Ingham, 1971; Ingham 1984). When examining speaking rates for children, we focus on ranges of acceptability that are slower than those for adults.

How do we count the number of syllables as the client is speaking? The basic method for calculating involves a pen or pencil. As the client is speaking, the clinician makes a pencil mark, line, or stroke to identify every syllable. At the same time, the clinician starts a stop watch when the client begins talking and stops the watch when the client finishes speaking. Typically when the client pauses, the clinician notes the time in seconds, resets the watch, and attempts to take another sample. For example, a client produces 20 syllables in 10 seconds. Remembering our formula, we divide 20 by 10 and multiply by 60. In this case the answer is 120 spm. Peters and Guitar (1991) provide an alternate method for counting the number of syllables. These authors suggest the use of a simple calculator on which the clinician can press 1+1 and use the = button to count the number of syllables. As the client is speaking, the clinician pushes the equal button for each spoken syllable while starting and stopping a stop watch. The same formula can be used to calculate these speaking rates. A more advanced method for calculating the speaking rate involves a computer and a rating program that was developed at St. Vincent's Hospital (Sydney, Australia) and is available in the United States from the author. This program was developed as part of an intensive fluency therapy program that uses speaking rate as the primary goal for therapy. The computer program enables the clinician to calculate the client's speaking rate by depressing the space bar on the computer for each syllable and noting the resulting speaking rate on the video display.

On some occasions, we find it difficult to obtain a conversational sample with enough fluent segments to allow us to make a speaking rate measurement. On these occasions, we attempt to calculate the client's rate of speech during a reading task. Although reading rates are not the equivalent of speaking rates, we might use the obtained reading rate to give us some objective measurement of the client's rate of speech. During therapy, we are interested in discussing the relationship between the client's speaking/reading rate and his or her ability to use fluency skills. If we are unable to measure conversational speaking rate, we use reading rates as the next best available measurement. These reading rates may be used as a baseline measure for comparison with the changes that we might expect during therapy. It is our belief that many clients make excessive demands upon their speech production systems by attempting to speak at rates that exceed their ability to fluently coordinate their speech production systems. With objective information relative to the client's speaking or reading rates, during therapy we are able to discuss possible speaking rate modifications that can be made.

Starkweather (1987) discusses the concept of information flow and its relationship to speaking rates. Starkweather presented a passage that begins, "What I mean, what I mean is, that, uh, when you, you, go to the, uh, store because, uh, you, you want some. . . ." Starkweather goes on to state: "Words flow in this passage. Sound is continuously produced. What is not flowing is information" (p. 19) By examining Starkweather's example, we see that we can easily calculate the speaker's rate of speech. However, the client's ability to transfer information is impaired as a result of the disfluent nature of his or her speech. By examining information flow, we are able to make some determination beyond the number of syllables per minute as to how effective the client is at communicating. The number of syllables produced will be affected by the frequency, duration, and type of stuttering as well as the frequency and type of between-word disfluencies. When analyzing a client's conversation sample, we need to not only examine the client's ability to produce a given number of syllables per minute but also examine the nature of the client's ability to transfer information.

Consistency and Loci of Stuttering

Consistency of stuttering has been described as the tendency to stutter on the same words during repeated readings or repetitions of the same material. The adult clients are asked to read a paragraph five times in succession (e.g., The Rainbow Passage, Fairbanks, 1960) while children are asked to repeat or read a series of sentences (Neely & Timmons, 1967). During each of the readings, the clinician identifies every stuttering. The procedures for calculating consistency are best explained in tabular form and appear in Appendix A. When we identify a client who is consistent when stuttering, we agree with Johnson who suggested "that stuttering does not occur haphazardly or in a random or chance fashion but as a response to identifiable stimuli." (Bloodstein, 1995, p. 278).

When we determine that a client is consistent during the reading or repetition task, we try to determine the loci of those stuttered words. When the location of these words is identified, we then attempt to determine the attributes or characteristics of the consistently stuttered words. Loci has been explained in a number of ways. Brown (1945) identified four attributes of consistently stuttered words (phonetic factor, grammatical factor, word length, word position) while Quarrington (1965) suggested that the position of a word in a sentence and the predictability (information load) of a word accounted for the consistency of stuttering. We try, during our evaluation, to identify consistently stuttered words and to examine their attributes from a speech production perspective. We believe that by examining the manner in which a person stutters, we are able to develop a therapeutic strategy to deal with these consistently stuttered words. Our experience suggests that clients often develop sound or word fears that often translate into stuttering on the same sound or word. In addition, some clients develop inappropriate physiological strategies by which they begin to initiate words too quickly, start a word with too much physical tension, or begin to produce a sound or word and have difficulty moving to the next sound or word. When we can identify a speech production strategy that results in stuttering, we make note of these concerns and use these results when planning a therapy program.

Diadochokinetic Speaking Rates

To assess diadochokinetic speech rates, we model a series of monosyllabic (p ∧ , t ∧, k ∧), bisyllabic (p ∧ t ∧), and trisyllabic (p ∧ t ∧ k ∧) combinations (Fletcher, 1972) and ask the client to repeat these sounds as quickly as possible. Hall (1994) provides an excellent description of diadochokinetic speaking rates; "The purpose is to assess how consistently, accurately, and rapidly the patient is able to make the repeated movements. Diadochokinetic tasks place "stress" on the speech mechanism, because we rarely (if ever) use our most rapid possible rate of speech. But when the maximal movement or speech rate is attempted, you have the opportunity to observe how well the entire mechanism works as a whole and to assess how well the individual articulators function in the task" (p. 70)

The clients produce 20 repetitions of the monosyllables, 15 repetitions of the bisyllables, and 10 repetitions of the trisyllables. The clinician uses a digital stop watch to determine the client's speed of production. The results produced by the client can be compared to the norms provided by Fletcher (1972), although these norms do not extend below 5 years of age or beyond 17 years of age. In our opinion, the manner in which the client responds during this task is often more revealing and possesses greater clinical applicability than the comparison of age norms. It is difficult for us to suggest a chronological age by which the clinician can reliably assess diadochokinetic speech rates because the maturity level of the child and the child's ability to cooperate will affect the outcome. We have completed this task with children 3 years of age and have been unable to get 6-year-old children to cooperate. We are more concerned with our observations of the child's responses than obtaining an exact time for a specific production.

A typical response pattern for a child who stutters reveals that at the monosyllabic level, this child is often able to follow our model and complete the task with little difficulty. When we complete the bisyllabic task, we often observe some increased difficulty with initiating the first sound and occasionally with the fluent sequencing of sounds. When we ask these children to rapidly produce trisyllables, we often note the production of stuttering during the task, increased difficulty initiating sound sequences, and reversal of sound order (e.g., p $\wedge$ k $\wedge$ t $\wedge$). We interpret these problems to reflect the difficulties that the child experiences when attempting to maintain adult-like speaking rates outside of the therapy room. We believe that when the child is faced with a demand for faster speech, the child attempts to match the faster speaking rate but his or her speech production mechanism is unable to meet the demand. As a result, stuttering and coordination problems result. It is important to recognize that the previously described scenario may be observed in totality for one child but to a lesser degree with another child. For some children who stutter, these diadochokinetic tasks do not appear to cause any problem at all.

VTC: 00:06:53:08
00:09:37:00

Articulation and Language Skills

We approach the evaluation with the idea that we are evaluating the total client. This perspective enables us to examine the client's stuttering relative to other speech and language concerns as well as environmental and emotional influences. With children, we recognize that our evaluation time is limited and that the major focus of the evaluation needs to be on the child's stuttering. However, we do attempt to examine the child's articulatory skills using a speech sound inventory (e.g., *Structured Photographic Articulation Test Featuring Dudsberry, SPAT-D*) and compare these findings to the child's articulation during conversation. When a child exhibits articulatory problems, we note the nature of the problem and further determine whether a phonological analysis needs to be completed as part of the child's evaluation. Additional testing is often scheduled at a later date because we may not be able to complete all of our speech and language testing on the same day.

For younger children, we may screen language development by assessing the child's receptive vocabulary using the *Peabody Picture Vocabulary Test* (Dunn & Dunn, 1997) expressive language using the Mean Length of Utterance (Brown, 1973), and on some occasions, assess both receptive and expressive language using the *Preschool Language Scale* (Zimmerman, Steiner, & Pond, 1992). If the results of our testing lead us to suspect that a child has language concerns, we often schedule a second day of testing.

When dealing with older children and adults, we typically determine speech and language skills during our conversational interactions with the client. On those rare occasions when a speech or language concern is detected, we schedule a second appointment to investigate the nature of the client's additional problems and its potential impact on the client's stuttering.

Summary

With the information that we obtain by examining the client's speech abilities, we are able to determine whether the client is stuttering, the characteristics of the client's stuttering, and any other potential speech and language problems. However, because stuttering is multidimensional and influenced by both the environment and the client's awareness of and reactions to speech and the environment, we continue the evaluation by examining the contribution of the environment toward the development of stuttering.

Communicative Environment

Our evaluation of both children and adults includes a focus on the communicative environment in which the client must function. We believe that the communicative environment has the potential to contribute to the development of stuttering in young children and to the maintenance of stuttering for both children and adults. Our best information can be obtained by interviewing the parents, older children, adolescents, and adult clients and also by observing parent–child interactions. In the next section, we will discuss the clinician–parent interview and the clinician–client interview. Our focus with young children is to determine the nature of stuttering onset and subsequent stuttering development. For the older client, our focus is directed toward the relationship between the client and his or her communicative environment.

General Interview Information

We begin our discussion of the interview process by referring back to the section that deals with case history information. Our interview is generally structured along the same lines as the general headings of the case history form. These include history of the speech problem, speech and language development, medical history, general development and daily behavior, and academic and social history. In the case of the adult client, we obtain information on the aforementioned factors but tend to spend the greatest amount of time discussing the client's emotional perspectives associated with stuttering and his or her reactions to these concerns.

When interviewing parents or adult clients, our initial focus is directed toward the onset, development, and present status of the client's stuttering. When evaluating young children, the information obtained in response to our questions will be crucial to our decisions on the presence of a problem, the continued development of the problem, and the need for immediate enrollment in therapy. On the other hand, developmental history and age at onset with older children, adolescents, and adult clients plays a much lesser role in clinical management. With these clients we obtain information about the development of their stuttering and the possible effects of stuttering on social, academic, and work-related activities.

We will begin by focusing on the parent interview and the information that we believe is important to obtain relative to the client's stuttering development and the client's interaction with his or her communicative environment. A second section will follow that focuses on the adult client and information to obtain during an adult interview. To assist the reader, we have included a list of questions relative to stuttering and stuttering development in Appendix B.

Parent Interview

The goal of the parent interview is to obtain all of the relevant information associated with the child's stuttering to help determine the presence of a problem and the type of management required. To begin, we ask the parents a general question, "Why are you here today?" The information provided has the potential to reveal the parent's perceptions of the problem (e.g., "We're here because our son stutters and we just don't know why this is happening to him.") as well as to provide information about other therapy programs attended (e.g., "I'm here because her other speech pathologist was unable to help her stuttering."). Parents also may reveal that they are attending the evaluation because other family members encouraged the evaluation but the parents don't understand the importance.

When interviewing parents of preschoolers, we remind ourselves that the information we obtain will assist in our decision as to whether the child might grow out of the problem or continue to stutter. As a result, our initial questions are targeted toward the onset and development of stuttering. Our initial questions include the following: (1) When did the problem begin? (2) How has the problem changed since the onset? (3) Is there a family history of stuttering? The responses to these questions open a number of doors for additional questions and help us to formulate a management plan for the child. When obtaining this same information for the older child, adolescent, and adult, we recognize that the information is important but not to the same degree as the child, who has the potential to spontaneously recover from the problem. Our parent interview continues with questions on the types of disfluencies exhibited by the child, the parent's perceptions of the child's stuttering, and the child's reactions to the stuttering. As we noted, our interview is structured to follow a general pattern, from stuttering development to speech and language development to the medical, social, and academic history. However, interviews rarely follow in as orderly a manner as this text would lead you to believe. We often view a clinician who brings a list of 100 questions to the interview. The clinician is prepared to follow the script of questions to obtain as much information as possible. At times, a parent may respond to question number 3 and include information related to question number 27. A clinician needs to be skilled enough to note this information and then determine whether to follow the sequential list of questions or deviate to obtain information that may or may not be available again. An illustration may help to clarify this issue.

Technique—Interviewing Parents

We ask Mr. and Mrs. Brown to describe when their son Matthew began to
stutter. Our goal is to determine when Matt began to stutter and how his
problem has changed over time. Mrs. Brown responds: "Matthew began
stuttering when he was 3 years of age. We were living in Texas at the time
and had a bilingual nanny for Matt. I think his stuttering began during the
summer." We have a number of options to follow regarding this interview.
The first option is to follow the line of questioning so that we obtain
information that we believe to be important relative to stuttering onset
and development. However, the mother has revealed an important piece
of information regarding a bilingual nanny who interacted with Matt at
the time. The clinician has to be flexible enough to either change the
direction of the conversation to determine the potential impact of the
bilingual communicative environment on Matt's speech, or retain that
information for later questioning. Because this information was provided,
we believe that the clinician needs to take advantage of this situation. We
are comfortable detouring away from our line of questions to inquire
about the potential impact of a bilingual caregiver, recognizing that we
need to eventually return to our original line of questions. Our point in
this example is to not highlight our opinion of bilingualism and stuttering. Rather, we want to encourage clinicians to remain flexible during the
interview and open to the sharing of unexpected information. We have
found that as clinicians gain skills at interviewing, they are less likely to
rely on a list of questions and are more likely to be open to sharing information with parents and clients.

VTC: 00:14:51:19

As we obtain relevant information about the child's stuttering, we transition to questions about the child's speech and language development. Our
goal is to evaluate the total child rather than "the stuttering child." It is
important to understand the stuttering in the context of the child's speech
and language development, medical history, and motor, academic, and social
development. We attempt to determine whether any aspect of the child's
development has been influenced by the child's stuttering or whether some
aspect of development has impacted the child's stuttering. Of course, we
continue to bear in mind that the information obtained is the parents' perception of the problem.

In the section to follow, we discuss the parent interview with specific attention focused on speech and language development, medical history, general development, academic and social development. In each of the sections, we discuss some questions that attempt to relate the client's stuttering to the heading provided.

Speech and Language Development. Our questions regarding speech and language development typically evolve from the discussion on the client's history of stuttering. We question parents regarding their child's comprehension, his or her first words, and the general course of the child's speech and language development. Our questions might include: "Does your child have any problem with speech sounds?" and "Does your child seem to understand everything that you ask?" When a parent states that his or her child has a co-occuring problem (e.g., multiple sound errors) we need to examine in depth the nature of the child's problem and the parent's associated concerns. When questioning parents regarding other speech and language disorders, we are looking for potential interactions between stuttering and phonology or stuttering and language comprehension or expression. When we obtain this information, we will be better prepared to provide management suggestions that deal with all of the client's communicative problems.

Medical History. The clinician questions the parents regarding their child's medical history. We remember that the case history form is sent to the parents so that the evaluation can be efficiently completed. By examining the case history form before the evaluation, the clinician can note the presence of any potential areas that need further investigation. For example, a parent may report a difficult labor and delivery without providing additional information. The clinician recognizes that a difficult labor and delivery may have little impact on the infant or it might result in some neurological problems. As a result, a parental report of difficult labor and delivery warrants further investigation. In a similar manner, any medical condition that has the potential to impact speech and language development requires further investigation. This might include high prolonged fevers, hospitalizations, or frequent middle ear infections that may delay speech and language development. On the other hand, we often examine a case history form that reveals nothing remarkable. In this case, we might ask the parents if there is something in their child's medical history of which we need to be aware. In many of these cases, the parents state that their child is in good health with no known medical problems, and we then move on to another line of questions.

General Development. The clinician obtains information about the child's major motor milestones (e.g., sitting up, walking) and activities of daily living (e.g., toileting, feeding). The clinician will compare the development of the child in question to the normative data for a child of similar chronological age. For those children who are delayed in some aspect of their development, we might encounter a child who attends physical and/or occupational therapy or is just slow to develop at this time in their life. The clinician's goal is to determine how the child's general development has impacted the development of the child's stuttering.

Academic and Social Development. Questions in this area are focused on the child's attendance in preschool or kindergarten programs and the child's ability to interact with other children. Our general focus is aimed toward the child's ability to be successful in school and to develop friendships and social relationships. A more specific focus is aimed toward the potential impact of the child's stuttering on academic and school behavior.

When asking these questions about preschoolers and kindergarten children, we are attempting to determine whether the child's peers are reacting to the stuttering and what the child's reactions are in turn. When a child's peers are observing and reacting to his or her stuttering, the situation has the potential to cause the child to react in a manner that ultimately results in increased stuttering and increased avoidance of speaking. We ask parents whether their child is aware of the stuttering. When a parent indicates that his or her child is aware, we ask the parent to describe how they know this. For a number of young children, the parents might describe their child's look of frustration or the occasional comment from the child who states "I can't say that" and walks away in mid-sentence. When parents of a young child describe these looks of frustration and the child's reactions to stuttering, we see this as an additional sign of stuttering development and one good indicator for enrollment in therapy.

Parents of older children and adolescents also share negative experiences related to their child's speaking. Parents have related their child's reluctance to read out loud in class and answer questions when called upon. Sometimes, parents report that their child will provide an incorrect answer in class because the correct answer was too difficult to say. Many of these parents are extremely concerned by the reactions received by their child and their child's subsequent reactions to talking. In addition, the parents express a lot of frustration with their inability to help their child.

Our experience with older children and adolescents suggests that we not only obtain information from the parents on their child's academic and social experiences, but also need to gain the perspectives of the clients themselves about their stuttering, their peers, and their school environment. On many occasions, clients are willing to share information with us that they do not make available to their parents. The comparison of the two perspectives is often enlightening. At times, the parents' perspective coincides with their child's perspective but at other times, we receive very disparate views. The clinician needs to learn to sift through the information and use this information when attempting to develop a management plan.

Observing Parent–Child Interaction

To maintain consistency in our discussion of younger children who stutter, we have chosen to include the discussion of observing parent-child interactions at this time, prior to our discussion of the adult interview. With younger children who stutter, the communicative models provided by the parents appear to be more influential in the continued development of stuttering from parental communicative models used with older children and adolescents. As a result, we focus a portion of our evaluation on the interactions between parent and child.

Our goal for observing parent-child interactions is similar to our goal for the parent interview. We are attempting to examine the child's communicative environment and to determine the possible influences of the environment upon the child's speech development. When examining the parent and child interacting, our purpose is not to point a finger at parents and hold them responsible for their child's problem. As primary communicative models for their children, parents provide environments that have the potential to influence their child's speech development. For stuttering, we examine those interactions that we believe place time or linguistic demands upon the child. While making these observations, we not only examine the parents communicative interactions with the child but also examine the child's reactions to the parents. We recognize that every child brings a unique temperament and set of personality characteristics to the situation. Our job is focused on documenting the characteristics of the parental interaction and describing the child's responses. In this section, we will discuss some typical communicative characteristics of parents, and in a later section, we will discuss the child's responses.

We emphasize that we do not believe that parents cause stuttering in children. As we have indicated previously, we believe that some children are born with a predisposition to stutter and their communicative environment can contribute to further development of the problem. By observing parent/child interactions, we can identify those communicative behaviors that have the potential to influence a child and provide the parents with management suggestions for changing their behavior. During our observation we obtain a conversational sample of the child's speech and use this sample to measure the characteristics of stuttering (e.g., frequency of occurrence, most frequently occurring disfluency type). The results of these measurements can be compared with conversational samples taken during clinician/client interactions and similarities and differences can be noted. In addition, we try to examine the parents' speaking rate and turn-switching pauses (the time from the termination of a child's utterance to the onset of the parent's response) during interactions with their children (Zebrowski, 1994b). For some children we find that as the child attempts to maintain adult speaking rates, this time demand increases the child's likelihood of producing stuttering. The faster speaking rate appears to result in difficulty maintaining speech fluency. For turn-switching pauses, in some families the listener often begins to talk before the speaker has concluded. With normally fluent speakers, this shortened time between speakers may cause some annoyance but does not appear to disrupt speech. With some young children who stutter, the shortened response time appears to create a sense of urgency to initiate speech in a fast manner. The child responds in a hurried manner and these rapid initiations may make it more difficult for the child to maintain fluent speech. During our observation of parent/child interactions, we attempt to examine those parental responses that may increase the time demands on the child. In addition to increased time demands, we also look at the type of questions that parents are asking, the manner in which questions are asked, and the vocabulary used during the interaction. At times we observe parental expectations for more adult-like speech and language development despite the fact that we are often observing preschool and kindergarten children. Parental expectations for speech and language may exceed the child's abilities at the present time. The parents' behaviors often result from a desire for their child to succeed. Rarely are parental behaviors associated with any malicious thoughts by parents. However, the speech-language pathologist needs to assess the parent/child interaction from the perspective of the child who is stuttering. Despite the fact the other children in the family may not have been affected by the parents' fast rate of speech or expectations for adult-like language, the child in question may be more sensitive to these time and linguistic demands.

Our observations of parental behaviors also include verbal and nonverbal reactions to the child's stuttering. Because of our belief that stuttering is a multidimensional problem, examining the parents' behavioral reactions to their child's stuttering enable us to view the child's responses to the parents responses. Parents are often unaware of their reactions to their child's stuttering. Some of the more typical responses include filling in words for the child or talking before the child is finished (turn switching pause). However, we have also observed parents holding their breath, holding a rigid body position, and staring at their child in response to stuttering. We recognize that these behaviors do not cause stuttering and, unlike Johnson and associates (1956), we don't believe that stuttering onset occurs because of the parents' behavior. However, if we note that a child appears to be reacting to a parent's reactions, we will talk with the parents about their reactions (many parents are oblivious to their reactions until the clinician calls attention to the behavior) and plan some management strategies to assist the parents.

We find that the parent-child interaction can be extremely valuable for planning a therapy program for young children who stutter. We are able to examine the characteristics of the child's stuttering with familiar listeners while at the same time we can observe the communicative characteristics of the parents' speech when they interact with their child who stutters. Finally, we can also observe the child's awareness and reactions to his or her parents so that information obtained during this part of the evaluation can used to develop a management program for the child.

Adolescent and Adult Client Interview

The focus of the section to follow is an exploration of the interview with the adolescent and adult client. We believe that some of the questions used during this interview also can be used when interviewing older children.

Motivation and Purpose

We begin our interview by discussing the client's motivation for attending therapy. Our first questions often include: "Tell me why you're here today." and "Why have you decided at this time to seek help for your speech?". Our clinical experiences have included clients who believe that their careers have been halted because of their speech and clients who have had a number of bad therapy experiences and are looking for a better therapy experience. It is our belief that the clients who will be most successful are those who attend therapy with a specific goal in mind. On occasion we encounter clients who move from therapy program to therapy program until they find a clinician who tells them what they want to hear. In most cases we try to discourage this type of client from attending our therapy program because we believe we will reach a point in therapy at which our answers are insufficient and the client will terminate therapy and move on to another program.

In most situations, adult clients are attending therapy for a specific reason. These reasons include being able to ask questions in class or believing a promotion at work would be available if there was greater fluency. With adult clients, we have adopted the philosophy proposed by Neilson and Andrews (1993) when describing the criteria for enrollment in intensive therapy: "The client must evidence strong personal motivation to achieve fluency. There is little prospect of lasting gain for those who undertake the program principally to please their family, their employer, or a lover" (p. 145).

Fluency and Stuttering

Our primary interview focus with the adolescent or adult client is to determine the relationship between the client's stuttering and his or her daily activities. We recognize that any situation in which the client has to communicate has the potential to be related to stuttering. However, we also recognize from years of clinical experience that environmental influences affect every client in a different way. It's not the environmental situation that causes a problem, it's the manner in which the client reacts and responds to the environment that ultimately affects the client's stuttering. We will discuss the client's awareness and reactions at length in a later section.

With adolescent and adult clients, we ask the client to provide information relative to his or her family history of stuttering and the history of their own stuttering development. With these clients we know that the chance of spontaneous recovery is long past; however, the client can provide their perceptions relative to their stuttering development. These perceptions can ultimately be valuable when providing therapy with a client. For example, an adult client may relate some family history as passed down from mother to son. The client's mother may have explained that the client's stuttering began when his pet dog ran away from home when the client was 4 years of age. The client may have believed this story for 21 years because he had no reason to question its validity. Additionally, the client's mother may continue to manifest some guilt because she was responsible for the dog running away. We will need to educate this client about the onset and development of stuttering and make the client aware that his mother is not responsible for his stuttering. While this preceding scenario may sound far-fetched, we continue to be amazed at the amount of misinformation that exists on the development of stuttering.

We continue our questioning of clients by obtaining information on their previous past stuttering therapy. With adult clients, the information provided often sheds some light on the client's perspectives on therapy and the client's potential for success in therapy. We may encounter a client who has attended a number of therapy programs only to leave when the work was too demanding or when the client did not agree with the clinician. On the other hand, we are amazed to meet adults who have well-developed stuttering problems and have never been identified as having a problem and have never attended a therapy program. Questions about stuttering history are extremely valuable for planning therapy with the adolescent and adult client.

On rare occasions, we encounter adult clients who exhibit no stutterings during the evaluation. This period of fluency may result because the client only stutters during specific situations or the client is very good at avoiding words, substituting words and revising thoughts. For some clinicians, this absence of stuttering would result in the observation, "I don't think you have a problem because you're not stuttering." From our perspective, we have emphasized to the reader that our belief is that stuttering is multidimensional and includes more than a focus on the client's stuttering or fluency. This client may reveal that despite a lack of stuttering during the evaluation, there are specific times during the day or situations in which he/she must communicate that results in stuttering. Additionally, some clients will report that they anticipate stuttering on words and have learned a variety of avoidance techniques to remain fluent. These clients often report that they are tired of all of the mental activities that are required for avoiding and revising and would like to deal with their problem. We believe the client. The client would not go to the time and effort of seeking an evaluation unless he or she believed that a problem existed. As we do with any adult client, we explore the perceptions of his or her communicative environment and its relationship to his or her speech. It is also important to discuss the client's emotional and behavioral reactions during these situations so that an effective management program can be developed. During the evaluation of a school teacher, we noted no stuttering during the entire evaluation. The client explained how she stuttered when lecturing to her classes and very often avoided words, substituted words and revised her lecture as a reaction to her stuttering. We continued our evaluation of this client and subsequently enrolled her in a therapy program that was designed to meet her specific needs.

VTC: 00:14:51:19

Medical History

Obtaining a medical history for the adolescent or adult client is an attempt to rule out conditions that may result in disfluent speech other than stuttering. Some examples include a history of alcoholism, substance abuse, neurological damage, and psychological problems. In the event that the client has a past history of problems that might be associated with disfluent speech, the clinician will need to explore this situation. When a client has no such history, the clinician should attempt to determine the client's past medical history and present health status and relate this information to the potential impact on the client's present day stuttering. Additionally, the clinician may inquire about the client's use of prescription and nonprescription drugs because these may have an impact on the client's speech skills and emotional well-being.

Client's Expectations

We continue our interview by exploring the client's expectations for therapy and the type of results the client expects from therapy. We attempt to determine if the client's perception of the therapy process and the goals set are realistic. Within the university clinic we have, numerous times, encountered seniors in their last semester of school who have arrived at the realization that they are graduating in a few months, will have to complete a number of job interviews, and free speech therapy is available at the university speech and hearing clinic. For these clients, we are able to complete the evaluation and provide some basic information about the nature of therapy. We also explain that we cannot provide an effective treatment program given the amount of time they have allotted for therapy. We discuss a number of options with these clients but try to be realistic with them about a course for therapy. Of course, we suggest that stuttering therapy can be provided at the university clinic when they graduate. We often encounter other adult clients with unreal expectations of therapy. Many adults are used to a medical model of treatment that typically involves the client's identification of a problem, an evaluation by a physician, and a subsequent prescription to deal with the client's problem or alleviation of symptoms. For adults who believe that therapy will be a 2-week or even 2-month process, we need to spend a lot of time explaining the amount of effort and time that is required to change their speech and associated attitudes.

On the other hand, many clients are more realistic in their therapy expectations. These clients have no preconceived ideas about the time or work required. When these clients are presented with facts, they are usually agreeable and willing to begin therapy. We find that by obtaining information relative to the client's history of the problem and perceptions of stuttering, we can better plan a management program that includes a focus on both the client's speech and the attitudes associated with his or her speech.

Summary
In summary, our primary focus when interviewing an adult is to determine the relationship between stuttering and the daily environment. Information is obtained to help in the identification of a client's stuttering, to determine the client's perceptions of the problem, and to determine the potential environmental influences on the client's speech. In the section to follow, we will examine the client's reactions to his or her stuttering and the environment.

Behavioral Reactions, Cognitive Awareness, and Reactions to Stuttering and the Environment

Behavioral Reactions
To understand the problem of stuttering, it is not sufficient to only focus on stuttering and the environment without also examining the client's reactions and awareness of stuttering and the environment in which he or she must communicate must also be examined. We will begin our discussion by focusing on those behaviors produced in association with stuttering. Zebrowski (1994b) stated that "Associated behaviors are thought to reflect a child's awareness at some level that he is doing something 'different' when he stutters." Schwartz and Conture (1988) suggested that associated behaviors (e.g., head turns, eye opening and closing) reflect a client's attempts to cope or adapt to stuttering. It has also been suggested that the greater number and variety of associated behaviors produced reflects a more developed (Schwartz and Conture, 1988) or more severe (Riley, 1980) problem. More recently, Conture and Kelly (1991) reported that two associated behaviors, eyelid blinking and eyeball movement to the side, are produced more often by children who stutter when compared to normally fluent children. As a result, the speech-language pathologist might use the occurrence of these associated behaviors as possible prognostic indicators for continued development of stuttering. A number of investigators (Schwartz, Zebrowski, & Conture, 1990; Yairi, Ambrose, & Nierman, 1993) have reported that children close to stuttering onset produce behaviors in association with their stuttering. It has been suggested these behaviors indicate that right from stuttering onset, children appear to be aware that they are stuttering and start to react behaviorally to their stuttering. For some children these

associated behaviors increase and vary as the problem develops. Although more research will be needed to understand the occurrence of associated behaviors, we do have some initial information to assist in our decisions to enroll a child in therapy.

For older children, adolescents, and adults who stutter, associated behaviors also are viewed as behavioral reactions to stuttering. These behaviors often add to the complexity of the client's problem by making the client's stuttering appear more severe or more developed. To the casual viewer, associated behaviors often get the listener's attention before the listener is aware that the person has a stuttering problem. When questioning older children, adolescents, and adults who stutter, it is important for the clinician to determine the client's awareness and perceptions of these associated behaviors. For some adults, associated behaviors contribute to their negative feelings about communicating because they believe that these behaviors call attention to their problem and set them apart from other speakers. However, a large number of adults who stutter appear to be oblivious to the production of associated behaviors and have not developed any reactions or feelings about these behaviors. Thus, it is the clinician's responsibility to not only identify associated behaviors produced by clients but also discuss the client's perceptions and reactions to these behaviors.

In addition to the nonspeech behaviors that are often associated with stuttering, we occasionally identify a client who uses between-word disfluencies in response to stuttering. In some extreme examples, the between-word disfluencies are so pervasive that they easily mask the production of stuttering. These occurrences are best demonstrated in the example below.

The mother of an adolescent client telephoned and indicated that her son's stuttering was characterized by frequent repetitions. We scheduled an evaluation for the following week. Although we spent some time interviewing the mother, we also conducted a thorough interview with the client as we often do with adolescent clients. During the client interview it was obvious that he was producing a significant number of phrase repetitions. In fact, prior to the production of most short-duration, inaudible sound prolongations, the client would typically say "I have, I have, I have, I have, I have, I have, I have . . . to go." In the previous example, the client produced a 250-msec inaudible sound prolongation on the word /to/ but preceded the stuttering with 7 phrase repetitions. To the untrained listener, this client was producing frequent repetitions of words while to the trained speech-language pathologist, this client produced an inaudible sound prolongation preceded by 7 phrase repetitions. We interpreted the phrase repetitions as the client's attempt to anticipate stuttering and to use these phrase repetitions to help him get through the stuttering. Unfortunately for the client, the multiple phrase repetitions added to the client's disfluency. We explained to the client that these phrase repetitions often are viewed by the listener as signs of nervousness or uncertainty and even as a sign that a stuttering was upcoming. These multiple phrase repetitions occurred throughout the client's speech. While the aforementioned example is an extreme case, it is not unusual for a client to precede a stuttering with an interjection such as "um" or "uh" or a whole word such as "He was was was e-e-eating." Because these associated behaviors add to the perceived severity of the client's speech and have the potential to interfere with communication, the evaluating clinician needs to be able to identify these behaviors.

Cognitive Awareness of Stuttering— Reactions to Stuttering and the Environment

When we ask clients to tell us why they are being evaluated, we are attempting to determine clients awareness of their stuttering. For the young client, we are trying to determine whether he/she even knows what stuttering means and *how* stuttering is discussed within the child's communicative environment. For some children, the word stuttering is never mentioned at home because to mention stuttering in the child's presence is believed to make the problem worse. For other children, stuttering is a word that is not addressed in the child's presence as if the mere mention of the word will lead to a life of shame and heartache. Some children have been made more aware of their stuttering by their parents and respond "I'm here because I stutter." When questioned further by the clinician, "What does stuttering mean?", the child is unable to respond but indicates that his or her parents said that he/she stuttered. When we ask a child to tell us "Why are you here today?" we are attempting to determine a strategy for counseling both the parents and the child. We want parents to know that talking about stuttering will not make a child's problem worse. In fact, a major focus of all of our therapy is to help the client understand stuttering so that it no longer appears to be that unpredictable big black cloud that appears out of nowhere and causes speech problems.

We also question older children, adolescents, and adults about their stuttering. We try to determine whether the client is aware when he/she might stutter and why the stuttering might occur. Many clients have listened to neighbors, friends, and coworkers who have provided a variety of explanations for the occurrence of stuttering. "You're too nervous, you talk too fast, you talk too slow, you were born different, you weren't born different" and on and on. We believe that the client's perceptions of their problems can lead to beliefs that prevent a client from growing and developing. If the client believes that stuttering is a permanent condition with little chance for improvement, he/she might make a career choice based on this information. When a client has difficulty communicating on the telephone, the client develops strategies for using the telephone or avoiding the telephone. As a result, a large focus of our client interview with adults and to a lesser degree with older children and adolescents is the client's awareness of stuttering and subsequent reactions to the problem.

When we address the clients' awareness and reactions, we often ask the client to tell us how their stuttering "gets in their way." By asking a question in a general manner, the clinician can sometimes determine those people, words, or situations that stand in the forefront of the client's consciousness which result in the greatest reaction by the client. The clinician needs to remember that there is no one typical response produced by all persons who stutter. Any and all situations in which communication is required has the potential to be a concern for a person who stutters. For some clients, situations may not be a problem but the client may react to sounds or words. Words may be substituted, and sounds or words may be consciously avoided. The clinician should attempt to observe any obvious sound or word avoidance in addition to questioning the client about this issue. We also should point out that the frequency and type of stuttering produced by a person who stutters does not determine the degree to which a person reacts or avoids situations or words. We have known many adult clients whose frequency of stuttering was relatively low and whose type of stuttering did not prevent communication. However, these individuals were just as likely to avoid communicating on the telephone, speaking in a restaurant, or saying his or her name as the person with twice as many stutterings. The degree to which a person who stutters reacts to his or her stuttering appears to be related more to the characteristics of the client's personality than the characteristics of the client's stuttering. Importantly, we need to examine both characteristics and to determine the level of interaction between the client's personality and his or her stuttering.

When evaluating most adult clients, we use two questionnaires that enable us to gain additional insights into the client's views of communication and the degree to which the client understands and accepts responsibility for his or her actions. We ask each adult client to fill out the *S24 Modified Erickson Scale* of communication attitudes (Andrews & Cutler,

1974) (Appendix C) and the *Locus of Control of Behavior Scale* (Craig, Franklin, & Andrews, 1984) (Appendix D). The results of the S24 scale provide the examiner with information on the clients' attitudes toward communicating. Results of this measure can be compared to results for clients who were beginning therapy, completing therapy, and fluent adults. As will be noted in Chapter 7 exploring the adult intensive fluency therapy program, positive changes in communication attitudes are seen as one prognostic indicator for continued therapy success (Andrews & Craig, 1988). In a similar manner, the Locus of Control of Behavior Scale provides the examiner with some insight into the clients' beliefs in their ability to control their behavior and environment. Positive changes in this measure also are viewed as a prognostic indicator for continued therapy success. It is important to note that questionnaires are administered for two purposes. The paper and pencil task itself provides information that is comparable to other groups of individuals who have also taken this measure. Second, we can examine the responses to individual test questions so that we can direct our questioning during our interview, to explore in depth the nature of the client's concerns for communicating at work, at school or in social situations. When a client's results suggest that he or she is extremely negative about communicating, we try to compare these results with our finding from the client interview. If the client is truthful, his or her responses to our questions will be consistent with the attitudes reflected on the S24 scale. When the results are inconsistent, we have to determine whether the client was providing us with information that he or she wanted us to believe or whether the client exhibits inconsistent attitudes about communicating. Similarly, the Locus of Control of Behavior Scale provides the clinician with information relative to whether the client believes that life events are within the client's control or out of the client's control. Depending upon the clients' responses, additional information can be obtained through questioning. Subsequent therapy can be directed toward teaching the client to adapt a greater sense of responsibility for his or her actions.

Summary
In the preceding section, we described a number of methods for determining a client's awareness and reactions to stuttering and the communicative environments. Results of questionnaires can be used to help the clinician to further investigate the client's concerns during the interview, while results of the interview and questionnaires can be used to plan a therapy program for the client.

Making Sense of the Results—Young Children

When we complete our evaluation of young children, our goal is to determine whether these children exhibit stuttering, whether they grow out of their problem, and whether they require therapy. As we have noted previously, when a child is exhibiting 3 or more stutterings per 100 syllables of conversational speech, we believe that the child is stuttering. To determine whether the child will grow out of his or her stuttering, we examine the time from the onset of the problem and generally use one year post onset as a guideline for determining if a child will spontaneously recover. As the young child gets further away from the onset of stuttering and does not demonstrate positive changes toward fluency (i.e., decreased frequency of stuttering), the likelihood of spontaneous recovery occurring decreases significantly. Another important consideration is the family history of stuttering and the recovery of family members from stuttering. For the child who has a family history of stuttering and relatives who continue to stutter, therapy is more likely to be recommended than for the child with no family history. Two additional factors to be considered in the continued development of stuttering include the contribution of the child's communicative environment towards stuttering development and the child's awareness and reactions to speech and the environment. The more factors that we can identify as potential contributors toward stuttering development, the more likely we are to suggest enrollment in therapy.

Making Sense of the Results—Older Children, Adolescents, and Adults

As with younger children, our initial goal is focused on determining whether these clients exhibit at least 3 stutterings per 100 syllables of conversational speech. In the majority of cases, these clients have been identified by parents, other clinicians, or themselves as already having a problem, and our results are used to confirm or refute the initial diagnosis. Because stuttering is seen as a multidimensional problem, it is imperative for the clinician to not only examine the results as they relate to frequency and type of stuttering. The clinician also needs to examine the nature of the client's communicative environment and determine how this environment impacts both the client's stuttering and the client's ability to complete daily activities. As a result, the case history information and interview results provide information that will be an important component of the therapy process. Additionally, by exploring the client's communicative environment, the clinician can also examine the client's awareness and reactions to both his or her speech and the environment in which he/she must function. Therapy programs for older children, adolescents and adults will need to address both the client's speech and their attitudes and reactions associated with stuttering.

SUMMARY

Within this chapter, we have addressed the evaluation of stuttering from a multidimensional perspective. Although some clinicians have reduced their evaluation procedures to a measurement of frequency of occurrence, we believe that an evaluation of stuttering must consider the speech abilities of the client, the client's communicative environment and its interaction with the client and finally, and the client's awareness of, and reactions to, his or her speech and the environment. When a clinician uses this multidimensional focus to evaluate stuttering, the clinician will be able to develop a management plan that has the greatest potential for long-lasting changes in fluency and changes in associated attitudes and beliefs. It is our belief that this comprehensive approach to the problem provides the client with the most potential for success.

▶ 3

Fundamental Therapy Procedures for All Clients: Speech Modification

In the following chapter, we will provide a description of the speech skills that we teach to enable a client to improve his or her fluency. We believe that these basic skills transcend age groups and can be included in this introductory chapter to stuttering therapy. In subsequent chapters, the skills that have been presented in Chapter 3 will be reintroduced, discussed, for clients of differing ages and stages of stuttering development. The concepts remain the same even though their applications change.

PHILOSOPHY

We believe that the majority of children and adults who attend stuttering therapy want to learn to be more fluent. These individuals are very interested in learning methods for changing their speech in order to gain control over behaviors that appear to be random and unpredictable. Stuttering is not a randomly occurring event. We try to teach our clients that by understanding how they stutter and the behaviors that lead to stuttering, they can gain a greater sense of control over their speech. An increased sense of control adds to clients' feelings of confidence, which ultimately assists in fluent speech production. When an individual gains additional insights into the problem and understands that speech can be controlled, the ability to control speech becomes an important component of the therapy process. We should note that clients' abilities to make progress in therapy relate in part to their ability to (1) understand the requirements of speech and attitude change and (2) consistently return to therapy and resume at the point where the previous session was terminated. Those clients who lack the cognitive skills to understand the requirements of therapy and those clients who inconsistently attend therapy often have difficulty with our type of therapy program.

Stuttering therapy requires that the client changes in two ways to establish, transfer, and maintain fluency. These two changes include (1) changes in speech production where the client learns to replace older, bad habits with new methods of communicating and (2) changes in attitudes and perceptions about stuttering so that the client understands that he or she is responsible for his or her own behavior. Taking responsibility for speech change has been identified as one important predictive factor for determining a client's ability to continue to use his or her fluency skills 1 and 2 years after the completion of therapy (Craig & Andrews, 1985; Craig, Franklin, & Andrews, 1984). Within the therapy room we teach clients to change their speech and counsel them on these changes. As the client begins to demonstrate changes in speech and attitude within the therapy room, activities are assigned to assist in the transfer of fluency outside of the therapy room.

BASIC SPEECH MODIFICATION PROCEDURES

Conture (1990) stated that time and tension are the two elements of speech production that need to be changed to become more fluent. When we examine the myriad suggested stuttering programs, we note that the majority of these programs contain elements of either time modification, tension modification, or a combination of time and tension. Examples of individual programs that focus on time modifications include metronome conditioned speech retraining (Brady, 1971), speech changes associated with delayed auditory feedback (Goldiamond, 1965), gradual initiation of phonation (Webster, 1980), and the smooth speech techniques of Neilson and Andrews (1993). Modifications of tension include "pull-outs, preparatory sets, and light articulatory contacts" (Van Riper, 1973), Conture's (1990) directions for changing physical tension levels, and Williams (1971) suggestions for "holding back" and "moving forward." As a result, the clinician must decide on a focus for therapy.

In the sections that follow, we will discuss our therapy program with its emphasis on both time and tension modification. Upon initial inspection, our program may be viewed as a fluency shaping program because our initial focus in therapy is directed toward teaching the client to become more fluent. However, unlike some programs that ignore or minimize the emotional perspectives associated with stuttering and the communicative environment, we place a great deal of emphasis on the client's emotions and emotional reactions associated with stuttering. We believe that we have taken the best information from fluency shaping programs, combined this information with the best information from stuttering modification programs, and developed a comprehensive therapy model that can be adapted to meet the needs of most clients. When clients complete our therapy program, they exhibit improved speech fluency and more positive attitudes and beliefs about speech. When these changes occur, we believe the client has the best chance for long lasting fluency. Read on.

DAY ONE IN THERAPY

All of our clients are first taught the anatomy and physiology of speech production. Although some clinicians may argue that knowledge of speech production is not a prerequisite for becoming fluent, we believe that the informed, knowledgeable client is the client who is most successful in therapy. In the following description, we provide one possible method for explaining speech production to an older client. In subsequent chapters of this book, we will provide modifications to the descriptions in this chapter so that the reader will see the potential applications of this general chapter to specific groups of persons who stutter.

In addition to understanding how speech is produced, it is also important for the clients to understand the different types of disfluencies that they produce. We discuss the different types of disfluency with our clients (see Chapter 1), including both stuttered and normal disfluency. We explain to our clients that although the early stages of therapy will focus on establishing speech fluency, understanding different types of stuttering and knowing the manner in which stuttering interferes with their ability to remain fluent will help them to better understand the relationship between fluent speech and their speech production mechanism. We explain to the clients that when they fail to use their fluency skills they may produce a stuttering. Understanding the speech production mechanism and the manner in which they stuttered will help them to redirect their attention toward methods for modifying their speech.

Technique—Speech Production Mechanism

The speech production mechanism can be divided into three separate systems. These systems include the respiratory system or the breathing system, the laryngeal system for making sound and the articulatory system for shaping the sound into speech. In Figure 3–1 you can see that we highlighted the lungs, the area in the neck called the larynx or voice box, and the lips, tongue, teeth, and jaw, which make up the articulatory system. In order to produce speech, you first take in some air and your lungs fill up. In order to use that air for speech, you have to close your vocal folds to make some sounds or leave your vocal cords open for other sounds. Now, the way in which you close your vocal cords can affect whether you stutter. One goal of our program is to teach you to produce speech in a gradual manner so that you are less likely to have problems. Our experience has shown that clients often have difficulty when they attempt to begin speaking in a rapid manner. By starting in a gradual manner, you can assist the speech process by enabling your speech muscles to work smoothly, not lock up and move on to the next sound. Once you get your vocal folds opening and closing in a smooth manner and vibrating, the air moves through the vocal tract and gets shaped by your lips, teeth, tongue, and soft palate, your articulators. Once again, smooth and connected movements of your muscles will result in fluent speech while increased physical tension and rapid initiation of movements for speech can result in stuttering. In summary, you are the one in control of how you use your muscles. Usually, you don't think about this type of muscular control but it is available to you if you think about it. Understanding how we produce speech and remembering to think about speech production will allow you to gain more and more control of your own speech.

VTC: 00:59:49:26

SPEAKING RATE AND FLUENCY

In Chapter 2 we discussed speaking rate measurement and its importance relative to the diagnosis of stuttering. If we examine the stuttering therapy literature, we will note that a number of therapy programs use speech rate

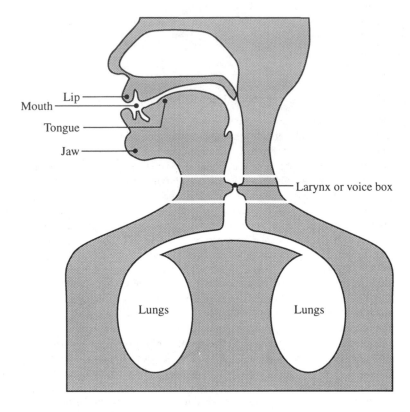

FIGURE 3–1. **The anatomy associated with speech production.**

reduction as the primary therapy goal. The clinician focuses his or her attention on the number of words per minute or number of syllables per minute (spm), and therapy is directed toward the reduction in words or syllables. In our therapy program, we also focus our attention on speaking rate modification but only as part of a more comprehensive approach to the problem. In our view, speaking rate reduction is the prerequisite behavior that is necessary to learn fluency skills associated with phonatory and articulatory modification. Historically, we know that devices such as the metronome (e.g., Brady, 1971) or delayed auditory feedback (e.g., Goldiamond, 1965) enable clients who stutter to slow down their speaking rate and become more fluent. It has been reported that the resulting fluency is a function of articulatory and phonatory changes (Wingate, 1969) rather than the fact that the client is saying fewer words or syllables. However, the fluent speech that results from these devices is often described as sounding unnatural, with the client being extremely reluctant to substitute unnatural sounding speech for stuttered speech. It is our belief that we can teach the client a set of speech skills that result in articulatory and phonatory changes and normal-sounding speech. To learn these skills, the client must first slow down his or her speech production system to integrate the changes necessary for fluency. Perkins (1973) described this process as "slow motion speech" by which the client is taught to prolong his or her speech. In the same manner that a golfer must slow down his or her swing and analyze that swing into its component parts, a clinician will teach clients to slow down their speech production system (produce fewer syllables in a given period of tme) to learn a new set of speech skills. However, like the golfer who ultimately increases the velocity of his or her swing to hit the ball and improve the efficiency of the game, the client in therapy must learn to integrate these fluency skills so that he or she can achieve normal speaking rates and improved fluency.

When a client has learned to control his or her speaking rate and recognizes his or her ability to complete the task, the client will now have a number of available options that were previously unavailable regarding speech fluency. In other words, a client who can be fluent at both slower and faster speaking rates can choose which option, according to the nature of their conversation. These options are typically discussed with adolescent and adult clients. During the later stages of therapy and beyond, clients who learn to control their speech can choose how fast or slow they would like to speak. If the client decides that his or her effort to be fluent is not worth the outcome, the client may choose to speak at a faster rate, recognizing the increased likelihood of stuttering. When a client understands that he or she has a number of available speaking options, he or she is able to deal with stuttering in a more realistic manner.

As we move to describe our methods for teaching fluency, it is important to note that, the skills, strategies, and concepts discussed throughout this book are rarely taught in isolation. Our approach always involves a number of simultaneous activities. However, when presenting these ideas in the text, we need to describe these ideas as independent entities. In actuality, our techniques are uniquely linked to the other aspects of therapy.

FLUENCY SKILLS

In order for a client to become more fluent, he or she learns to modify his or her speech production mechanism to integrate the necessary fluency skills. Instead of teaching a client to follow a beat or prolong words in a sentence, we teach a set of fluency skills within a reduced speaking rate environment.

The skills learned at a slower speaking rate serve as the foundation for later fluency when the client is encouraged to continue using these skills in situations requiring more naturally occurring speaking rates. Our goal is the replacement of stuttered speech with fluent speech. Through the teaching of these fluency skills, we work with the client to not only become fluent, but maintain normal loudness, prosody, and rhythm. We don't not want to substitute a new set of fluency skills that the client will not use. Our discussion of fluency skills includes (1) initiating speech in a gradual smooth manner, (2) phrasing, (3) increasing vowel duration within a word, and (4) connecting across word boundaries.

Our clinical experience indicates that our focus on fluency skills enables the clinician to help the client to modify his or her speech in a manner that best serves the individual client. As each client is different, our attention toward specific fluency skills will be different for each client. We typically begin teaching fluency skills by modeling smooth speech for the client during reading or simple speaking activities. With adolescents and adults, we often teach fluency skills during reading. As Perkins noted (1973) for a delayed auditory feedback (DAF) therapy program, "Reading is preferred during early stages of shaping because it usually permits more attention to perfecting the motor skills of speech." For most younger children and older children, we provide a fluency model while describing a picture using a simple sentence. When the client reads or describes the picture following our model, we note the client's strengths and weakness relative to the fluency skills we teach. For some clients, gradual initiation of phonation is a strength while connecting across word boundaries is weak. We then identify those skills that the client must focus on and continue to work on these skills. While we might note a weakness in using a particular skill, it is important to recognize that the client will need to address all of these skills in order to improve fluency. We might emphasize one skill but will work on all of the skills. We begin our discussion by examining speech initiation.

VTC: 00:26:24:21

Initiating Speech in a Slow Smooth Manner

When a client is instructed to begin speaking in a less hurried, slower manner, he or she has an increased opportunity to produce fluent speech. Guitar (1987) provided an excellent analogy that can be used to delineate this concept. Guitar suggested that initiating speech in a fast manner is similar to a person attempting to quickly remove his or her two fingers from a Chinese finger trap. When this task is quickly attempted, the person is unable to remove his or her fingers. When finger removal is attempted in a slow gradual manner, the fingers easily slide out. One might speculate that persons who stutter develop a time and tension threshold. When speech is rapidly initiated, this threshold is exceeded and the client is no longer able to produce speech in a smooth, coordinated manner. As a result, the client may produce a stuttering. When clients are taught to use fluency skills for gradual, smooth initiation of speech, they are better able to remain below this threshold and produce the word fluently. We encourage our clients to begin every sentence and phrase following a pause using a gradual initiation of speech. As will be noted throughout this book, this skill, like all of the skills that we teach, are first taught during less complex activities. As the client begins to master this skill, more complex activities are introduced.

Technique—Slow and Smooth Speech Initiation

Our experience has shown that many clients try to start talking in a fast manner. As a result, their speech system appears to be unable to coordinate in as fast a manner as the speaker would like. Starting fast often results in "getting stuck." "If you remember to take a small breath prior to starting to talk and slowly let the air out, you can get your vocal folds to come together in a gradual manner and speech can begin. By using this technique, you will be able to smoothly move through the first sounds in the word to the rest of the sentence. The air in your lungs provides the energy to vibrate your vocal folds. If you try to talk after you let out a lot of your breath, you'll lose the necessary energy to vibrate your vocal folds as well as your ability to start in a gradual manner. Take a breath and slowly let out a little bit of air. As the air begins to move, slowly begin the sound."

VTC: 00:26:40:17
00:42:40:11

Phrasing

A second fluency skill that we emphasize is phrasing, chunking, or grouping five or six syllables together. Phrasing is a skill that requires the client to group a number of syllables together, pause, and continue with another group of syllables. In contrast to the metronome that requires one word per beat, phrasing enables a client to approximate more natural sounding speech. We recognize that during the early stages of therapy, phrasing may sound unnatural to the client who is used to attempting 20 syllables per phrase. However, it is the client's attempt to produce 20 syllables per phrase that partially accounts for stuttering. Using phrasing appears to enable clients to gain a sense of control of their speech production mechanism that results in more fluent speech.

We often note that many clients use a strategy to produce as many syllables as possible in as short a period of time as possible. When questioned regarding this strategy, the client often states that he or she doesn't know when a stuttering will occur and as a result, he or she tries to say as many syllables as possible before the occurrence of the next stuttering. In most cases, this strategy results in a fast speaking rate, difficulty understanding the client, and increased stuttering.

During the early stages of therapy we discuss with our clients the need to break up their sentences into shorter phrases consisting of four to six syllables followed by a short pause that is followed by another five- or six-syllable phrase. Our clinical experience has shown us that a client learns to use his or her respiratory system in an efficient manner when producing four to six syllables and, when combined with slow gradual initiation of the sentences and phrases, the client appears to be reducing the articulatory demand associated with speech production. The client is producing fewer syllables and appears to have better control over his or her speech production system. This increased control results in increased fluency.

When we teach phrasing, the client is encouraged to slowly initiate speech and produce four to six syllables per breath. After each phrase, the client is encouraged to take another breath and restart the process. It should be noted that the client is cautioned to not take excessively deep breaths or exaggerate his or her breathing. We don't want to add additional associated behaviors to the problem. We want to encourage a skill that maximizes the client's ability to be fluent yet looks like part of the normal speaking process.

It is important to note that as a client learns to be more proficient at phrasing, he or she gradually learns that it is possible to increase their speaking rate and produce more syllables per breath. However, for many clients, even when we do work at increasing speaking rate, we encourage the clients to continue to pause between phrases. This skill will result in fewer stutterings and more opportunity for the client to control his or her speech production mechanism.

Technique—Phrasing

"In order for you to be able to coordinate your speech system in a smooth manner, it will be easier if you only try to produce four to six syllables on a breath. Remember, you start off in a smooth, gradual manner, and then try and produce a phrase with no more than six syllables. When you finish with one phrase you pause, take a breath, and start again."

VTC: 00:38:27:07
00:52:22:02

Connecting across Word Boundaries

Connecting across word boundaries involves two skills. These skills focus on modifying articulation to move easily from one word to the next and continuity of voicing within a phrase. Neilson and Andrews (1993) discuss phrase continuity that combines airflow, articulatory movements, and sound.

We often encounter clients who use a lot of physical effort to produce words. This effort is often exhibited as over articulating a word or a hard glottal attack. Our clinical experience has shown that when a client over articulates the final consonant of a word (e.g., /t/ or /p/), he or she experiences difficulty moving on to the next sound. When a client who stutters feels the need to over articulate and precisely say all final consonants, we often find that the client has difficulty moving from one sound to the next.

We discuss the need to connect the words in a phrase by using light articulatory contacts across word boundaries. Although Van Riper (1973) and others have encouraged light articulatory contacts for initiating words, we view the need for this skill as a bridge between the end of one word and the beginning of the next word. It is believed that by blending the words, the client is better able to make smooth articulatory transitions between words. When clients learn to connect across word boundaries we encourage them to combine this skill with slow and smooth speech initiation to maintain fluency throughout the sentence.

In addition to modification of the final consonant, we also encourage the client to "keep his or her voice on" when connecting words within the phrase. We are not encouraging the client to maintain continuous voicing across all phrases nor do we encourage the substitution of voiced sounds for voiceless sounds. Our focus is phonatory modification within each phrase. Although the client is encouraged to keep his or her voice going across word boundaries, the speech-language pathologist recognizes the physiological impossibility of this statement. When one word ends in a voiceless consonant and the subsequent word begins with a voiceless consonant (e.g., I ate candy), the client is not really producing continuous phonation. The client begins to learn that the change in voicing combined with articulatory modification results in fluency. "Thinking of a multiword phrase as simply one big word often helps clients to achieve continuity skills" (Neilson & Andrews, 1993, p.150)

Technique—Connecting across Word Boundaries

I'd like you to try to connect the words in each phrase as you go along. Try to keep your voice going across the words and avoid emphasizing the final sounds in the words. You want to use your voice to blend the words so that you have smooth movements from one word to the next. Remember, we are going to focus on phrases and, specifically, one phrase at a time.

VTC: 00:32:00:20
00:46:56:07

Increasing Vowel Duration

When we teach fluent speech skills, specifically teaching connecting across word boundaries, we have found that encouraging clients to lengthen their vowels assists in the phonatory and articulatory changes that are needed for increased fluency. Clients are encouraged to slightly lengthen their vowels where appropriate or, in more practical terms, "put more expression in your speech." When done in the extreme, the client's speech sounds abnormally slow and lengthened. When done correctly, the client's speech becomes more fluent, sounds natural, and is more expressive. We try and maintain our own internal model for acceptable vowel duration and continually compare the client's speech production to our own internal model. By examining the video, the reader can observe how we teach clients to lengthen their vowels and what we believe to be acceptable vowel duration.

Technique—Increasing Vowel Duration

As you begin each phrase, I want you to make the vowel longer if the word begins with a vowel. When the word begins with a consonant I want you to focus less on the initial consonant by smoothly moving toward the vowel and trying to make the vowel longer. You are going to use your voice to connect the words and this will happen if you make the vowels longer. You can think of this skill as putting more expression in your voice and the vowels will automatically get longer.

VTC: 00:32:00:20
00:46:56:07

Clients' Perceptions of Therapy

During the early stages of therapy, our clients interpret our approach to therapy as "slowing down." A client often enters therapy and states, "Everyone tells me that if I could just slow down I'd be more fluent." As we previously explained, speech rate modification enables the clinician to teach fluency skills in an environment where the client can effectively learn to change his or her speech. However, we believe that our goal is to not only teach the client to use the fluency skills to become more fluent, we also want the client to understand how to use these skills and why they work. By teaching our clients to understand how and when to use their fluency skills, clients are learning that they are responsible for their own fluency. When a client understands that he or she is in control of his or her own speech, the clinician is providing the client with a set a tools that the client can use throughout his or her lifetime. As the ancient Chinese proverb states "Give a man a fish and he eats for a day, teach a man to fish and he eats for a lifetime."

Additional Considerations

When teaching any and all of the above skills, the clinician needs to remember that the goal of this entire process is teaching fluent speech that sounds normal. Without the focus on normal-sounding speech, the client is likely to reject the techniques, despite the fact that they stutter less. In fact, some clients will opt for normal sounding stuttered speech rather than learn fluent speech that is not within an acceptable range of normalcy. To accomplish this task, the clinician needs to remember that intonation, rhythm, and loudness (Neilson & Andrews, 1993) need to be addressed as part of normal sounding speech. When teaching fluency skills, the clinician will need to not only focus on the specific skills (e.g., connecting across words), but the clinician will also need to be aware of the client's loudness, rhythm, and intonation. If a client is producing smooth speech while connecting words, the clinician must also determine whether the client's speech sounds natural. If the client is perceived to be using a monotone voice or speaking at a low intensity, the clinician should not reward this behavior. The clinician needs to be aware of every aspect of the client's speech so that the result of therapy is normal sounding fluent speech.

Accepting Responsibility for Change

Throughout the entire therapy process, a major focus of treatment involves requiring the client to accept responsibility for the changes that occur in therapy. A clinician does not want a client to think that the only reason he or she continues to be fluent is that he or she entered the therapy room. Whether dealing with a young child or an adult, a client is taught to accept the responsibility for change. Responsibility for change is associated with learning to use fluency skills within the therapy room, completing homework assignments that assist the use of fluency skills both within the therapy room and at home, and completing more complex assignments that strengthen the client's fluency as therapy progresses. We believe that during the early stages of therapy, a clinician assumes 90% of the responsibility toward a client's success in therapy. However, as therapy continues, we believe that there is a gradual transfer of responsibility from clinician to client so by the later stages of therapy, the client assumes 90% of the responsibility for change, and the clinician acts as an advisor toward the client's continued success.

We start to teach responsibility for change beginning on the first day of therapy and continuing throughout our entire program. A client is never led to believe that his or her speech changes because he or she sat in the therapy room and talked with Dr. Schwartz. The following example will illustrate the process.

If stuttering continues to be some black cloud of doom that remains unpredictable, clients will continue to believe that changing their behavior is beyond their control. As Williams (1957) observed:

> When a person begins thinking that a certain way of behaving is "part of him," or "just the way he is," it represents a relatively basic orientation that is reflected in the way he talks about him-

self. It implies that he is a certain kind of person. He believes that he may change certain ways of acting but that he cannot change the fundamental "him." (p. 391)

Technique—Teaching Responsibility for Change—Early Stages

We begin by not only teaching the clients the necessary skills to become fluent but we also teach the clients the necessary vocabulary to remain fluent. We tell clients, "To become fluent, you will need to start slowly, connect the words with your voice, and break the sentences into phrases." We encourage clients to internalize the modeled vocabulary and use these statements to describe the changes noted in their speech. During individual therapy we often pause from an activity requiring 20 fluent sentences and ask the client, "Why was that sentence so smooth?" During the early stages of therapy, clients often respond, "I don't know." We then ask, "Do you think your speech was smooth because I waved my magic wand?" The client typically responds, "My speech was smooth because I started slowly and connected the words." To which we respond: "That's right, you connected all of the words and the whole sentence was smooth. Great job." Following another two or three sentences, we will repeat the process until clients are able to consistently indicate that fluency occurs because of something they're doing. In a similar manner, clients learn that they get stuck or stutter when they're not using their fluency skills. We don't set up these parameters to blame clients for not using fluency skills. We want clients to understand that they are capable of controlling a behavior that was previously viewed as random and unpredictable. We want our clients to understand the behavioral requirements of becoming more fluent so that they can use these skills to become their own clinicians when they are away from the therapy room.

VTC: 00:54:03:14

When clients see stuttering as a fundamental component of their make-up, they continue to manifest the belief that they will always stutter and have no control over their problem. We work with our clients to change that perspective.

VTC: 01:22:00:26

When clients fail to use their fluency skills, do we criticize them for their inability to be fluent? Do we punish a client for stuttering? Hardly. Our clients know that the focus of therapy is fluency. We do encourage our clients to achieve the highest levels of fluency possible. However, we are also realistic with our clients and indicate that fluency skills like other tasks (e.g., golf, tennis, riding a bike, playing a video game) all require a lot of practice. We advise clients that some people are better at learning fluency skills than others. We encourage the client to work to become as fluent as possible. Most clients learn to be fluent within the therapy room. Difficulty with fluency skills are typically associated with transfer of fluency beyond the therapy room. Because as each client differs in their level of fluency outside of the therapy room, we modify our expectations for fluency by discussing with the client their perceptions and goals for fluency beyond the therapy room. Throughout the entire therapy process, the client is reminded that they control their own fate. When clients exhibit some initiative toward the internal control of their speech, this behavior is rewarded with a positive comment or encouraging statement so that the client will continue to take responsibility for his or her stuttering and fluency.

The transfer of responsibility during the therapy process takes place both within the therapy room and when the client is away from therapy. When the client is interacting with the clinician, it is easy to question the client about the changes that are occurring. However, it is the client's willingness to work on his or her speech when away from therapy that provides us with the most information about taking responsibility for speech changes. We believe that clients who continually fail to complete homework assignments are those clients who are not accepting responsibility for change. It will be the clinician's decision as to a course of action regarding the continuation of therapy. Sometimes we are confronted with difficult decisions on the continuation of therapy. Clinicians need to be realistic. Will a client learn to change his or her speech on a consistent basis when the only attempts made to change speech occur within the therapy room? We think not. As a result, clinicians need to determine how many times a client can fail to complete a homework assignment before continuation of therapy is discussed. We don't have an easy answer, and these decisions must be made in view of the individual circumstances of each client. It would be easy to make a rule that states, "If you fail to complete your homework assignment on three successive occasions, therapy will be terminated." We would encourage clinicians to determine why the homework is not being completed before such decisions are made. It may be possible that a client's failure to complete homework may be related as much to the nature of the assignment as the client's reluctance to work beyond the therapy. On one occasion, we encountered a 25-year-old male client who was always very cooperative in therapy and often completed his homework assignments with regularity. However, when we asked the client to use a tape recorder to record various conversations beyond the therapy room, this client returned to therapy on a number of occasion without completing the assignment. We recognized that the nature of the assignment was difficult for this client and after a number of discussions during the therapy session, we modified the assignment in such a way that the client was willing to begin work with the tape recorder. Eventually, as the client discovered the benefits of practicing with the tape recorder, he was more willing to complete the homework assignments although never quite comfortable with the tape recorder. This situation reminds us that we need to examine why a client may fail to complete his or her homework before we decide to terminate therapy.

SUMMARY

In the preceding chapter, we documented a general therapeutic philosophy with specific techniques for treating children and adults who stutter. Regardless of the age of the client, we use these basic techniques to teach the client to replace those habits that interfere with communication with newly learned skills that facilitate fluency. We believe that the goal of all of our therapy programs is spontaneous fluency (Peters & Guitar, 1991), meaning that fluency is produced without conscious effort. However, we have done therapy long enough to know that individual clients achieve varying levels of fluency. It is our job to help the client become as fluent as possible and with the appropriate emotional perspective, which will assist the client in remaining as fluent as possible following the completion of the therapy program. In the chapter that follows we will discuss some basic ideas on counseling and follow this with our approach toward therapy as a function of the client's age, emotional maturity and awareness, and reactions to stuttering and the environment.

► 4

Counseling Persons
Who Stutter

We often ask our students the question, "Who should provide the counseling for persons who stutter?" Are speech-language pathologists qualified to provide counseling? Unfortunately, many speech-language pathologists immediately respond no. For some reason, the school-speech language pathologist who provides suggestions for parents of a preschooler with articulation problems does not see this interaction as counseling. In another situation the clinician working in a hospital with the family of a person who has had a laryngectomy does not view this interaction as counseling. In our view, the speech-language pathologist is the most skilled person available who understands the relationship between the clients' communicative disorder and their daily behavior outside of the clinic. Because we view counseling as a significant part of our therapy program, we train clinicians to deal with the client's speech problem, the behaviors and emotions associated with the speech problem, and methods for interacting with families to encourage family members to best understand the relationship between stuttering and emotions.

We also offer a word of caution. The experienced clinician recognizes the difference between those problems associated with the client's stuttering and a more generalized problem that transcends communication and affects a person's general emotional state. For example, we questioned a client regarding his wife's reactions to his attendance in therapy. We thought that a supportive environment at home would assist the therapy process while negative reactions to the client's attendance in therapy could restrict the client's growth in therapy. The client indicated that his wife was unconcerned that he was attending therapy. The client continued this discussion by reporting on his marital difficulties, his wife's sexual problems, and the continuing saga of his relationship. As clinicians we can empathize with the client although we realized that these matters were well beyond our scope as speech-language pathologists. We discussed therapy options with the client including a variety of counseling services available and our willingness to make a referral. We advised the client that we would need to address those issues related to the client's communication while additional emotional matters would need to be discussed with a person better trained in marital counseling. We believed that it was important to exhibit a level of concern for the client's problems while maintaining a professional demeanor that affirmed our lack of training in this area. We indicated to the client that if he desired, we could share our information with other professionals if the client gave permission. The decision to share information between professionals is made by the client.

While the aforementioned case description examined an adult concern, we have encountered pervasive emotional concerns with both children and adolescents. In all cases, we try to recognize the limits of our training and the severity of the client's emotional reactions. Although the occurrence of pervasive emotional problems is less common in younger clients, being aware of their presence can not only assist the client's progress in speech therapy but also can assist general emotional development, social skills development, and academic success. As we discussed regarding adult clients, children and adolescents with problems that go beyond the skills of the speech-language pathologist need to be addressed by other professionals. We try to encourage parents to give permission for the sharing of information, although the final decision is left with them.

On a rare occasion, we encounter a client who we believe will only succeed in speech therapy if he or she also attends psychological or psychiatric counseling. We find that these clients often do well in our clinic because they put the full focus of their attention on the technical aspects of speech modification. The problems begin for these clients when they are asked to discuss their feelings associated with their stuttering and their emotional reactions when they attempt to use their fluency skills in situations beyond the clinic room. We are not talking about normal reluctance to share the personal feelings associated with a lifetime of stuttering. We are talking about a client who is experiencing many difficulties in all aspects of his or her life (e.g., socializing at work, interacting with peers, succeeding in school, getting along with family members). Our experience has been that the demands of daily functioning require so much of the clients' attention that they are unable to integrate fluency activities into their daily routine. As hard as we try to teach the transfer of fluency skills in gradual steps of increasing difficulty, the client continues to have difficulties outside of the clinic. For many of these clients, the early stages of therapy go very smoothly because the activities are discreet and focused within the clinic. As therapy progresses, we begin to see fewer and fewer advances. After exploring the many reasons why the client is failing to progress, we often come to the conclusion that the client's emotional perspectives are getting in the way of therapy success. On these rare occasions, we have strongly suggested to the client that additional counseling therapy is necessary. When a client decides to seek additional help, the results of this therapy often assist the client towards progress with fluency therapy. When our strong suggestions fail, we believed that it was necessary to provide an ultimatum that stuttering therapy could not continue unless the client was willing to seek additional help. This decision by the speech-language pathologist to terminate therapy unless there is psychological counseling is not easy to make and should not be made in any rushed manner. This decision is typically made when a client reaches some impasse during his stuttering therapy. The client may not be following through with homework assignments, complaining about his inability to progress beyond the therapy room, and is generally at a standstill regarding progress. It is the clinician's responsibility to be monitoring the client's progress to recognize whether the client's failure to progress is a function of the inappropriate selection of homework assignments, normal emotional reactions to difficult communicative situations, or a pervasive emotional concern that affects many of the clients interactions outside of therapy. When we encounter clients with emotional difficulties beyond communication, a dual counseling approach may be the only approach to help them succeed.

STUTTERING AND COUNSELING

Our years of clinical experience have led us to conclude that attitudes and beliefs about stuttering do not change merely because a client has learned to become more fluent. There is no question that teaching a client to improve his or her fluency skills results in a more positive outlook on communication. However, the clients' learned reactions associated with their stuttering continue to exist despite this new found fluency. As a result, it not only becomes necessary to teach the client to use his or her fluency skills in emotionally demanding situations, it is also important to counsel the client on his or her perceptions of stuttering as well as the relationship between perceptions, stuttering, and communication outside of the therapy room. In the same manner that we approach the teaching of fluency skills in a systematic manner, we also address the clients' emotional perspectives in a similar way. During our initial client interview and our continuing discussions during therapy, we attempt to determine the clients' perceptions regarding their speech and the relationship between perceptions, stuttering, and daily functioning. It is important to note that we continuously reassess the clients' perceptions as they are learning fluency skills within the clinic. In this manner we are providing a dynamic form of therapy that adjusts to the client's emotional growth and development.

The amount of time that we spend counseling our clients typically increases with the age of the client. In general, we spend more time counseling our adult clients than we do our preschoolers. However, it is important to recognize that it is not unusual to talk about beliefs, emotions, and reactions with preschoolers and school-age children. On occasion we have spent more time counseling a 6-year-old boy than we have with many adults. A lot of the information in this chapter is modifiable and applicable for all age groups. It is a mistake to believe that young children are not aware and not reacting to their stuttering.

Until recently, very few academic training programs provided any formal coursework in counseling. Counseling involved on-the-job training in the clinic and was often taught by a clinical supervisor who may have developed her/his own method for counseling clients. This on-the-job training appeared to be sufficient for some clinicians in certain settings, although a number of clinicians always believed that they carried around a gaping hole in their bag of clinical training. As a clinician who had progressed beyond a doctoral degree without a formal course in counseling, I took it upon myself to examine my clinical style and the style of those clinicians who I admired and respected. I then began an examination of available books and articles that discussed counseling methods and ways to approach clients. From this exploration, I realized that my counseling approach was most closely associated with the area that psychologists refer to as cognitive-behavioral counseling.

Our approach to counseling persons who stutter can generally be classified as a form of cognitive therapy. "Cognitions are thoughts—including beliefs, assumptions, expectations, attributions, and attitudes. Cognitions often maintain our behaviors. Cognitive-behavioral therapy changes cognitions that are maintaining conditions of psychological disorders," (Spiegler & Guevremont, 1983). We are not implying that all persons who stutter exhibit psychological disorders. However, we have found that for many clients who stutter, there are many learned reactions, beliefs, and expectations that are related to their stuttering. As a result, our counseling focuses on directing the client's cognition in a manner that helps to facilitate and maintain fluent speech.

Our approach to counseling has borrowed ideas from a number of sources. We have been most influenced by the writings of Vaillant (1977) and Ellis (1977). In order to best understand the influence of Vaillant, a short description of his work is in order.

ADAPTIVE MECHANISMS

In 1937 the William T. Grant foundation initiated a longitudinal investigation of how normal people develop by focusing on those factors that were responsible for success and good health. The investigators in this study were interested in the development of individuals across their lifetime. The investigators chose to study 268 men from Harvard University (Seligman, 1990) who were selected for characteristics that included good health, independence, and men recognized as being "sound." These individuals were studied across their lifetime with interviews and questionnaires directed toward the investigation of emotional and physical health. As the designers of this study began to age, they enlisted George Vaillant to continue their investigation. Vaillant focused on the lives of 95 of these men and reported on the results of 30 years of investigation in his book *Adaptation to Life* (1977).

Adaptation to Life (Vaillant, 1977) is a book that describes the many adaptive mechanisms that individuals unconsciously use to deal with the emotional demands in their life. Clearly, this is not a book that deals with persons who stutter. However, if a speech-language pathologist is expected to counsel persons who stutter, knowledge of the adaptive mechanisms that persons use should be helpful toward counseling adult clients and helping them to become fluent speakers.

In the introduction to *Adaptation to Life* (1977), Vaillant indicated that the major focus of his work can be summarized in a quote provided by Frank Barron, a psychologist who had extensively studied college students (1963). "Soundness is a way of reacting to problems not an absence of them." We must enter therapy believing that all of our clients confront adversity. It is the manner in which our clients deal with that adversity that determines their emotional well-being. Not only should we focus on the mechanisms that enable a client to be successful, we should work with our clients to help them determine how to redirect those adaptive mechanisms that prevent them from growing emotionally and becoming more fluent.

Vaillant (1977) writes, "In fact, a major thesis of this book is that a man's adaptive devices are as important in determining the course of his life as are his heredity, his upbringing, his social position, or his access to psychiatric help." As speech-language pathologists, we need to follow this direction and learn to identify the manner in which a client reacts to his or her stuttering. With such knowledge, we help the client to identify the adaptive strategies that are associated with stuttering. With this knowledge, the clinician can reward the client for making the correct choice or counsel the client regarding his or her use of an inappropriate adaptive mechanism. Therapy focuses on redirecting the client's focus toward strategies that will result in more positive growth.

The adaptive mechanisms described by Vaillant (1977) are presented in four levels: (1) psychotic; (2) immature; (3) neurotic; and (4) mature. Vaillant reported that the healthiest of individuals use more of the mature adaptive mechanisms. Those individuals who exhibited more psychotic and immature mechanisms not only exhibited emotional difficulties but also had more physical problems as well. It is not in the scope of this book to detail all of Vaillant's findings. It is the author's desire to direct the reader to a valuable resource that can assist the speech-language pathologist to better understand the choices that clients make in response to adversity and to train the reader to become a clinician who can counsel clients rather than a technician who follows a set of rules.

We would like to provide one good example using Vaillant's descriptions of adaptive mechanisms. First we provide one clinical example of how a client uses repression (Level 2, Immature) as an adaptive style for dealing with stuttering. We will then describe and contrast two adaptive mechanisms, repression and suppression, and provide a clinical example to demonstrate how a client might use these mechanisms.

Repression is described by Vaillant as "seemingly inexplicable naivete, memory lapse, or failure to acknowledge input from a selected sense organ. The feeling is in consciousness, but the idea is missing" (p. 385). Our experience with adults who stutter can amplify this definition. On numerous occasions we encounter an adult who stutters and when questioned as to how he or she stutters, the client responds, "I don't know." Our first thought is that this client stutters throughout the day but is unable to describe how the stuttering is produced. We wonder if this client is unwilling to share this information with us or is embarrassed to discuss it. However, upon further questioning we realize that many clients are faced with daily stuttering and have no knowledge of how to modify their speech or deal with their problem. If this client spent a lot of time focusing on stuttering, it may be difficult to get through the day. We speculate that by using this adaptive mechanism, repression, the client is able to put aside signals from sensory organs and get through the day in spite of stuttering. One problem arises when this client begins a therapy program. The ability to recognize the occurrences of stuttering is an important component of therapy. In therapy we may spend a considerable amount of time discussing the manner in which the client is producing speech by getting him/her to focus on those things that he or she has been avoiding to this point in time. Initially, a client who represses sensory input may have some difficulty focusing on those sensations that he or she has tried to avoid for quite a few years. Additionally, when a client is not using his or her smooth speech skills during therapy, we might question the client as to "what happened when you spoke." Our goal is to get the client to become more in tune with his or her own speech so that he or she believes that he or she has the necessary controls to be fluent. For the client who has been repressing these feelings, therapy may take longer. It may be necssary to focus on those behaviors that the client is using so that they can be modified. On occasion, the client may begin to stutter more. The clinician will need to explain to the client that being more in tune with how speech is produced will help the client to make better progress in therapy. By identifying the adaptive mechanisms that the client is using, we are better able to counsel the client and help the client develop more positive adaptive mechanisms.

In the previous paragraph, we examined one definition of repression. A second definition of repression suggests a convenient memory loss, a naivete. We can contrast this definition of repression with the more mature adaptive mechanism, suppression. Suppression has been described as "the conscious or semi-concious decision to postpone paying attention to a conscious impulse of conflict" (Vaillant, 1977, p. 386). Vaillant reports that an individual says, "I will think about it tomorrow, and the next day one remembers to think about it" (p. 386). As part of our transfer program, we often ask a client to complete a homework assignment that is similar to an activity being working on during the therapy session. For example, we may be working with two different clients who are working on the same activity during therapy. Each client is required to describe 20 pictures and tape-record this activity at home. When the first client returns to therapy he reports that he really wanted to do his homework but was so busy with his other school work that he forgot to complete the assignment. The clinician emphasizes to the client the importance of homework, and the client declares that it will definitely be completed and the tape recording will be brought in for the next session. During the subsequent session, the client reports that he was really busy with his school work and forgot to complete his stuttering assignment. This client appears to be using the immature mechanism repression. The use of repression in this example prevents the client from progressing in therapy. The client verbalizes a desire to do the homework and make improvements in speech and yet fails to follow through with the task. In the second case, an adolescent reported that he had to study for a number of tests in addition to his therapy homework. The client reported that he had to put all of his attention into studying for his exam. However, the client realized that when he was taking a break from studying, the time was ideal for completing his speech homework. As a result, the client used a mature adaptive strategy that enabled him to put his focus on studying for his exams and then when he took a break, was able to remember to refocus his attention on his speech homework. In this manner, the client identified that he had a number of important tasks to complete but by addressing the tasks on a case-by-case basis, the client was able to return to his speech homework and get both of his assignments completed. We note that for the first client, our goal in therapy may be to teach the client better time management skills, methods for organizing his homework schedule, and taking responsibility for his actions outside of the therapy room.

The aforementioned descriptions are just two examples of how adaptive styles can be examined as part of stuttering therapy. We strongly encourage readers to examine Vaillant's book and use this information to strengthen their knowledge of the methods that people use to adapt to difficult situations. By learning how people adapt, a clinician can determine appropriate intervention strategies to help the client grow and develop. In the section that follows, we present a second component of our approach to counseling with clients who stutter.

A RATIONAL APPROACH TO STUTTERING THERAPY

During our early clinical experiences with persons who stutter, we recognized that many of these clients developed attitudes and beliefs regarding their stuttering that often prevented them from becoming more fluent and that inhibited their emotional development. For these clients, therapy not only included teaching fluency skills but also required counseling for those attitudes and beliefs that prevented further emotional growth. We began by questioning the clients' perceptions of themselves and their stuttering and offered challenges to this way of thinking. As we continued to grow as clinicians, we recognized that many of the philosophies outlined by Albert Ellis (1977) in his development of rational emotive therapy (RET), could be modified and adapted as part of our therapy program. In their introduction to *A New Guide to Rational Living* (1975), Ellis and Harper state that the rational emotive approach follows:

> *the humanistic, educative model which asserts that people, even in their early lives, have a great many more choices than they tend to recognize; that most of their "conditioning" actually consist of self-conditioning; and that a therapist, a teacher, or even a book can help them see much more clearly their range of alternatives and thereby to choose to reeducate and retrain themselves so that they surrender most of their serious self-created emotional difficulties (p. X).*

This philosophy of choice and the "self-created emotional difficulty" are our primary focus with persons who stutter. The fact that a client stutters is not the problem. The clients' perceptions of their stuttering and the behaviors that follow these perceptions will determine many of the clients' life choices. Depending upon the client, we have observed personal, social, academic, and career choices that were all associated with clients' stuttering or their perceptions of their stuttering. Sometimes the client makes positive choices, and these result in positive emotional growth. At other times, a client makes choices that impair his or her ability to emotionally develop, and it is at these times that the counseling speech-language pathologist can help the client to focus on those areas that can be modified.

Stuttering (A), Thoughts (B), and Emotions (C)

In the aforementioned title, the reader can see that we have provided three labels, ABC, to stuttering, thoughts, and emotions. This ABC label is derived from Ellis's (1977) model for rational emotive therapy that describes the relationship between thought and emotion. Ellis developed this model in an attempt to deal with emotional disturbance. In our case, we are adapting this model to deal with the irrational and rational beliefs that are exhibited by persons who stutter so that we may counsel these individuals and help to reshape their belief systems.

Ellis's model begins with (A) the activating experience or event. In our discussion, the majority of activating events will relate to the client's stuttering at a specific point in time. For example, "I went to a party and I stuttered when I had to introduce myself." As Ellis described the model, the client tends to jump to point (C), the emotional and behavioral consequences of the experience at point A. In our case the client reports that he's depressed because he stuttered on his name. The client also reports that he won't go to other parties because he doesn't want to be depressed and generally withdraws from these social situations. In this RET model, clients "falsely tend to assume *that A causes C* " (Ellis, 1977, p. 6). In reality, according to this RET model, the emotions and behaviors associated with (C) are the result of (B), the beliefs that a client has about the problem. In our case it is the client's beliefs that if he or she stutters at the party it would be terrible, "I would be so embarrassed by my stuttering that I don't think I'd want to stay at the party." Dryden (1990) described beliefs as a persons cognitive evaluations of real world situations that are either rigid or flexible. When beliefs are used in a rigid manner, they are called irrational. Irrational beliefs can be observed during client interaction when the client uses such expressions as, "I have to be fluent, I can't let them see me stutter or I should have been fluent." When a client is using irrational beliefs, he or she often reaches irrational conclusions like "I'll never be fluent, everyone hates me because I stutter, or I don't think I'll ever stop stuttering." When a client is using rational beliefs, his or her thinking tends to be more flexible and typically does not evolve into irrational conclusions. With a rational belief system, a client recognizes that a negative event has occurred and evaluates the occurrence of the event but does not generalize the event to every other event or life situation. Using a rational belief system a client will note, "I stuttered at that party but it was only a momentary loss of control. I'll do better next time." Dryden (1990) suggested that inappropriate negative emotions lead to psychic pain and discomfort, self-defeating behavior, and, in general, prevent an individual from reaching his or her goal. On the other hand, appropriate negative emotions make the person aware of the problem, stimulate the person to develop appropriate behaviors and generally result in the "successful execution of behavior necessary to reach one's goals". As clinicians, it is our job to help the client to identify those irrational beliefs. When the client learns to identify these beliefs, we teach the client methods for disputing beliefs and dealing with the beliefs and emotions associated with stuttering.

In an attempt to explain the concept of rationality, (Dryden, 1987) defines rational as "that which helps people to achieve their basic goals and purposes" (p. 7). The clinician is taught that a client has the power to control his or her "thoughts, emotions and actions" which he or she uses to achieve his or her basic goals. As a result, the term irrational is defined as "that which prevents people from achieving their basic goals and purposes" (Dryden, 1987, p. 7).

Rational versus Irrational Emotional Responses

One of the major therapy focuses in RET involves a process in which a clinician helps the client to actively dispute his or her irrational beliefs. It becomes the clinician's job to identify the presence of irrational beliefs, to sort out rational beliefs from irrational beliefs, and finally to challenge the client's irrational beliefs by questioning and debating the statements made by client.

As mentioned previously, irrational beliefs are often associated with terms such as *must, have to,* and *should have.* The client's thinking is in absolute terms and the client often takes these beliefs to a worldwide conclusion. To the client the event was the worst experience possible, something horrible, an event that was intolerable. It is in these situations that the client is exhibiting irrational thinking. As previously described, Dryden (1990) stated that rational beliefs are associated with appropriate negative emotions while irrational beliefs are associated with inappropriate negative emotions. To assist in our ability to identify rational from irrational beliefs, we might examine appropriate versus inappropriate negative emotions. Dryden (1990) has paired appropriate, rational emotional responses with inappropriate negative emotional responses and defines these emotions as follows:

> Concern vs. Anxiety *Concern is an emotion that is associated with the belief 'I hope that this threat does not happen, but if it does, it would be unfortunate', whereas anxiety occurs when the person believes, 'This threat must not happen and it would be awful if it did (p. 9–10).*

As clinicians, we would examine our clients' statements regarding their stuttering and attempt to determine whether the emotions associated with their stuttering were appropriate or inappropriate. During the early stages of therapy a client reports that he or she is required to give a presentation in front of a group of co-workers. The client indicates to you that if he stutters it would be terrible. "I just can't stutter in front of my co-workers." When examining this statement we would note that our client was exhibiting anxiety related to his or her stuttering and we would view this emotional reaction to be inappropriate. Because this inappropriate negative emotion is associated with some irrational belief, we would begin to challenge our client's belief system by asking the client, "Why would it be so terrible if you stuttered in front of your co-workers?" We would question our client as follows:

> *Clinician: Why would it be so terrible if you stuttered?*
> *Client: I would be embarrassed.*
> *Clincian: Why would you be embarrased?*
> *Client: Because they saw me stutter and they think I'm stupid.*
> *Clinician: You mean you never stutter at any other time at work?*
> *Client: I do stutter and I know that they think I'm stupid.*
> *Clinician: How you do you know? Have you questioned them about your stuttering? Is it possible that some of them don't even hear your stuttering?*
> *Client: I suppose so.*
> *Clinician: Perhaps not everyone thinks you're stupid. Some of them might think that you have a stuttering problem and you're a pretty strong person for getting up in front of the group and speaking.*

From the above discussion, the reader will note that the clinician is attempting to redirect the client's thinking by challenging the client's beliefs and perceptions about the problem. We don't expect the client to immediately agree with our assessment of their irrational beliefs and associated emotions. However, we present an alternate way to look at the client's stuttering so that the client begins to recognize that he or she actually has some options regarding their beliefs about stuttering. With continued therapy, both client and clinician work together to change the irrational thinking. Importantly, we do not negate the clients' negative emotions associated with their stuttering. We recognize that the client stutters and doesn't like to stutter in front of a group. However, when the clients recognize that stuttering in front of the group is something they dislike but is not the end of their existence, the clients will be open to an increasing number of strategies that will assist fluency development, and subsequently they will be better equipped to modify their negative perspective associated with this situation.

A second pair of appropriate and inappropriate emotions is defined by Dryden (1990):

> Regret vs. Guilt *Feelings of regret or remorse occur when a person acknowledges that he has done something bad in public or private but accepts himself as a fallible human being for doing so. The person feels badly about the act or deed but not about himself*

because he holds the belief, 'I prefer not to act badly, but if I do, too bad!' Guilt occurs when the person damns himself as bad, wicked, or rotten for acting badly. Here, the person feels bad both about the act and his 'self' because he holds the belief: 'I must not act badly and if I do it's awful and I am a rotten person.' (p. 10)

When a client can report to you that he or she stuttered during a conversation and although he or she didn't like the fact that he or she stuttered, he or she continued talking without concern, this client is exhibiting appropriate negative emotions associated with rational thinking. Our goal for most clients is to get them to a point where their stuttering is regretful but nothing more. However, when many clients first enter therapy, they view their stuttering as something awful, a behavior that makes them a rotten person, and a behavior that has to be hidden. Our experience suggests that the client who perceives that stuttering in public is something awful and they too are awful, will often develop a number of avoidance strategies that enable the client to hide the problem. The dilemma that arises however, is the fact that when a client continues to use these avoidance behaviors, he or she continues to foster the growth of guilt. Clients recognize that they have postponed the negative emotions associated with stuttering but now believe that they are awful because they are not confronting their problem, which leads to additional guilt. The result is a continuous cycle of inappropriate negative emotional development where the clients not only feel guilty for stuttering but also feel guilty for not stuttering.

A third pair of emotions is defined by Dryden (1990):

Sadness vs. Depression *Sadness is deemed to occur when the person believes, 'It is very unfortunate that I have experienced this loss but there is no reason why it should not have happened.' Depression on the other hand is associated with the belief, 'This loss should not have occurred and it is terrible that it did' (p. 10).*

A client returns to the therapy session having completed a homework assignment and reports that he's depressed because he should have been fluent during his telephone conversations. When the client makes fluency demands upon him- or herself and believes that the ability to control his or her speech is beyond his or her control, the client often develops feelings of hopelessness, which lead to the conclusion that "I will never get better." Our job as counseling clinicians focuses on teaching the client to accept responsibility for his or her successes and failures at being fluent while viewing his or her "failed" homework as a skill that has yet to be mastered. In this manner, the inability to be fluent is related to the clients' speech skills rather than an external force that controls their speech. It is acceptable to be sad because you had difficulty with a homework assignment. It is not acceptable to be depressed because depression will prevent you from developing the necessary fluency skills to move forward in therapy.

The fourth definition provided by Dryden (1990) includes:

> Annoyance vs. Anger *Annoyance occurs when another person disregards an individual's rule of living. The annoyed person does not like what the other has done but does not damn him or her for doing it . . . In anger, however, the person does believe that the other absolutely must not break the rule and thus damns the other for doing so (p. 12).*

An adolescent male client reports to you that his best friend never lets him finish talking, "He's always finishing my sentences for me." Your client states that he's really angry with his friend and won't be contacting him in the near future. This client blames his friend for not letting him talk. The client often interprets his friend's behavior as insensitivity to stuttering. Our goal in therapy is to teach the client that it is acceptable to not like his friend's behavior. However, the client's anger creates a situation where he is likely to lose a friend without having shared his feelings with his friend. The anger displayed by the client creates a situation where communication between the two parties may be very difficult. We ask our client, "Is it worth risking your friendship by remaining angry with your friend?" We talk with our client and explain that his friend may not even be aware of interrupting and its effect upon the stuttering. Rather than remain angry, which will close a door on the friendship, we tell our client that it's acceptable to be annoyed with his friend but communicating his feelings will help to straighten out the situation.

The final definition provided by Dryden (1990) includes:

> Disappointment vs. Shame/Embarrassment *Feelings of disappointment occur when a person acts 'stupidly' in public, acknowledges the stupid act, but accepts herself in the process. The person feels disappointed about her action but not with herself because she prefers but does not demand that she act well. Shame and*

embarrassment occur when the person again recognizes that she has acted 'stupidly' in public and then condemns herself for acting in a way that she should not have done (p. 10).

During the early stages of therapy, quite a few clients report that their stuttering leads to feelings of shame and embarrassment. A client may develop some internal standard for how his or her speech should sound. When clients are unable to meet that predetermined expectation, they go beyond being disappointed and begin to believe that they acted stupidly, that their listeners perceived them as being stupid, and anytime stuttering occurs in public, listeners will make judgments about their speech. For the speech-language pathologist, it becomes a continuing focus in therapy to challenge the clients' perceptions about their speech. We must help the clients recognize that they are often their own biggest critic, and the majority of the listening public is so focused on their own problems that they are oblivious to the clients' stuttering. When this counseling approach is combined with teaching the client methods for becoming more fluent, we ultimately begin to see positive emotional growth.

SUMMARY

In summary, this chapter has focused the reader's attention on the need to include a counseling component as an integral part of stuttering therapy. We recognize that the information presented is limited in scope and does not encompass the entire gamut of counseling. Our purpose has been to point the reader in a number of positive directions to begin his or her own inquiries about counseling. We expect the reader to develop his or her own counseling approaches and hope that this chapter begins the process. The information provided in this chapter is best suited for the adolescent and adult client although modifications to meet the needs of younger clients are possible. Throughout each of the remaining chapters, aspects of counseling will be integrated into the discussion. We strongly believe that clinicians need to be aware of their clients' beliefs and emotions associated with stuttering. Additionally, we strongly urge all clinicians to find a time and place to not only teach clients to become more fluent but also learn to talk with their clients and counsel their clients so that stuttering therapy can be a rewarding and long-lasting experience.

▶ 5

Young Children Who Stutter

The decision as to the type of therapy program that is best suited for the young child who stutters is made by the speech-language pathologist following the diagnostic evaluation. It is our intent to explore the available therapy options. In this chapter we will discuss stuttering therapy for the child whose evaluation results indicate that some form of intervention is necessary. Our focus is on the child who has started stuttering prior to age 6 and has typically not completed kindergarten.

For the children under discussion, we believe that there are a number of therapy options available. These options include the following: (1) indirect therapy that typically focuses on parental/environmental changes; (2) group therapy that typically involves both parent and child; and (3) direct, individual therapy with parental participation. It is important to recognize that the many strategies and skills that we teach parents as part of indirect therapy are the same skills that we use in parent-child group therapy or during parental participation with individual therapy. The skills remain the same while the manner in which they are taught may differ. We believe that the parents are an important component to the therapy process, and we include the parents in all of the therapy that we provide.

Our discussion will focus on indirect therapy, the parent-child fluency group, and direct therapy. Each section includes a definition, the characteristics of the child best suited for this approach, the activities provided, and the role of the parents.

INDIRECT THERAPY

Definition

In our clinical view, indirect therapy is any therapy where we do not talk with the child about his or her speech problem and do not attempt to teach the child to make changes in his or her speech. Indirect therapy most typically involves working with parents and other caregivers in an effort to modify communicative demands and to facilitate fluent speech within the child's daily environment. In addition, indirect therapy may involve shaping communicative interactions between the parent and child so that the positive aspects of talking are addressed without ever mentioning or addressing the child's stuttering. Indirect therapy is provided because it is believed that the child will become fluent as a result of modifying the communicative environment, a naturally maturing speech-motor production system, and a child's lack of reaction to his or her speech or the communicative environment.

We recognize that when we work with very young children, it is often possible to have the parents change their style and method of communicating with their child and also make environmental modifications at home that will result in the child exhibiting increased speech fluency. However, our clinical experience reveals that as children get older and the problem continues to develop, parental participation in therapy continues to be important but environmental modification by itself will not result in increased speech fluency.

The Child Best Suited for Indirect Therapy

When we recommend indirect therapy for a child, our belief is that we can change the child's speech by encouraging changes in the child's communicative environment without directly talking with the child about his or her stuttering. In most cases, these children have been stuttering for less than a year, and their stuttering and associated behaviors have not changed significantly since the onset of their stuttering. These children have not developed strong emotional reactions to their speech problems and do not appear to be behaviorally or cognitively aware that a problem exists.

One key factor for determining which child is best suited for this program is the time from the onset of the problem. When making our decision to provide indirect therapy, it is usually the child who is closest to stuttering onset who will benefit most from indirect therapy. When stuttering persists for 12 months post onset, it is more likely that this child will require a different type of therapy. Our philosophy is one that promotes prevention of continued stuttering development through intervention. We don't believe that our intervention makes the problem worse. Unlike Johnson's notion that calling attention to stuttering results in stuttering (Johnson, 1959), we believe that by working with the parents, we help to create environments that facilitate the development of fluent speech.

Modifying Parental Communication

Indirect therapy involves helping parents to identify and modify those aspects of their communication and daily activities and routines that may have a negative impact on their child's developing speech fluency. It is not that we believe that parents are producing pathological behaviors that cause their child to stutter. Instead, we look at normal routine activities that may have a negative impact on those children at risk for continued stuttering. As a result, we often conduct two or three preliminary therapy sessions to initially assist parents and then encourage the parents to remain in contact with our clinic. We typically schedule a follow-up evaluation 3 to 6 months after these initial sessions.

Our discussions with parents focus on the relationship between communication and the child's perception and reactions to time. We explain that any activity that the child interprets as a time demand has the potential to disrupt speech. These time demands can be related to communicative activities that occur among family members or to time demands associated with more general environmental issues such as getting to appointments, number and variety of extracurricular activities, and the families' ability to follow a daily routine. We must point out that these time demands may only be a problem if the child who stutters reacts to the situation by producing more stuttering. As much as we'd like to be able to identify one or two factors that serve as precipitators of the child's stuttering, we recognize that every child who stutters is different and each child responds in his or her own unique manner. As a result, we will first discuss some suggestions that parents can implement to modify their own communication at home. A second focus will be directed toward modification of various family activities that can have a positive impact on the child's speech.

VTC: 00:45:13:01

Parents Modifying Their Speaking Rate

In our the discussion to follow, modification of speaking rate generally means slowing down. However, if we ask parents to explain their perception of slowing down, we usually come up with some idea that the ideal speaking rate s. . . o. . . u. . . n. . . d. . . s l. . . i. . . k. . . e t. . . h. . . i. . . s. We like the idea of modifying speaking rates so that parents realize that a change needs to made but the resulting speaking rate does not have to be pathologically slow. We advise parents that the speaking rates that they use to communicate with other adults and even other children in the family may be very appropriate for those situations. However, when the parents are communicating with a child who is experiencing speech difficulty that is affected by time, then it makes sense that parents modify their speaking rate to have a positive effect on their child's speech. We might envision mom and dad with child in hand walking quickly to cross the street. Both parents are able to keep in step and generally both adults have fluid smooth walking skills as they proceed. However, the young child in hand may be tripping, falling, and generally having a difficult time keeping up with his or her parents. During most situations like this, the child is often expected to maintain the same rate as the parent. As adults, we have to be taught and reminded that at times we need to modify our behavior to meet the needs of our children. When a parent learns to modify his or her speaking rate when communicating with his or her child, we believe that the child perceives a lessened time demand to produce speech. As a result, for many of the children receiving indirect therapy, rate modification often results in a reduced time demand. The child senses this reduced demand and is able to coordinate his or her speech production system in a manner that results in fluent speech.

We instruct the parents regarding modification of their speaking rate in a manner similar to that described in Chapter 3 for working with clients. The following discussion should illustrate our interaction with the parents:

Technique—Modification of Speaking Rate

We begin by asking the parents to explain to us how they might modify their speaking rate. Most parents typically respond, "Well, you just slow down." The clinician responds, "OK, show me." When the parent responds the result is typically the same rate as they had previously produced or an

---

extremely exaggerated slow speaking rate. We ask the parent to try again or to follow a model that we might provide. When the parents are able to make some type of modification in their speaking rate, we ask them "What did you do to slow down." The typical response is, "I don't know, I just slowed down." We then ask the parents to explain the process for slowing down. When we fail to get a response we explain the following. "There are a number of ways to modify speaking rate. You could pause after every word but this typically sounds unnatural." We usually provide an example. We then explain that we could pause after a phrase and use natural pauses in our conversation to assist rate reduction. This technique of pausing between phrases results in more natural sounding speech. When modifications sound natural, parents and/or clients are more likely to make the modifications. In addition we point out that we can lengthen words by slightly elongating the vowel. This vowel elongation reduces the speaking rate because each word will now take a little longer to produce. We also demonstrate to the parents that they can begin speaking in a relatively slow smooth manner rather than rushing to begin each and every sentence. We demonstrate to the parents that when these techniques are combined, we can have natural sounding speech that is relatively slower than the conversational rates that they previously used. We note that continued use of rate modification by the parents can have a positive effect on the child's developing speech fluency.

Modification of Turn-Switching Pauses

We previously described a turn-switching pause as the time from the completion of the speakers' utterance to the onset of the listeners' response. During adult interactions, we often note that adults begin talking before a speaker has completed a thought. Although this type of behavior may result in listener annoyance and/or increased speaking rate by the listener, the speech of the adult listener is typically unaffected by this behavior. However, when an adult fails to provide a young child who stutters with enough time to respond, that child may interpret the situation to be that the adult wants the child to respond quickly, because time is a precious commodity. For the child who has difficulty producing fluent speech in a fast manner, this adult behavior may lead to more stuttering and a child's increased awareness of his or her problem. The following situation will illustrate a method for teaching parents the necessary skills for providing their child with enough time to respond.

Technique—Modifying Turn-Switching Pauses

During a conversation with the parents, you indicate that there are some issues that they need to address regarding adult conversational behaviors that may be inappropriate when interacting with a child who stutters. "We are going to talk about the type of conversations you and your son have at home. During the conversation, I may stop you to point out some areas that need to be addressed." During the subsequent conversation, the mother starts talking before you are finished. The clinician states "Can you tell me what dinner time. . ." to which the parent interrupts, "Dinner time is quite hectic." "Did you notice what you did as I was talking?" asks the clinician. "You started talking before I was finished and this interrupting made me feel uncomfortable. I wanted to jump right back into the conversation. Can you tell me how your son would respond if you interrupt his speech in the same way?" The parents begin to think about their son's stuttering and observe that they often hear more stuttering when their son is talking with them. We sit down with the parents and discuss a method for modifying this time-demanding behavior. We explain to the parents that they can control the flow of the conversation by waiting at least 1 second after their child finishes before they begin talking. We note that this change will not be easy to make; however, if the parents can work on this interruption, they can help to create an environment that will facilitate fluency at home. We tell the parents that it is all right to interrupt each other when they communicate and even interrupt their other children if they desire. However, for a child who appears to be sensitive to time, providing enough time to respond can have a positive effect on the child's developing speech fluency.

Rewarding Fluent Speech

Too often we encounter parents who are so focused on their child's speech problem that they fail to recognize that the majority of their child's speech is fluent. This fact has long been recognized by some of the outstanding clinical writers in our profession. For example, Bloodstein (1995) in the newest edition of *A Handbook of Stuttering* writes:

> *Finally, everything possible is done to strengthen the child's anticipation of normal speech and self assurance as a speaker. The chief method used is to give the child every opportunity to experience fluency and to gain a sense of enjoyment, adequacy, and suc-*

cess in speech situations. During periods of relatively fluent speech the child is encouraged to speak as much as possible. During episodes of unusual difficulty, the parents may be trained to provide successful speaking experiences through the use of choral speaking, singing, recitation of nursery rhymes, rhythmic speaking, or puppetry. (pp. 435–436)

It is interesting to note that for many parents, the suggestion to focus on their child's fluency is an eye-opening experience. These parents have been so concerned that they have caused their child's speech difficulties that they lose their objectivity and focus all of their attention on the relatively low number of difficulties that their child is experiencing. When parents begin to examine their child's speech in a more objective manner, they often note the long fluent strings of words and phrases that their child is exhibiting and then learn to positively reward the child for fluency. We are not suggesting that parents stop their child, indicate the number of fluent words and say "Great fluent speech." Instead, we encourage parents to change their focus from worrying about the few difficulties that the child experiences to the relatively large amount of time their child is not having a problem. Parents are encouraged to use expressions such as "I really like how you said that" or "You are a good story teller" or "I really like how you talk." We remind the reader that our discussion is focused on the child receiving indirect therapy. We reward fluent speech without really making a specific request of the child. We want the child to foster the idea that communication is fun. When parents change their focus from stuttering to fluency, the child often responds in a very positive manner and fluency results.

Modifying Situations and Schedules within the Family

In addition to the speech modifications made by the parents, family members can modify the communicative environment at home in an effort to help the child to develop fluent speech. Parents may report a regular routine with a quiet lifestyle, a generally chaotic routine, or something in between. Time demands can be associated with any environment. We don't like to point a finger at parents to suggest that their lifestyle caused their child's problem. Within a family, each child will react in a different manner to communicative demands. We recognize that children, whether they stutter or not, exhibit individual differences. As a result, parents are encouraged to describe their daily routines so that both parent and clinician can identify common daily occurrences that might have a negative impact on the child's fluent speech development. The majority of behaviors and situations that we will discuss are normal routine behaviors in most families. In fact, the reader will be able to recognize these same behaviors in their household. We are not suggesting that parents of children who stutter produce abnormal, pathological demands and that these demands account for stuttering. In reality, it is typically our normal conversational interactions that may be more difficult for the child who stutters. As a result, we need to help parents identify those behaviors that can be changed, instruct them in the methods for making these changes, and then discuss the best times to implement these changes.

When we deal with parents regarding environmental change, we often encounter parents who believe that they have caused their child's stuttering. As Conture (1990) has described, we need to help parents distinguish between causal behaviors and maintaining behaviors. We agree with Conture that the behaviors that we help parents identify are those behaviors that help to maintain the problem rather than cause the problem. It is our belief that if we can identify conditions within the environment that may have a negative effect on a child's speech, we can teach the parents to modify these conditions. When we provide indirect therapy, we believe that when parents make the requested changes, fluent speech will develop.

When the clinician and parent discuss environmental modifications, we suggest to the parents that they not think of completely abandoning their existing lifestyle in an effort to help their child. Our goal is to help the parents identify one activity or one behavior that can serve as their initial focus. In the case of the parent who is chronically late, we might suggest that he or she plan to leave 15 minutes earlier for an appointment. When a parent completes this task, he or she begins to recognize that change is possible. We encourage the parent to make an effort to leave 15 minutes early for their next appointment and the following appointment. We suggest that a consistent focus on one behavior will ultimately result in change. It is our expectation that as the parents begin to make changes that affect time demands at home, the child will respond positively to these changes.

We must also point out to the parents that, on occasion, parents will make all of the modifications that we request in an attempt to help their child's speech and the child continues to stutter. When stuttering continues to occur despite all of our efforts to change parental behavior, additional therapy may be warranted.

Demonstrating Speech and Environmental Modifications

After we've spent some time with parents discussing the possible changes in their speech and exploring the communicative environment at home, we believe that it is important to show the parents some potential ways to make these changes. A practical demonstration of the modifications under discussion can be designed in a multitude of ways. We like to structure our therapy session where we set up a play situation to observe parent-child interactions. We like to use materials that help to facilitate conversational interaction. These materials often include a play garage or farm with associated figures. Our experience has shown that when we provide books in this situation, we often get limited conversational interaction.

Initially, the clinician will sit off to the side or observe from behind a one way mirror, observing the parents' ability to modify communication as they interact with their child. If the parents have integrated the information from our previous discussions, we will note attempts to modify their speaking rate, modification of interrupting behavior, and consistent praise for fluency. In some cases, as the parents are making these changes, they may begin to see changes in their child's speech. These changes might include a slower speaking rate, fewer stutterings, or decreased duration of the stutterings. Being realistic we recognize that most parents will require some time to integrate these modifications into their communicative interactions. In fact, some parents will catch on right away while others will require an extended period of time.

The clinician has the opportunity to either observe the parents throughout the entire interaction or participate in all or some of the activities. Some clinicians may choose to take notes and videotape the session for a later discussion with the parents. We take a more interactive approach towards teaching and typically jump right into the interaction with the parents. If the parents are having difficulty modifying their speaking rates, we might provide a model that is slightly exaggerated so that the parents can follow our lead without our providing direct comments on their speaking rates. When parents continue to interrupt their child, we might ask them to remain quiet for a short time while the clinician interacts with their child and models the appropriate behavior for the parent. When the parents are not providing enough positive verbal reward for fluent speech, once again we might model the behavior. As we point out throughout this book, we believe that instruction is best facilitated when we immediately identify the behavior in question and then encourage and model a change. In this manner, the parent can immediately identify the behavior in question and then try to modify this behavior. When we complete this session with the parents, we encourage them to implement these communicative modifications at home. We encourage the parents to contact us with any questions that they may have and indicate to the parents that change both in their own speech and their child's speech is a gradual process. It is important that the parents recognize that the purpose of indirect therapy is to modify those time demands that may disrupt a child's speech while they are working to prevent further development of the child's stuttering.

In reality, change does not occur instantly, and sometimes environmental modifications may have little effect on the child. We explain the realities of therapy to the parents and indicate that our best approach is to try to make modifications. As clinicians, our goal for indirect therapy is to provide monitoring of the child's speech and associated reactions. This monitoring can be regular telephone contact with the parents or may involve periodic reevaluation. For some children environmental modifications may result in long-lasting fluency. For other children, environmental change is insufficient and additional intervention becomes necessary. We continue to use 1 year post onset of the problem as our focal point for direct therapy. When we have provided indirect therapy and the child exceeds 1 year of stuttering, we usually suggest a more direct approach toward fluency.

PARENT-CHILD FLUENCY GROUPS

The parent-child (PC) fluency group serves a number of functions. The clinician is able to work directly with children who are stuttering while their parents can receive instruction regarding the nature of their child's problem, share similar concerns with parents of other children who stutter, and learn techniques and strategies for facilitating fluency outside of the clinic.

Structure

Our discussion of the PC fluency group will primarily be based on our clinical experiences within a private practice environment. Additional observations will come from a PC fluency group within a university clinic environment. We recognize that many speech-language pathologists function in different clinical environments that may or may not be similar. It is not our intention to encourage the reader to duplicate our structure. We are attempting to share with the reader a number of ways in which therapy has been provided using the PC fluency group format. We understand that many clinicians will be working by themselves and do not have access to graduate student clinicians or a second colleague to assist. However, it is our hope that the procedures provided will encourage the reader to explore the manner in which they are presently providing therapy and pick and choose those aspects of our program that will fit within their existing service delivery model.

Our PC fluency group is typically conducted one time per week for 50 minutes. Within our private practice environment, our PC fluency group is usually scheduled for 6 P.M. The ideal number of children for our fluency group is four. Our clinicians have conducted groups with a maximum of six children although as the numbers increase, it becomes increasingly more difficult to provide each child with the necessary amount of time to work at developing fluency.

It is our expectation that the child will not only learn fluency skills within the clinical environment but that his or her parents also will learn to facilitate fluency outside of the clinic. Thus, an optimum view of our program would reveal that a child gets one weekly in-clinic therapy session and six out-of-clinic therapy sessions per week. In reality however, we often hear from parents about the difficulties of finding time to practice speech during the week. We suggest to the parents that even one day of practice between in-clinic therapy sessions will be beneficial to their child. We will discuss these concerns at length later on in this chapter.

In our private practice environment, groups are conducted during the early evening. We structure our group so that one clinician is responsible for working with the children while a second clinician works with the parents. On some occasions, we have simultaneously conducted two groups of children (different ages and maturity levels) with two clinicians while a third clinician worked with the parents. While our waiting room appears to be somewhat chaotic immediately prior to therapy, our ability to conduct two groups of children and integrate all of the parents into one group has proven to be an effective and efficient method for providing service.

Within the university setting our group is conducted somewhat differently. This group, Turtle Time, is part of our graduate training program and includes a master's level graduate supervisor and a number of graduate student clinicians. The group is conducted for 90 minutes during one day with a number of preschoolers in attendance. The group is often conducted like a preschool class where children learn fluency skills within a language-learning environment. In this group setting, the parents have the opportunity to observe, to discuss issues with the clinicians and other parents, and to participate in home assignments. The setup of this group is quite different from our private practice group although the focus is generally the same.

The Child Best Suited for a PC Fluency Group

The child who is recommended for the PC fluency group has typically been stuttering more than 1 year and has begun to exhibit some awareness of his or her stuttering. This awareness might be manifest as a number of associated behaviors or a comment such as "I can't say that." It is believed that these children will not outgrow their stuttering without some type of intervention. As we previously discussed, the age of the client typically ranges from 2 to 6 years of age. Because of the many developmental differences (e.g., physical size, emotional maturity) that occur in children within this age range, we tend to divide the group by age and emotional maturity. We typically create a cutoff that places children younger than 4 in one group while older and mature 4-year-olds are grouped with children 5 and 6 years of age.

Children's Group Therapy

Our goals for children are similar to our goals for adults. We expect the child to learn a set of skills that will result in increased fluency and then internalize these skills and take responsibility for these skills so that fluency can be transferred and maintained outside of the therapy room. We generally take a direct approach to therapy by modeling and demonstrating fluent speech skills for the child and asking the child to follow our models by producing fluent speech. By following our general therapy descriptions in Chapter 3, we see that for all clients, we begin by talking about speech production and how we produce speech.

Obviously, a discussion of speech production with young children is limited to the simplified descriptions of our breathing, our voice box, and our mouths. However, one group activity can involve the coloring of a simple diagram of the speech production mechanism and identification of the component parts. Children can be asked to identify these same body parts in themselves and other group members, and discussion can lead to the identification of places where their speech seems to get stuck and won't come out. As we have previously pointed out and will continue to do so throughout this book, we do not believe that talking about stuttering makes the problem worse. We believe that an educated client, whether 3 years of age or 80 years of age, has the best potential for learning to be fluent and remaining fluent.

We don't see the need to hide information from any of our clients. When we have completed a discussion of the speech production system, we begin to introduce the clients to the speech production skills that will result in fluency.

Teaching the Concepts of Fast and Slow

We have developed a program that expands upon Conture's (1982) descriptions of turtle speech and rabbit speech. We believe that a prerequisite toward understanding the skills for fluent speech involves understanding the concept of fast and slow. Although it is possible to develop a number of analogies that may help to solidify the concepts of fast and slow with young children, we are often drawn back to the rabbit and turtle because they appear to be two animals with whom even the youngest child can relate. Within our clinic, we have collected a number of rabbit and turtle puppets that serve us well during our therapy sessions. Our initial therapy focus may involve a number of activities for identifying the concepts of fast and slow. At times we start with nonspeech activities to demonstrate fast and slow. On one occasion, my graduate student Marilyn Poole suggested that by rolling a ball across the floor, we could demonstrate fast and slow. This activity worked so well for Marilyn that I have included the game ever since. We often go to opposite ends of the therapy room and ask the child to follow our model. We roll the ball fast and the child follows. We often point out to the child, "That was really fast, did you see how the ball was flying around the room?" We then roll the ball slowly and point out to the child how it is easier to get the ball to the other person when we roll it slowly. Interestingly, despite all our attempts to identify the benefits of slow versus fast, when the children are questioned regarding their favorite, fast or slow, of course they respond, fast. We do not let the child's response deter us from continuing to teach fast and slow. In fact, the child's response clarifies for us the notion that while it is important to teach children how to slow down in order to learn fluency skills, we also need to recognize that in the end, these children would prefer to be communicating at relatively normal speaking rates. When we are sure that the child understands the basic concept of fast and slow, we begin to focus our attention on more speech-related activities.

Like other therapy programs for older children and adults that believe that identification (Conture, 1982; Van Riper, 1973) is a prerequisite for therapy, we developed a number of identification games so that the child learns to identify the fast speech of Mr. Rabbit and the slow speech of Mr. Turtle. As the child learns to identify fast and slow speech in these animals, we begin to discuss the idea that when we use rabbit speech we often get stuck, but when we use turtle speech our speech is smooth. The concepts of turtle speech and rabbit speech are continued as we begin to provide models for the children.

Teaching Turtle and Rabbit Speech

Our PC fluency group is set up for the child who we believe will be able to quickly understand the concepts of fast and slow speech and subsequently integrate these concepts and follow our speech models to produce fluent speech. We begin teaching fluency skills during less complex activities (e.g., single-sentence picture descriptions) and continue through to conversational activities. These activities can include game playing, following a recipe to bake cookies, or role-playing. The clinician can vary the activities while continuing to model fluent speech. During the process of teaching fluency skills, we have found it beneficial to set up a number of speech rules for the children. These speech rules serve two functions. First, we have a number of rules that remind the child about speech production strategies that enable them to remain fluent. These rules are that (1) we start slow and (2) we connect the words with our voice. In addition, we use Conture's (1982) suggestions for modifying behaviors associated with communicative interaction. These pragmatic behaviors involve (1) listening when others are talking, (2) waiting your turn, and (3) not talking when others are talking (Conture, 1982). By teaching the child how to produce fluent speech and then making the child aware of methods for reducing communicative demands in a group situation, we are providing the child with a set of skills that will serve as the foundation for fluent speech beyond the therapy room.

During the first few therapy sessions, we discuss the speech rules with the group of children and then create a large poster that we can review before every therapy session. Because the majority of children are unable to read, we will need to put some symbol on our list of speech rules so that the child is reminded of the nature of these rules. For example, when we discuss starting slowly, we often use an analogy of a child who is ice skating or roller blading. We note that when we start fast with our skates, we often slip, fall, and fail to move. When we start skating more slowly, we observe that we are able to skate smoothly and continue moving. For the rule of starting slowly, we might put up a picture of a child ice skating as a reminder for that rule. Likewise, the clinician and the children can discuss each of the rules and determine what symbol or figure might best represent each rule.

Because the focus of all of our therapy includes the child's understanding of the behaviors that result in fluency, we review the rules at the beginning of each therapy session and may stop a child during some interaction and ask the child why or why not he or she had produced smooth speech. Our expectation is that these children will be able to state to the clinician that their smooth speech occurred as a result of the changes they made or behaviors they produced. Obviously the language that the child uses may be very different. However, our expectation continues to be that the child understands that he or she is in control of his or her behavior in contrast to thinking that Dr. Schwartz waves a magic wand and makes me fluent.

We often find it necessary to develop activities that emphasize the speech rules. When we discuss the rule of *waiting our turn*, we often use a turtle puppet or turtle hat as a method of identifying which child is allowed to talk while the other children wait their turn. We might ask a question and then give the puppet or hat to a child. The group is instructed that the only person who is able to answer the question is the person with the turtle. In this manner, we are able to continually remind the children that they can only talk when in possession of the turtle and when not holding the turtle, they must wait their turn. To add variety to the game, we might pick one child to distribute the turtle so that this child may gain a sense of control and understanding of waiting to speak.

Throughout the above described activities, we often ask the clients to tell why their speech has changed. In the beginning we often get responses like "I don't know." As this response is similar to the responses that we hear from older children and adults, we understand the need to teach these children that they are responsible for the changes that occur in their speech. As a result, we might question the child, "Did you get stuck?" or "Were you using your turtle speech?" When the child is unable to respond appropriately we might ask a second child. If the second child answers correctly, he or she might be rewarded. We want these children to understand that they are in control of their speech and that they posses the ability to make the necessary changes. This concept is important whether the clinician is working with a 3-year old child or a 30-year-old adult. Taking responsibility for the necessary changes will make it easier for the child to transfer fluency beyond the therapy room.

As the children learn to use their fluency skills in the therapy room, we recognize that their fluency is extremely fragile and is often disrupted as conversational demands increase. As a result, a major focus of therapy involves strengthening the child's fluency skills so that he or she can meet the conversational demands outside of the therapy room.

Transferring Fluency beyond the Therapy Room—Toughening up Fluency

Clinicians who have worked with children or adults who stutter will be able to relate at least one experience where they have worked with a client who was totally fluent within the clinical setting but as soon as their client stepped over the therapy threshold to leave the therapy room, his or her fluency broke down. In the past we believed that once a client was fluent in the therapy room he or she was ready to be dismissed from therapy. We now recognize that transferring fluency beyond the clinic room needs to be an active process in which the child learns to use his or her fluency skills in progressively more demanding communicative situations.

As kids are learning to be fluent during the therapy sessions, we are also encouraging the parents to work with their child at home using activities that are similar to the activities that we address within our clinic. We point out to the parents that working with their child to establish fluency at home does not mean that they have to create therapeutic environments at home. We encourage the parents to set aside a time where the parent and child can work on fluency skills without the distractions of television, video games, or other kids at home. For example, when a child is just starting in our PC fluency group we might practice our Turtle Speech while looking at pictures. In the clinic we might model a sentence for the child and the child responds with fluent speech. We suggest to the parents that they might select a book, magazine or even a family photo album where the parent can provide an appropriate fluency model and the child can respond. As the tasks get increasingly more difficult in the clinic, we encourage the parents to modify the activities at home to reflect the activities that we are conducting in the clinic. In this manner, the child is given the opportunity to modify his or her speech in a number of different environments. As the tasks increase in complexity, we expect the child's fluency to strengthen so that he or she is less susceptible to the demands of the environment and is better able to maintain fluency in view of these increased communicative demands.

In addition to the work that parents are doing to strengthen the child's fluency skills beyond the therapy room, we introduce a variety of activities that are focused on increasing the communicative demands on the child within the therapy room. These increased demands can result from the clinician speaking at a faster speaking rate, interrupting the client, minimizing the turn switching time, or even sitting more closely to the client. We attempt to use these demands in a systematic manner to strengthen the fluency skills of the child so that when the child confronts communicative demands outside of the therapy room he or she will be better equipped to maintain his or her speech fluency.

Increased communicative demands can be used during two different types of activities. When the child has first learned to master fluency skills within the clinical setting, the clinician can introduce a faster speaking rate or interrupt the child to determine the possible impact on the child's fluency. In this manner, the clinician is attempting to simulate the potential demands that a child may face outside of the therapy room so that the clinician can determine which child is more sensitive to these demands and which child is more likely to struggle outside of therapy. With this knowledge, the clinician can develop additional clinical activities for strengthening fluency and identify those children who will need additional work at remaining fluent. In addition, the clinician can help the parents to identify the potential problems that the child may face when he or she leaves the therapy room.

A second type of activity that we use involves group activities where the children are told that we are going to try to make them get stuck and their job is to continue to have smooth speech. We tell the children that when they leave the therapy room they will be talking with people who are speaking quickly and interrupting their speech. We tell the children that we know that when they talk with these people it's more difficult have smooth speech. As a result, we are going to play a game and their job is to stay as smooth as possible. The following description will help to illustrate this activity.

Technique—Toughening Up Fluency

We are going to play a game today that is a little different than the games we usually play. When we usually play speech games, we try to have slow smooth speech and try to not get stuck at all. All of you have done such a good job that I usually hear smooth speech all of the time in here. Now, I know that when you leave here, some of you have trouble using your smooth speech. Sometimes when you're outside you don't connect your words or forget to start slowly. I know that when you talk to some other kids or grown-ups, using your smooth speech becomes more difficult. Well, we know that when you talk to some other people they may be fast talkers or you may feel like you have to talk fast to keep up with them. When you try to do this, you get stuck. In our game, I am going to be a fast talker and you are going to try to use your smooth speech as best as you can. I am trying to get you stuck and you have to show me that you keep your smooth speech.

The game proceeds where we intentionally increase our speaking rate and often interrupt the child while he or she is talking. When a child appears distressed by the activity, we will back off from the demands as we will be defeating the purpose of the activity. For many children, the challenge to remain fluent while facing communicative demands is seen as an accomplishment that they can boast about to their parents. These children enjoy the competitiveness of the activity and are not bothered by the increased demands. If children exhibit stuttering, we encourage them to continue and point out how well they did. Additionally, we might tell the child that before therapy they would have had 10 or 15 stutterings but today they only got stuck once or twice. We are not looking to discourage our clients. We try to identify their accomplishments and continue to work from that point forward.

With some children, the demand situation that we just described is clearly the wrong activity. Modifications in the selection of activities will be necessary to toughen up their speech. The clinician will need to determine whether the activity benefits the majority of the group or whether the activity should be suspended until the one child experiencing difficulty is ready to participate. The activity can have positive benefits if the clinician can find the appropriate time.

We do not view these activities as harmful to the child. Our goal is to create some of the communicative demands that a child might encounter outside of the therapy room, within therapy. The child is taught to use his or her fluency skills as the communicative demands increase. We don't punish, berate, or focus in any negative way if a child is unable to complete the activity. These results help us to identify the potential difficulties the child will face during communicative interactions outside of therapy.

Weaning a Child from Therapy

There is no one rule or formula to follow on decreasing a child's attendance in within-clinic therapy. The time always arises when the clinician observes that the child is generally fluent within the clinical setting and the parents report good fluency skills at home. At this time, we often discuss with the parents the need to space out our in-clinic speech therapy sessions so the child learns to rely more on his or her own fluency skills and less on the reminders that we provide in the clinic. Because most children are attending group therapy once per week, our first attendance change will be for the child to attend group therapy every other week. In this manner, we are not totally separating the child from therapy and yet the child will be required to monitor his or her own speech for a longer period of time away from the therapy room. We always counsel the child's parents that if they have any concerns about their child's speech during the 2-week period they are free to contact our clinic. In addition, if the parents note that their child is having some increased level of difficulty because he or she is not attending as regularly, the parents can contact our clinic and we will discuss a course of actions with parents.

As the child continues to remain fluent outside of the clinic, our goal is to extend the time period between sessions. We typically require that the child continues to exhibit the same or better fluency skills for a period of time (1 to 2 months) before we recommend a further reduction in the number of in-clinic sessions. We eventually move to one time per month and then one time per 6 months. In the same way that a physician may require a yearly checkup, we will follow a child's progress for 1 to 2 years with a telephone call to the parents or an in-clinic session to determine the status of the child's speech. At the end of this time, we will wish the child well and dismiss him/her from therapy.

Parental Group Therapy

All of the programs that we provide for young children and older children include parental participation. We have come to recognize that the more people within the child's environment who participate in the therapy program, the better chance that child has to become fluent and remain fluent. Because parents are the primary models for communication in the young child's environment, involving parents in the therapy program can be extremely beneficial. Parents can learn to provide communicative models outside of the clinic that facilitate the child's fluency skills while at the same time modifying the communicative environment at home to provide the child with additional environments in which he or she is able to use his or her newly learned fluency. As a result, while the children are participating in group therapy, we also conduct a group therapy session for the parents. The parental therapy group can serve both an educational and therapeutic function for these parents. The educational component of the parent group focuses on the sharing of information about the onset and development of stuttering, strategies for modeling fluent speech outside of therapy, and strategies for communicative modifications at home that will facilitate the development of fluent speech. The therapeutic function of the group enables parents to express their concerns about their child's speech and general development with a group of people who are faced with similar circumstances. In addition, parents are able to report to other group members about their successes and failures when trying to implement our recommendations for speech changes at home.

Educating Parents

We try to conduct our parent group at the same time that the children are receiving therapy. It is not mandatory for both parents to attend our group sessions although we do require consistent, regular attendance by at least one parent. Our group is comprised of parents of children who are at various stages in the therapy process. Because of the diverse nature of the group relative to the amount of time spent in therapy, we are able to make use of the knowledge obtained by some parents because of the time their child has spent in therapy. As a result, these parents may be called upon during our interactions to share information with parents of those children who have just begun in therapy. Interestingly, we were conducting one parent group with parents of children who were all relatively new to therapy. In this case, we contacted a parent of a child who we had dismissed from therapy and asked her to participate with these new parents. During the session, the new parents not only benefited from the knowledge shared by the returning parent but also recognized that the returning parent's child had been dismissed from therapy because he was now fluent as a result of therapy. We recognized that we can discuss many therapy successes with parents who will listen with some degree of appreciation. However, when a parent returns to the parent group to share her knowledge of the problem and the success story of her child, parents view this type of situation to be far more rewarding than our presentations of clinical success.

When a parent participates in our group therapy session, we attempt to encourage a relaxed atmosphere so that information sharing takes place. We recognize that our role in this group should be a facilitator of conversation rather than a lecturer. However, because we are viewed as the expert, the parents look upon us to provide information. As a result, the clinician who will conduct this parent group has to find the right balance between providing objective information and listening to opinions and comments of the parents in the group. The listening component continues to be the behavior with which we continually struggle. As clinicians we get so used to being the source of information that we forget about the insights, needs, and participation of others.

Very often the parents who participate in the group bring a lot guilt to the situation because they believe that they caused their child's problem. When we explain to parents that they are not responsible for the child's problem, we can almost visualize the weight of the world being lifted from their shoulders. We have in fact observed audible sighs of relief when we've shared this information with parents. We try to provide objective information on our current thinking relative to the onset and development of stuttering and let other parents discuss how they view the problem and how they have worked out their concerns for their child.

Responding to Common Questions

Our experience working with the parents of young children who stutter has led us to develop a list of common questions that we are often asked to answer during our group interaction. In this section, we will present a question and a suggested answer to that question. While the list is not all inclusive, we believe we cover a lot of the concerns expressed by parents of young children who stutter.

Is Stuttering Genetic?　"We know that stuttering tends to run in families. If you have a relative who stutters, there is a greater likelihood of finding additional persons in your family who stutter. In addition, we know that the recovery rate of relatives is also a factor that must be considered. When we are trying to determine whether a child will continue to stutter, relatives who have not recovered increase a child's potential for continued stuttering. One final point: We know that stuttering runs in families but we also know that there is not a direct pattern of transmission from father or mother to child. Unlike disorders such as hemophilia or Huntington's chorea, the best we can say is that if there is a relative who stutters, the likelihood of finding additional stuttering in a family increases.

Will My Child Always Stutter?　The most common response to this question is "I don't know." However, we never this leave this question unanswered because parents are seeking information from as, the professionals. We explain: "We know that the greatest amount of recovery occurs during the first year following the onset of the problem. Once a child reaches 1 year post onset, the likelihood of spontaneous recovery where your child just stops stuttering, decreases dramatically. At best 80% of those children exhibiting stuttering will outgrow the problem. At worse, 20% of the children fail to outgrow the problem. Given the possibility that at least 20% of the children exhibiting stuttering will continue to stutter 1 year post onset, it is extremely important to enroll these children in therapy as soon as possible. In our case, we do not wait a year to enroll a child in therapy. We complete our evaluation and based upon some specific predictive criteria (e.g., frequency of stuttering, type of stuttering, parental awareness and reactions, the child's awareness and reactions) we typically enroll these children in therapy. We work to prevent the problem from continuing to develop and to ease the concerns of the parents. However, given all of the above information, there are some children who in spite of our best efforts, continue to stutter."

How Should I Respond When My Child Stutters?   "We believe that the best method for responding to your child's stuttering is to maintain the conversation, keep eye contact, and provide the child with enough time to respond. As we have explained previously, we don't believe that you have caused your child's problem. However, some of your reactions to his or her stuttering can help to perpetuate the problem. This idea was suggested by Conture (1982), a well-respected author and clinician. As we have discussed and will continue to discuss, when a child perceives some type of time, linguistic, or emotional demand that is beyond his present capability, his or her speech seems to break down in response to that demand. As a result, as parents, we can attempt to make modifications in the manner in which we communicate with the child. We will ask you to learn some modifications that help to facilitate fluency outside of the therapy room. However, despite the fact that we may make all of the necessary changes to our own speech and the environment, some children will continue to stutter."

What Can I Do to Help?   "To begin with, sometimes doing nothing works just as well doing something that you're unsure about. During the early stages of therapy, we can focus on some aspects of your communication that can be modified. However, until your child becomes more familiar with the skills necessary for fluency, we will encourage you to do nothing, in terms of direct work with your child. Initially, you will find it difficult to make the changes that we will ask regarding your own communication. These suggestions will occupy a lot of your thinking. In terms of working with your child, the best approach in the beginning is to not comment about his or her speech. We don't believe that calling attention to your child's speech is a bad idea. In fact, in the future we will encourage you to discuss fluency skills with your child. However, until your child's learns a mechanism for making the necessary changes in his speech, it is best that you concentrate on the changes that you can make in your speech and observe whether the changes that you make have any impact on your child's speech."

My Other Child Stutters—Did My Second Child Catch It?   "There is no evidence to indicate that stuttering can be transmitted by contact with another person who stutters. We often observe large families where there is a child who stutters but all of the brothers and sisters are fluent. We know that stuttering occurs more in families with a history of stuttering. In your case it appears that both of your sons are predisposed to stutter. It is best to have your second child evaluated and make some determination about the nature of his problem based upon that evaluation."

What Should I Tell His or Her Grandparents?   "We believe that it is important for all family members to be aware of the child's stuttering. This increased awareness is not suggested to make the child an object of pity who receives special treatment. Instead, we believe that with the knowledge that a child has some problems with communication, grandparents can be made aware of the communicative strategies that they use and the potential impact of their communication upon their grandchild who stutters. We often suggest that parents discourage grandparents from requesting that their grandchildren perform, recite poetry, or generally increase a child's communicative demands. We are not suggesting that children avoid conversations with their grandparents. Instead, we can advise grandparents in the same manner that we have advised parents regarding the nature of stuttering and techniques for facilitating fluency outside of the therapy room."

Encouraging Environmental Modifications

In addition to providing parents with information related to the onset and development of stuttering, we often discuss with the parents methods for modifying the child's communicative environment at home. It is our belief that if we can create an environment at home that is less demanding upon the child's speech production system, then as the child learns fluency skills within the therapy room, the transfer of these skills to situations outside of therapy will be maximized. We immediately recognize the reader's concerns that environmental modifications may have little or no effect on the speech of some children. However, we believe that our approach to therapy will target those situations and environments within our control so that if and when the child is in a position to use his newly learned fluency skills, we will have worked to maximize his or her chances within that environment.

When we first discuss communicative changes with the parents, we emphasize that these changes should occur in some gradual manner rather than complete implementation within all of the environments at home. Too often we encounter overzealous parents who believe that if 10 minutes of practice at home is good, then 30 minutes of practice is even better. This type of thinking continues to escalate to the point where the parents believe that they should be modifying their communicative environment all of the time. While our ultimate goal for therapy may be a consistent change in the child's communicative environment, we don't believe that we need to start out with anything greater than 5 to 10 minutes per day. We try to discuss with the parents the types of changes that we expect to occur and then discuss the best time for implementing the changes. The discussion on modifying situations and schedules within the family that we included at the beginning of this chapter provides the necessary information that we share with the parents. Issues related to modification of speaking rate, modification of turn switching pauses, and rewarding fluent speech continue to be our focus with children attending the PC fluency group.

Parents Sharing Experiences with Parents
In addition to the discussions related to the onset and development of stuttering that take place during our parent group sessions, we also note that parents have the opportunity to share their experiences related to their attempts to change their own speech and modify the communicative environment at home. As clinicians we understand the difficulties associated with behavioral change. However, the parents experience a range of difficulties that may be new to them. These difficulties often result in frustration that the parents can bring to the parent group session. Because we have a number of parents whose children are at various stages in their stuttering program, it is not uncommon for a parent to identify with the frustrations expressed by another parent and subsequently relate some story or comment about his or her own difficulties and how he or she was able to overcome the problem. The real benefit of our parent group is that a frustrated parent can receive emotional support from both the clinician and other parents. Using this combined counseling approach we are often successful at dealing with most of the concerns raised by parents.

In addition to dealing with the parent's frustrations regarding behavioral changes at home, we often encourage each of the parents to spend some time in the therapy room observing and participating with the clinician. When the parent returns to the parent group, we encourage that parent to share his or her observations with the group. Our discussion might focus on a particular fluency skill that the clinician was teaching or the manner in which the clinician dealt with behavior problems in the group. We find that different parents focus on different aspects of our therapy program, and these observations provide a variety of topics for our group discussion.

Our clinical experience suggests that parental participation in the therapy program is a major factor for successful fluency therapy. Without the participation of parents and other persons within the child's communicative environment, the speech-language pathologist is expecting the child to spend 60 to 120 minutes per week in therapy and be able to use his or her newly learned skills outside of the therapy room. Experience indicates that this generalization of skills occurs for the child who is the exception to the rule. The majority of children who attend our PC fluency group require a lot of practice and encouragement both within the therapy and at home to make lasting changes in their speech. Parental cooperation with the speech-language pathologist can result in these long-term changes.

DIRECT INDIVIDUAL THERAPY

Definition

Direct therapy involves a therapy program where we work directly with the child to teach him or her a number of speech skills that will result in fluent speech production. When a young child is enrolled in direct therapy, it is our belief that indirect therapy and/or environmental modification will not be sufficient to help the child become fluent. This program is very similar to the program that we conduct with older children and adolescents, although the manner in which we deal with these children is modified to meet the needs of their age and emotional development.

The Child Best Suited for Direct Therapy

The focus of this chapter continues to be the child who has not completed kindergarten. The child who is best suited for direct therapy has begun to demonstrate an awareness of his or her stuttering. The child's awareness often results in changes in the type of stuttering (an increased number of sound prolongations) and an increase in the number and variety of nonspeech behaviors associated with stuttering (Schwartz & Conture, 1988). In addition, parental reports may include mention of a child's avoidance of certain sounds, words, or situations. Occasionally, a parent may note his or her child's comment such as "I can't say that." As we have previously indicated, the child and parent are both involved in the therapy process.

Providing Direct Therapy

In our discussion of the PC fluency group, we indicated that the early stages of therapy include a focus on the anatomy associated with speech production and activities that focus on increasing the child's awareness of both his or her speech production and stuttering. As part of our direct therapy program, we include a similar focus in therapy and all of the aforementioned descriptions are applicable during the early stages of direct therapy.

The major difference between the child attending the PC fluency group and the child attending direct therapy is that the child attending direct therapy appears to be reacting cognitively or behaviorally to his or her stuttering, and it is believed that this child will need to be instructed in a systematic manner on the necessary skills to become fluent. The child attending direct therapy typically does not generalize fluency skills as fast as the child in the PC fluency group. As a result, the focus of therapy is instruction on fluency skills and the systematic use of these skills during progressively more difficult tasks. We assume that the reader will be able to apply our previous discussions regarding fluency skills both in Chapter 3 and the earlier portions of this chapter when working directly with a child. As such, our discussion to follow will focus on the necessary tasks for teaching fluency skills during progressively more complex tasks.

VTC: 00:46:50:18

Tasks for Teaching Fluency

The idea of using progressively more complex tasks during fluency training is attributed to Ryan (1974) who developed his program, Gradual Increase in Length and Complexity of Utterance. Further development of this idea was reported by Costello-Ingham (1993) who termed her program, Extended Length of Utterance Program. We tend to favor the idea that in order to teach a client to be fluent during conversation, it is necessary to begin with relatively simple, less complex tasks and then progress to longer more complex tasks. It is at this point where we would like to differentiate our program from the programs proposed by Ryan and Costello. Costello notes: "The length of children's utterances can be controlled by the use of clinician models, written stimuli, or the presentation of pictures or topics that evoke responses of the desired length." During this program, the clinician will present a desired model and request the child to verbally reproduce the model. When a child produces a fluent response, the clinician rewards the child's fluency. Behaviorists such as Ryan and Costello expect that the child will repeat the next utterance in the same manner, thereby receiving additional rewards. In our program, we take a more direct approach toward teaching fluency skills. We begin by first teaching the child the necessary skills for fluency. When the child has mastered these fluency skills we reward the child for using these skills. During the Ryan and Costello program, the child is rewarded for fluency without learning why the fluency occurs. We believe it is important to take a more direct approach with the child. In this manner the child learns that he or she is responsible for the fluency that is produced so that when the child is away from the clinician and the therapy room, the child will have a set of internalized instructions for remaining fluent. Our approach is similar for the 4-year-old child and the 50-year-old client. The client will learn to use his or her fluency skills and take responsibility for the necessary changes.

When working with children, we begin with simple less complex tasks and gradually introduce longer and more complex tasks. For the child who has difficulty gaining the most basic understanding of the skills for fluency, we will often begin with a series of pictures where we model a carrier phrase such as "I see a ____." Every time we present another picture, the child is required to use the same sentence but substitute the object denoted in the picture. At this level, we are able to provide a consistent fluency model for the child. We discuss with the child how we are able to start slowly and connect the words with our voices. As the child learns to master fluency using carrier phrases, we progress to single-sentence picture descriptions, 2-sentence pictures descriptions connected with "and," 50-syllable pictures descriptions, 100-syllable picture descriptions, 50-syllable monologues without pictures, 100-syllable monologues without pictures, and ultimately conversations for progressively longer periods of time. Our goal is to reach fluent conversational speech. Not all clients require a progression through each of the tasks. However, we outline our perception of progressively more difficult tasks so the reader has an idea of one possible course for therapy.

We don't set out a specific number of sentences or number of attempts that convince us that a child has mastered a particular task. Instead we structure our therapy session in such a way that we are able to work at two or even three different task levels within the same therapy session. Let's consider a description of a typical 50-minute therapy session with a young girl who is working at single-sentence picture descriptions. To begin, we believe that record-keeping and monitoring a client's performance are an essential part of the therapy program. We are living in an age of accountability where we have to justify to a child's parents, the school, and insurance companies why a particular child needs to continue in therapy. As a result, it is imperative that we monitor the daily successes and failures of our client so that we know how much progress is occurring. We often determine that we can complete two to three different activities within a 50-minute therapy session. For the girl who is working on single-sentence picture descriptions, our expectation for mastery of this skill level is that the girl will consistently produce 20 to 30 fluent sentences during three consecutive sessions. When this client is able to complete this goal, we believe that she has mastered fluency for this task. Because these early tasks will serve as the foundation for all of the girl's subsequent fluency, our expectation for success at this level is the ability to fluently produce single-sentence picture descriptions with 100% accuracy. Our goal for success at this point in therapy is based upon the fluent production of a sentence. During this activity, we tally the number of fluently produced sentences relative to the total number of sentences produced and determine the percentage of fluent productions. At the sentence level, we find that focusing on task success rather than frequency of occurrence of stuttering, is a better way to focus the child's attention and a means to focus on the child's accomplishment. We recognize that some clinicians will balk at our requirements for fluency and even point out that we are placing excessive pressures upon this girl. In reply we return to our clinical experiences that reveal that most young clients respond to this fluency challenge and are very successful at working toward and achieving 100% success at the sentence level.

Our primary focus in our example is consistent fluent single-sentence picture descriptions. In our typical therapy session, we begin our session with a task that we know that the child has mastered or is close to mastering. In our example, we begin the therapy session using carrier phrases to help the client "warm-up her speech muscles." We explain to the client that we know that she is already successful at this task. We point out that because she is successful, she can use this type of activity as a warm-up for more difficult tasks that she may encounter at later stages in therapy. From the clinician's perspective, we expect the child to be fluent throughout this task. By beginning every session with a previously mastered task, the child is able to tune up her speech production system for more difficult tasks while at the same time gaining additional practice and confidence using her fluency skills. When the client completes 10 to 20 warm-up sentences, we then begin our work on single-sentence pictures descriptions. Because our client has already been working on this skill during previous sessions, we may set our goal for therapy at 85% to 95% success. Once again, the client's success is based upon the number of fluent sentences produced. Our therapy involves a flow of tasks rather than the completion of one task before starting another task. As a result, we often pause during the middle of an activity and introduce a more difficult task. The introduction of the more difficult task, in this case, two-sentence picture descriptions, enables the clinician to introduce the next more difficult task that will be addressed while at the same time the child is being tested to ascertain his or her ability to generalize his or her fluency skills to a more difficult level. After an attempt or two at the new task, we return to our task of single-sentence picture descriptions. We continue to pause throughout the task to encourage the client to become more familiar with the new two-sentence task that will be worked on during subsequent sessions. During our present session, we may ask the client to complete a second-single sentence picture description task with some additional activities that include two-sentence descriptions.

When our client is in the final stages of mastering single sentence picture descriptions, we begin to introduce the next task with an expectation for 60% to 70% success. During subsequent sessions, we begin the session with single-sentence picture descriptions as the warm-up activity, two sentence picture descriptions as the task to master, and fifty-syllable picture descriptions as the more difficult task that is being introduced.

In retrospect we see that the activities that make up our therapy session often begin with a task that has been mastered. This task serves as a speech production warm-up and a method that enables the client to strengthen his or her fluency skills within a non-demanding environment. We then continue working on our present goal until the client has reached the level of success that we prescribe for the task. During the early stages of therapy this level is often 100% success. While a client is mastering his or her fluency skills during the task, we begin to introduce more difficult tasks to determine the client's ability to generalize his or her fluency skills to a more difficult task and to introduce the client to tasks that will follow. When a client has achieved the desired goal and is working toward maintaining the consistency of this goal across therapy sessions, we introduce the next goal with a success rate that is consistent with the client's ability to be successful completing the task. This level of success is often 60% to 70% of the task. As the reader can view, our therapy sessions involve the evolution of tasks where simpler, less complex tasks, evolve to more difficult and complex tasks. We try to provide methods to gradually introduce more difficult tasks while at the same time providing time for the client to rehearse previously learned skills to gain the needed practice and additional confidence that is ultimately necessary for transferring fluency beyond the therapy room.

Parents and the Transfer of Fluency

We have already pointed out that the child who requires direct therapy will not become fluent if he or she is only provided with environmental modification. As such, the parental role for the child who attends direct therapy focuses on assisting the child's transfer of fluent speech beyond the therapy room and making environmental modifications that will help to facilitate the child's ability to remain fluent at home.

For the child attending direct therapy, it is important to include the parent in the therapy process. As discussed previously, parents are encouraged to make modifications in their communicative environment at home so that any fluency skills that the child learns will be more easily transferred to other communicative situations. Suggestions for rate modification, turn yielding pauses, and rewarding fluency continue to be important. In addition, parental observation and participation in the therapy process is even more important than previously discussed for indirect or group therapy. Because of the age and immaturity of these children, we find that a parent's encouragement and willingness to help the child practice his or her speech can facilitate faster transition of fluency skills into activities outside of therapy.

We discuss with the parents the need to establish a speech practice time at home where the activities that are practiced in the therapy room are also practiced at home. By focusing attention on the activities in therapy, we find that our subsequent therapy sessions often progress faster because the child does not have to relearn the skills that were taught during the previous session. In addition, the parents are learning to be better fluency models for their child so that during conversational activities like dinner or a drive in the family car, the parent is able to provide communicative models that will assist the child's fluent speech development. When we can get grandparents, teachers, and other child-care workers involved, we can expedite the transfer of the child's fluency.

A second activity that we use to help with the transfer of fluency is to include the child in direct therapy in the PC fluency group. As the child masters fluency in direct therapy, including the child in the PC fluency group will provide the child with an opportunity to practice his or her fluency skills with other children who have similar problems. In addition, the child will also benefit from the communicative activities that are facilitated through group interaction. We often recommend that this child continue attending one therapy session per week to work on his or her speech skills and also attend a second session with a group. As the child continues to improve, direct therapy may be discontinued and the child can continue with group participation. When the clinician notes that the child is consistently fluent within therapy, and the parents report that the child is consistently fluent outside of the therapy room, the child's participation in the group may be modified. We often reduce a child's attendance in the group from one session per week to one session per 2 weeks to one session per month to one session per 6 months and then dismissal. The amount of time that the child spends in this weaning process is a function of the child's ability to remain fluent as the number of sessions decreases. The parents working closely with the clinician can determine when to terminate therapy.

SUMMARY

We have attempted to describe a number of therapy options that are available for the young child who stutters. For the child who is closest to stuttering onset and showing no awareness of his or her stuttering, we have focused our attention on an indirect therapy program that is designed for environmental modifications through parental cooperation. For the child who has begun to show some development of stuttering as evidenced by changes in the type of stuttering, behaviors associated with stuttering, and awareness of stuttering, we have described a PC fluency group where the child learns skills for improving fluency while both the parent and child learn methods for facilitating fluency outside of the therapy room. Finally, for the child with the characteristics of a more developed problem, we have described direct therapy. In our direct therapy program, the child attends therapy to learn skills for improving fluency and for modifying his or her attitudes and reactions to speech and the environment. As this child begins to exhibit improved fluency skills, he or she can attend an individual therapy session to continue to work on fluency skills and attend the PC fluency group to practice his or her fluency skills in group situations. Some children will reach the point of only attending the PC fluency group as they progress toward fluency. Throughout our discussion we have attempted to promote the idea that parents, teachers, and other caregivers are all significant components in the therapy process. In the majority of cases, the more therapeutic involvement of persons within the child's communicative environment, the better chance for successful therapy.

▶ 6

Older Children
and Adolescents
Who Stutter

In the chapter that follows we will describe our therapy program for older children and adolescents who stutter. The therapy program presented can be adapted to meet the needs of both older children and adolescents. For those clinicians working with older adolescents, information within this chapter can be combined with information from the two chapters (Chapters 7 and 8) examining adults so that a more comprehensive program can be established. For both groups of children we will discuss teaching fluency skills as a method for establishing fluency. As the client begins to acquire fluency skills in the therapy room, we also will discuss methods for transferring fluency beyond the therapy room. It is important to note that we deal with the emotional needs of these clients beginning with the first day in treatment. As therapy continues, counseling the client and discussing relevant issues are part of every therapy session.

WHO ARE THESE KIDS?

Our discussion of older children focuses on those children who are still stuttering when they enter first grade (approximately 7 years of age). These children have typically been stuttering since the age of 3 or 4, and the likelihood of these children spontaneously recovering from the problem is unlikely. If we have had success conducting therapy with preschoolers who stutter, theoretically we should encounter very few older children who stutter. However, an examination of both the caseloads of public school speech-language pathologists and of private practitioners suggests to us that we are continuing to see stuttering in older children. How do we account for this phenomenon? We believe that there are a number of potential explanations for why we continue to see older children who stutter.

CHILDREN WHO HAVE NEVER RECEIVED THERAPY

We continue to be surprised by the number of older children who have never attended speech therapy prior to their seventh birthday. In view of our methods for preschool screening and our increased knowledge regarding the benefits of early intervention, we are often surprised to encounter children who have never attended therapy. How might we explain this phenomenon? For some parents, the suggestions of friends, neighbors, and relatives are strong enough to withhold treatment. Many parents have listened to their friends and neighbors advice, which suggested: "the problem will go away . . . My son stuttered when he was younger and he outgrew the problem . . . Your cousin Ralph stuttered for a time but he didn't need any therapy." In addition, when pediatricians, family physicians, and even speech-language pathologists recommend that stuttering should not be treated in preschoolers, we often encounter these children at later stages in stuttering development. These influences continue to be strong and as a result, we often encounter a child who has stuttered for three or four years before coming for an evaluation. In some instances, a parent will wait until a child is 9 or 10 years of age to seek help believing all the time that the child will outgrow his or her stuttering. Additionally, we sometimes see an adolescent who has not been bothered by a mild to moderate stuttering problem until he or she reaches high school. The client reports that he or she has been able to deal with his or her speech up to that point with little or no effort. However, as the child encounters the increased demands of high school, maintaining fluent speech is not as easy and his or her type of stuttering and frequency of stuttering often begin to change with his or her increased reactions to the problem.

CONSISTENCY OF THERAPY

The majority of older children and adolescents who continue to stutter fall into the category related to consistency of therapy. In our opinion, the key to successful stuttering therapy is consistent attendance followed by consistent practice followed by consistent attendance. Consistent, regular attendance in therapy enables the client to learn new skills, practice new skills, use those skills out of the therapy room, practice at home and then in the same week, return to therapy where those skills are reinforced through continuing practice with feedback provided by the clinician. When clients fail to attend consistently, progress is disrupted. For some clients this setback is minutes in duration during the subsequent therapy session. For other clients, the setback may last for days or weeks, until the client is able to catch up to previous levels of success.

What are the potential causes of disruption in the continuity of therapy? For school-age children in the United States, the nature of our school speech therapy programs appears to be the biggest disrupter of therapy. The school speech-language pathologist is faced with large caseloads that often result in a maximum of two 20-minute therapy sessions per week for a child who stutters. For some children this time may be adequate but for the majority of children who stutter, 40 minutes of therapy per week is insufficient. A significant problem arises when the clinician needs to group children together for expediency, given the makeup of his or her caseload. As a result, a child who stutters is often grouped in a 20-minute therapy session with a child who exhibits articulation problems. A skilled clinician may be able to address both issues simultaneously, although we wonder about the quality of therapy being provided. When a child is allocated two 20-minute therapy sessions per week, there are a number of additional problems faced by the clinician. A clinician is required to work around the child's classroom requirements, which oftentimes prevent him/her from attending one of his or her weekly therapy sessions. These classroom requirements include special classes such as music and art, special subjects such as math and reading, and weekly events that include classroom celebrations, field trips and so forth. If a child consistently receives twice-weekly therapy, it is often the exception rather than the rule.

Adolescents attending junior and senior high school face additional concerns regarding therapy. In an effort to maximize time and efficiently deal with a caseload, a school speech-language pathologist may find it necessary to provide therapy services at the junior or senior high school 1 day per week. Given the need for at least 60 minutes of weekly therapy for adolescents beginning in therapy, this type of program hardly meets the needs of the student. In addition, the school speech-language pathologist, whether visiting the high school 1 day per week or 5 days per week, often encounters the reluctance of the adolescent to leave his or her class room to attend therapy. Our experience suggests that even the most motivated high school student who stutters will be reluctant to attend therapy because of the perceptions of the other students. However, when parents can find alternative sources of treatment (e.g., private practice specialists) or therapy in school at the end of the school day, adolescents tend to be more successful when not confronted with the specter of their peers making judgments regarding their speech.

A lack of consistent therapy is easily attributed to the system in which we are expected to function. However, at times we find ourselves in a system that provides accommodations for older children and adolescents. Some programs enable a clinician to provide at least two 30-minute therapy sessions per week, and the clinician then is able to teach the client to change his or her speech in the therapy room. However, it is at this point where the therapy breaks down because the client is either dropped from therapy or referred to a specialist because the clinician is unsure how to proceed. In these cases, a child will continue to stutter for a variety of reasons. As noted in the previous chapter, parental involvement in therapy can play a significant role in the progress and course of treatment. When some clinicians begin to work with the older children and adolescents, they fail to recognize the continuing need to involve family members in therapy. We believe that the only method for effectively changing speech with older children and adolescents is to include as many family members in the therapy process as possible. We recognize that the role of the family has changed for this group of children but we don't see this as a reason to exclude a valuable resource from the therapy process. We will discuss the role of the family in therapy at length throughout this chapter. A second explanation for a lack of consistent therapy with this group of children has to do with the client's acceptance of responsibility and the client's self-initiated work on their speech outside of the therapy room. For many younger children, the parents are instrumental at this point in therapy. However, as the child gets older, we expect the child to become a more active participant in the transfer process. As will be discussed in this chapter and in the chapters dealing with adults, the need for an active transfer program is one key to successful therapy. In the majority of cases, fluency does not spontaneously occur outside of the therapy room.

Everyone, including parents, clients, and family members, would like to believe that because a client is able to be fluent within the therapy room, he or she should be able to be fluent outside of therapy. As clinicians, we also would like transfer to occur automatically. Unfortunately for most clients, the transfer of fluency is hard work that requires a lot of attention. When dealing with older children and adolescents we find clients who are often reluctant to allocate the necessary attention to their speech that will result in consistent fluency. We often discuss maturity as one explanation for a client's failure to progress and recognize that with maturation and environmental participation and support, we might begin to see changes.

CHILDREN WHO CONTINUE TO STUTTER

There is one client who is rarely discussed in the literature on stuttering therapy. If we examine our best case clinical scenario, we are talking about a skilled clinician who provides at least two 30-minute sessions per week on a consistent basis and a client who practices regularly outside of the therapy room. This client continues to stutter despite our best efforts to teach changes. We believe that two important factors can be identified as characteristics of these individuals. We find that the speech motor skills of these kids are slow to develop and generally at the low end of normal limits. Attempts to teach fluency skills are often slow and laborious. In addition, we sometimes find that a child has developed strong emotional reactions to his or her speech and the environment. As a result we find that the client learns the basic skills for being fluent, although any attempt to use those fluency skills beyond therapy result in problems for the client. For these clients, an alternate form of therapy may be necessary.

In our previous discussions, we characterized older children and adolescents who continue to stutter. We described the many reasons an older child or adolescent continues to stutter. In view of these facts, we are now faced with a client who will not outgrow his or her stuttering, has potentially developed strong emotional reactions to his or her problem, and may be reluctant to attend therapy. We are now faced with the question, "How will I develop a treatment program for these kids?" In the pages to follow, we will describe our therapy program in terms of teaching fluency skills, strengthening fluency skills using progressively more difficult tasks, transferring fluency skills beyond the therapy room, and encouraging parental involvement in the program. Counseling the client, building confidence, dealing with reluctance, and taking responsibility for changes are components of the program that are addressed during every therapy session.

INDIVIDUAL THERAPY

Teaching fluency skills to older children is quite a bit different than what was previously described for young children. Our clinical experiences suggest that the majority of these kids have been previously enrolled in some type of therapy program with little or no success. The kids that we enroll in therapy have not outgrown their stuttering and often exhibit characteristics of a well-developed stuttering problem. As a result, our focus in therapy is to address the fluency skills of these children and their attitudes and reactions toward their speech. Our therapy program focuses on teaching fluency skills that result in fluent speech. At the same time, we are talking to clients about their speech, their attitudes toward their speech, and their abilities to become fluent outside of the clinic. Within this framework, the child's parents are aware of the nature of the therapy program and are asked to participate at various stages as the program progresses. Within this book, we describe the individual components of the therapy program although, in reality, we are talking about simultaneous occurrences. Individual components of the therapy program will be described throughout the chapter. However, the following example will demonstrate how simultaneous attention to fluency skills and counseling may be required.

Is it unrealistic to set fluency goals for these clients? We think not. Our clinical experiences with older children and adolescents indicate that these kids would like to become as fluent as possible. We set fluency goals for our clients that we believe are attainable. We don't punish a client for not meeting fluency goals. However, clear, objective goals help the young client establish a focus for each therapy session. We believe that each client needs to understand the expectations for therapy and the kinds of changes we expect to see. What are the consequences when a client doesn't make changes or meet his or her goals? As clinicians we understand that goals may not be met for a number of reasons. These reasons include: (1) the clinician has chosen the wrong set of therapy techniques or started at level too difficult for the client; (2) the client takes a long time to integrate suggestions and skills for change; and (3) the client is failing to complete homework assignments resulting in a slowed down in-clinic therapy program. The speech-language pathologist must continually evaluate the tasks selected to meet the goals, the client's abilities to reach these goals, and the client's motivation to remain fluent when not attending therapy.

Technique—Fluency and Counseling

John, an 8-year-old with a moderate stuttering problem, is attempting to read fluently during the early stages of therapy. The goal for this therapy session is the fluent reading of 15 selected paragraphs. Although John is successful with his speech tasks and responding positively to verbal rewards, he pauses during the middle of the task and expresses concerns regarding the demands for fluency that are coming from his mother and father. The clinician faces a dilemma at this point. The client's goals for the session are established, and the client needs to continue to achieve these goals. On the other hand, the client has opened a door for the clinician regarding his emotions associated with his stuttering. We immediately recognize an opportunity to deal with the client's emotional concerns regarding parental demands. We note that our goals for the day do not include this type of discussion. However, we also know that many children this age are reluctant to share their feelings with the clinician. As a result, we stop our reading activity and focus all of our attention on the child's statement "Your parents are demanding fluency at home?" We believe that by immediately attending to the client's concerns, he will be more willing to share concerns in the future. Given John's concerns regarding his parents, we can schedule some discussions with his parents to deal with John's concerns. When John and the clinician have explored his concerns, the reading activities can be resumed.

Day One

The first day in therapy with older children and adolescents focuses on an orientation to speech production and stuttering and a discussion of the relationship between the two. Our description of the speech production system is a modification of our description in Chapter 3. We attempt to focus on the three systems required for speech production and explain speech production in a manner that is easily understood by the child.

Technique—Speech Production Mechanism

When we produce speech, we use our lungs, our voice box, and our mouth. These three things have to work together in order for you have smooth speech. The lungs fill with air, and this air provides the energy to make your voice box work. Your voice box controls the flow of air that goes into your mouth. When your voice box closes you make sounds with your vocal cords. These sounds can be vowels like /a/ and /o/ or consonants like /b/ or /z/. When you vocal cords are open, the sound usually comes from the moving air being controlled by your lips, teeth, and tongue. You make sounds like /s/ and /p/ by moving your tongue and lips. Kids who stutter can't move their vocal cords, lips, teeth, or tongue as smoothly as other kids. Because you can't move as smoothly, you sometimes get stuck and feel like you have to push harder and harder to get the sounds out. Pushing harder and harder just makes it more difficult to have smooth speech.

VTC: 00:59:49:26

We continue our Day One discussion with the kids by discussing the different types of stuttering that they are producing and where in the speech production system they might be "getting stuck."

Tasks for Teaching Fluency

We teach fluency skills within a framework that progresses from less complex activities to more complex activities. This framework can be viewed in Table 6–1.

The complexity of the activity is typically associated with the linguistic nature of the material, the amount of speech required by the client, the amount of fluency required for the task, and the demand placed by the clinician. As with all of our therapy programs, our goal is to teach the client to be as fluent as possible, sounding as natural as possible, with the least amount of effort. Do we always achieve our goals? We like to think that every client who participates in therapy continues to improve in a slow, continuous manner. We believe that as long as the client continues to attend therapy, some aspect of his or her speech or behavior will improve. We know that some readers will say that the preceding statement means that we will keep

TABLE 6–1.   **Overview for Establishing Fluency for Older Children and Adolescents**

1. Clinician educates the client regarding speech production and stuttering.
2. Clinician teaches fluency skills during reading.
3. Clinician teaches fluency skills during picture descriptions.
4. Client reads sentences and paragraphs.
5. Client produces one-sentence picture descriptions.
6. Client produces two-sentence picture descriptions.
7. Client produces 50-syllable picture descriptions.
8. Client produces 100 to 500-syllable picture descriptions.
9. Client produces 50-syllable monologues.
10. Client produces 100- to 1000-syllable monologues.
11. Client converses with clinician.
12. Client converses with clinician while clinician introduces increased conversational demands.

a client in therapy forever. However, we evaluate each client's progress after each therapy session. When a client is failing to progress, we question why. When a client has plateaued in therapy, we ask why. When we believe a client is ready to terminate therapy, we consult with the client and his or her parents to arrive at a decision that best meets the client's needs.

We see fluent conversation as the ultimate goal of therapy and, as result, our therapy program is directed toward that end. We begin with tasks that enable clients to focus their attention on learning fluency skills rather than conversational interaction. Our experience suggests that most of the clients in this age group find it difficult to learn fluency skills using only a conversational focus. As a result, we begin our therapy with either reading activities or pictures description tasks. By using reading or pictures, there appears to be a lessened linguistic demand that enables the child to focus on using the fluency skills without having to generate original thinking. When we begin this process, our goal is for the client to learn the skills for smooth speech by slowing down his or her speaking rate to the point where he or she can fluently read one sentence at a time or describe one picture. When we begin therapy, our focus is on fluency skills. When a client masters the fluency during these simple tasks, we change the nature of the tasks to become gradually more difficult. The client is expected to be fluent during longer reading and picture description tasks, which then leads toward monologues without pictures. As the client becomes more proficient at fluently producing monologues, he or she will be expected to learn to be fluent during conversational interactions both within the clinic and outside of the therapy room. With these goals in mind, we first focus on teaching the client the necessary fluency skills.

Reading

We will only use reading as a beginning activity when the client is a proficient reader. Typically, the level of oral reading skills necessary to use reading as a fluency activity begins in the fifth or sixth grade. When reading is inappropriate for a specific client, it becomes necessary to teach fluency skills using single-sentence picture descriptions. When we select material for reading, we often select material that is below the child's grade level so that the content will not pose a problem for the child. For example, for a child in the fifth or sixth grade, we might select a nonfiction book about whales that is geared toward a second- or third-grade child. By selecting this type of material, we can find a topic that might be interesting to the child and yet use the easier sentence structure and vocabulary to assist in the child's learning of smooth speech skills. When we work with adolescent clients, we select reading material that will enable the client to master his or her fluency skills. Sometimes this material may be below the reading level of the client and we find it necessary to explain why the material was chosen. As the adolescents begin to master fluency skills, we might change the reading material so that reading might serve a dual focus.

Our reading material may include a Stuttering Foundation publication *Do You Stutter: A Guide For Teens* (Fraser & Perkins, 1987). By selecting this publication, we believe that we can help the client to practice his or her fluency skills, but also provide a suggestion or insight into the stuttering problem. For example, we often use Guitar's (1987) chapter from the teen publication:

> *Notice how you tighten your mouth or your throat or your chest when you stutter? Why? Are you squeezing your muscles for exercise? No. More likely, you're struggling to get out of an uncomfortable situation. (1987, p. 62)*

VTC: 00:32:00:20

When we use a selection from this publication, we may choose to ask the client his or her opinion on the point the author was trying to make. On some occasions, the client's response provides a good opportunity to discuss a matter of concern to the client. As can be seen, we can not only address fluency during this task but also focus on the client's emotional perspectives regarding his or her stuttering.

It is important to recognize that regardless of the child's age, if the client is bored with the reading material, therapy will not progress and both client and clinician will perceive therapy sessions to be endless. As with many other types of therapy, it is important to select reading material that is meaningful to the client. To meet these ends, we often encourage a client to bring their own reading material from home. These materials range from popular series being read by classmates to popular magazines that reflect a client's interests. In our experiences, these magazines have ranged from *Boy's Life* to *Rock Guitar* and everything in between.

To teach speech fluency, we use the procedures described in detail in Chapter 3. The client is instructed to start slow, stretch the vowels, connect the words, and pause after three or four words. When these techniques are taught using reading, it is our belief that the client is taught these skills on a sentence-by-sentence basis. We begin our instruction by telling the client that we will stop him or her along the way if he or she is not using the necessary skills. Our goal is to not increase frustration but to have the client focus his or her attention on speech production rather than on the emotional reactions to speech. To accomplish this task, we often model a sentence for the client and ask the client to follow our model. If the client fails to use the necessary smooth speech skills, we immediately stop the client and identify the changes that need to occur. To the untrained observer, this method of instruction often appears to be negative as some clients are being stopped on a regular basis until they make the necessary changes. To the clinician who understands the rationale for stopping the client, he or she knows that there is no point to letting a client continue to use inappropriate strategies for producing speech. We recognize that our style is somewhat confrontational when we teach fluency skills. However, when we stop a client, we do not try to demean the client or berate the client. Our goal is to teach the client the new skills so that he or she can incorporate these techniques into his or her reading in as efficient a manner as possible. Our experience has been very positive with all of our clients, although we are sensitive to the client's frustration level and sometimes have to counsel the client on a balance between his or her speech skills and the emotional reactions associated with speaking and stuttering.

Technique—Teaching Fluency Skills During Reading

I am going to teach you fluency skills that will ultimately enable you to be fluent during conversation. In order to learn how to be fluent, we begin by teaching you to read fluently. We select reading because you don't have to come up with the words. The words are in front of you and you only have to focus on your fluency skills to be fluent. It is important for you to know that I will be stopping you along the way. You have to try to avoid getting frustrated or mad at me if I stop you. When I stop you, it's because you have not started slowly, you're not connecting the words or you're forgetting to pause. I know it's hard to remember all of these suggestions at once. However, if I don't correct you as we go along, you are going to think that you're correctly using your fluency skills when you're not. Because I want you to learn these skills, I'll be stopping you when it's necessary. You will need to continue to focus on producing smooth speech and not worry about the information that you're reading. Remember we are going slow so you can produce smooth speech. The way your speech sounds now is not the way it will sound when you are finished in therapy. I'm teaching you to slow down so that you will have enough time to make changes in your speech. When you learn to make the changes, you will gradually get faster and faster and your speech will sound normal. You'll have to be patient at this time.

VTC: 00:32:00:20
00:38:27:07

When we begin to teach fluency skills, we often use an analogy that the clients can understand. Because we believe that a slow speaking rate is merely an environment for producing fluent speech, we relate the following to the client.

During the first days of therapy, we focus on teaching fluency skills by working with the client on a sentence-by-sentence basis. Our experiences tell us that most older children and adolescents learn to master these basic skills relatively quickly (i.e., two to three therapy sessions), which enables us to reset our goals toward increasing the length and complexity of the tasks at hand. Clinicians reading this material will need to determine the nature of the therapy goal for individual clients. When a client has mastered smooth speech skills, we might then choose a goal that focuses on the number of fluent sentences read, the number of paragraphs read, the total number of

---

Technique—Analogy for Slowed Speaking Rate

When you are riding a bike down a hill and going pretty fast, it only takes a little movement of your hands and arms to make your bike go out of control. When you are going fast it only takes a little movement to be out of control. The same thing happens with your speech. When you're going fast, you don't have a lot of room to move or change what you're doing. If you're trying to learn various smooth speech skills and you're going fast, it will be hard to learn to incorporate these skills into your speech. Just as you're trying to connect the words, you will be saying the next word and may find it difficult to smoothly connect words. However, if you slow down your speech, you can learn to incorporate these skills into your speech as you go along. At slower speaking rates it is easier to remember to start slowly and connect your words. When you learn to gain better control while riding your bike, you can go fast down a hill and still control your bike. In the same way, once you learn how to produce smooth speech, you will be able to increase your speaking rate and still use your fluency skills. But for now, you need to slow down.

---

stutter free words, total pages, and so forth. For example, we might write a goal that states that the client will fluently read 20 sentences. For the same task we could state, "The client will exhibit 95% fluency while reading single sentences." In the first case, our goal was related to the number of sentences read while expecting 100% fluency. In the second case, our goal was focused on a fluency percentage related to all sentences produced. The choice of goal remains with the clinician. The ultimate goal is to increase the complexity of the task while the client continues to remain fluent. As the client learns to fluently read more complex material we then encourage the client to increase his or her speaking rates to approach more normal-sounding speech. As we noted previously, slowing the client's speaking rate during the early stages of reading enables us to teach the clients to use their smooth speech skills during this task. As clients become more proficient at producing fluent speech at slower speaking rates, the goal becomes to increase the clients speaking rate so that they can sound more natural, which is ultimately more pleasing to both client and the listener.

Daily Therapy Sequence

We would like to propose a daily plan for therapy that focuses on previously learned skills and new skills to be learned. This format relates to all therapy sessions but can be used when switching from one task that has been mastered (e.g., reading sentences) to a new task (e.g., reading paragraphs).

We find that the best way to begin our therapy session is to have the client complete a task where they have had previous success. In this example, we know that the client can fluently read single sentences and our new goal is reading paragraphs fluently. As a result, we ask the client to read 20 sentences as a warm-up for fluency. This warm-up serves a number of purposes. First, the client will be practicing those fluency skills that are fundamental for fluency within a context in which he or she can be successful. The client not only benefits from this fluency warm-up but also benefits from successfully completing a task. Our experience suggests that a client needs to continually build his or her foundation of positive communicative experiences in order to gain the confidence and skills necessary for maintaining long-term fluency. These positive experiences in therapy will help to serve that purpose. When a client completes his or her warm-up activity, he or she is now ready to use those same fluency skills in tasks of increasing complexity. The next portion of our therapy session is directed toward teaching the client to fluently read paragraphs.

Our goal for the client is to fluently read a paragraph. We expect the client to have some difficulty with this task and explain this to the client. As a result, we may reduce our expectations when we first teach the task and accept a success rate of 70% to 80% because the task is unfamiliar to the client. During this reading task we expect the client to continue to use his or her fluency skills in an appropriate manner, remain stutter-free, and complete 7 out of 10 paragraphs, thus a 70% success rate. We try to tie our goal to the number of successfully completed tasks rather than a fluency percentage. It may be important to remind the reader that while we set forth our goals of stutter-free speech, we are always trying to assess the client's reactions to the task at hand. We do not want the client to reach emotional extremes that prevent further progress in therapy. Unlike other therapy programs that set forth behavioral goals, we always explain to our clients the nature of our goals, the rationale for this goal, and also provide a lot of positive encouragement. We set targets for our clients to achieve so that we can demonstrate success. However, we are always aware of the potential problems when clients are trying to achieve goals to the exclusion of common sense.

Because we believe that it is important for the child to want to return to therapy to continue to work on his or her own speech, we try to end our therapy session on a positive note. In this regard we may select a final task for the client where he or she can once again achieve a good deal of success. In our above example, we may end with a short reading activity or introduce a counseling topic that we can deal with in a short period of time. It is our goal that the client leaves the therapy session with a positive attitude that results in the completion of his or her homework and his or her desire to return to therapy for the next session. On some occasions, it may be impossible to follow the above guidelines. However, in general, we like to begin with success, learn a new task and deal with the frustration during the middle portion of therapy and, finally, end the session on a positive note. If we are successful at therapy, the clinician and client both look forward to returning to therapy.

A Sequence of Reading Tasks

Our goal for clinical training is to develop clinicians who are problem solvers rather than recipe followers. We are discouraged by clinicians who want a set of rules for conducting therapy without having to question why or how the process works. On the other hand, we believe that it is necessary to provide the reader with a list of activities for teaching fluency skills during reading, recognizing that the listed activities are suggestions rather than doctrine for successful therapy. A possible sequence of activities might include those listed in Table 6–2.

Clinicians can use the sequence in Table 6–2 as a guide or develop their own sequence of activities. We strive to have our clients read with 100% fluency throughout the reading tasks. We view reading as the easiest task for most clients, and it serves as the foundation for most of the fluency that will be taught. As a foundation for fluency, we want the client's fluent reading abilities to be as strong as possible. We recognize that as the tasks increase

TABLE 6–2.   **Teaching Fluency during Reading**

1. Client learns fluency skills and reads one sentence at a time.
2. Client learns fluency skills and reads one paragraph at a time.
3. Client fluently reads ten paragraphs at 150 (+/– 20) syllables per minute.
4. Client fluently reads ten paragraphs at 160 (+/– 20) syllables per minute.
5. Client fluently reads ten paragraphs at 180 (+/– 20) syllables per minute.

in complexity, the client's ability to achieve the same fluency levels may decrease. The reader will note that at the same time that the clients are working at reading skills in the therapy room, we are encouraging the client to work on reading skills at home. For some clients, we are able to pay less attention to the specifically targeted reading rates (e.g., 160 spm) and focus more attention on reading at a comfortable rate without stuttering. On one occasion, we encouraged a client to speed up his reading rate to more closely approximate adult reading rates. However, the client indicated to us that he was comfortable at his present rate and believed that he was more likely to stutter if he went faster. Thus, we encourage clinicians to not be locked into any one reading rate but instead discuss with clients their perceptions on reading and then perhaps arrive at a mutually agreeable goal. We begin to work on transferring fluency skills during these early stages of therapy. Transfer will be discussed later on in this chapter.

For most clinicians, the question arises, "How do you know when a task has been mastered? If a client fluently reads 10 paragraphs during a session, do we believe that he or she has mastered this task and is ready to move forward to the next more difficult task? We often pose this question to our graduate students by asking them if 2, 4, 8, or 12 sessions are sufficient to determine mastery of a task. While we are sure that one session is not enough time to determine mastery, we believe that determining mastery of a task is a function of both the client's abilities and the clinician's perceptions. Additionally, if the clinician is following the aforementioned description of a daily therapy session, previously mastered skills are always reviewed during the subsequent session. As a result, the clinician can determine over the course of 2 to 12 sessions when to terminate the activity and move on to the next skill level. While it may appear that we are avoiding this issue, we are just reiterating the heterogeneity of persons who stutter and the need for clinicians to become problem solvers.

Keeping Our Perspective

We establish speaking rate goals for our clients with the idea that there is some idealized target that we attempt to reach, believing that this goal is correct for the client. However, it is often the case that a client produces speech at a slower than expected speaking rate that sounds natural and feels comfortable for the client. Do we continue to encourage the client to reach the faster goal and required number of paragraphs? Obviously the answer is no. We are thinking clinicians looking to teach our clients those skills that will be most beneficial. For many of our clients, we closely monitor their speaking rates until they develop their own internal model for an appropriate speaking rate. At that point we superficially monitor speaking rate while monitoring fluency skills during progressively more complex tasks. Remember, our goal is to not teach the client to slow down but rather to learn to use his or her smooth speech skills during conversational speech. It is often the case that a client will produce a stuttering during a task and we may stop our task to determine the reason for this occurrence. We are often able to identify a rapid initiation of a phrase or a lack of smoothness between words. When we identify this problem, we encourage the client to continue monitoring his or her speech so that he or she can more consistently use his or her smooth speech skills. We have found that the self-monitoring of speaking rate is slow for some clients and faster for others. For some clients, fluency occurs during reading with little effort and easily generalizes to more complex activities. For other clients, generalizing fluency occurs on a task-by-task basis at a much slower rate. It is the clinician's responsibility to determine the correct mix of speaking rate, fluency skills, and counseling to help the client to successfully move forward in therapy.

Some clinicians may question our goal of 100% fluency. We pursue our goal of 100% fluency, realizing that not all of our clients are going to meet that goal. Will failure to reach this goal result in termination of therapy or negative comments from the clinician? We hope not and make a conscious effort to discuss our goals with the client. We believe that most clients want to be as fluent as possible. To that end we work for total fluency. However, total fluency to the exclusion of the client's feelings, emotions, and reactions is short-lived fluency. We continue our pursuit in moderation recognizing all the time that, for some clients, 100% is not realistic.

Transfer Tasks for Reading

> *Transfer of behavior change involves the occurrence or acquisition of changes in behavior in situations other than where the previous learning took place. In stuttering therapy, this most frequently refers to communicative responses being made in the natural, real-life environment following changes in the clinical situation. (Speech Foundation of America, 1984)*

Many speech-language pathologists believe that the transfer of fluency from clinic to real world only occurs when the client has demonstrated 100% fluency during conversational activities in the clinic. In our program, the transfer program begins as soon as the client starts to monitor his or her own speech and is able to use his or her fluency skills with little or no instruction from the clinician. We are not suggesting that the client has perfect fluency or that the client has completely mastered all of the necessary skills in the therapy room. We view any homework activity as a form of transfer because the client has to use those skills that he or she has learned in therapy in another communicative environment. In essence, the client is learning to be his or her own clinician by taking increased responsibility for the changes that are occurring with his or her speech. When a client practices his or her speech on the days he or she doesn't attend therapy, we make the client aware that he or she is adding two or three extra therapy sessions per week by practicing on his or her own.

When a client practices on a regular basis, he or she is creating new behavioral patterns. These behavior patterns will serve a twofold purpose. First, the client is benefiting from the additional practice associated with his or her individual therapy and, second, the client is establishing behavioral patterns that will assist in maintaining fluent speech when the client has reduced or finished individual therapy.

Transfer of fluency during the early stages of therapy reflects the activities that are occurring within the therapy room. When a client is fluently reading paragraphs in therapy, the homework assignment will be to fluently read paragraphs at home. Most of the kids we see complain about homework and the need to practice outside of therapy. As a result, we often sit with the client and invite their parents into the therapy room to explain the need to practice between sessions. The parents are very receptive to their child's practicing and at times are overzealous in their supervision of the child's practice at home. These parental behaviors can be a problem and need to be extinguished as soon as possible. We advise parents that we don't want them to become speech-language pathologists at home. On most occasions, we suggest that the parents provide the child with a reminder to start. their speech homework but not sit with the child to monitor his or her successes and failures. The reader is now wondering how we determine whether the child is successfully completing the assignment. We have developed a number of methods for dealing with out-of-clinic assignments. We ask some to keep a daily log indicating the date, time, and any comments about their practice (see Appendix E). For the child who is reluctant to complete assignments, we are happy when the child returns his or her log indicating completion of the assignments. Of course, we are unable at this time to determine whether the child is using the correct techniques and remaining fluent. However, at this stage of transfer, completing the assignment is viewed as success. When we are unable to determine the child's successful use of fluency skills at home, the child's responses during the subsequent session in therapy often provide insight into the child's practice outside of therapy. When the child returns to therapy, it may be necessary to reinforce some of the previously taught fluency skills or move forward with a task of greater complexity. When the child begins to develop a regular homework routine and has mastered fluency skills in the therapy room, we find it useful to directly monitor his or her fluency skills outside of therapy. We encourage some children to continue to complete the log of their homework, although we add one additional factor. During a portion of the child's practice, we ask a parent to listen to the child's practicing and in a second column on the log, the parent is asked to provide his or her perspective on the child's smooth speech. In this way we are able to get the child's perspectives about his or her homework compared to the parent's perspective. With these results, we can often determine a potential source of conflict at home about a child's speech or verification that the child's perceptions are consistent with an external observer. At some point in therapy, the clinician will sit with both parent and child to discuss the parents' and child's expectations for fluency outside of the clinic environment. More recently, we have begun to use tape recorders to monitor the child's progress.

Our clinic has purchased a number of microcassette recorders that we provide to our clients to monitor their fluency skills outside of the therapy room. During reading activities we ask clients to record their reading at home, listen to their assignments, and then determine if they are using their smooth speech in the same way that we use smooth speech within the therapy room. If a client determines that his or her skills are not at the same level as his or her skills within the clinic, we encourage the client to determine those areas that can be improved so that during the next day's homework assignment those changes can be made. Most of the clients enjoy using the tape recorders because it enables them to take some responsibility for their own speech, and it doesn't require continual monitoring by their parents. However, for some clients, it becomes necessary for the parents to remind the child that they have to begin speech practice. Once the practice begins, the parents are free to continue with their own activities.

To conclude this section, we would like to share a very common experience that we encounter in the therapy process. Sometime during the first few months of therapy, a parent will express some degree of frustration with the therapy process. In the description that follows, we discuss counseling the parents on the course of therapy.

Technique—Parent Counseling Regarding Course of Treatment

"I just don't understand it. I sit in during therapy and observe how fluently my son can read. I know he can read fluently at home because I help him with his homework. At times in therapy I observed that he was using his fluency techniques during conversation. Last week we went to my parent's house to visit and my son was stuttering all the time. I encouraged him to use his smooth speech but he just got frustrated and walked away. Why can't he be fluent?" I explain to this mother, "I understand your concern for your child's speech and your desire to see him fluent with other family members. However, at present he really doesn't have the necessary control over his speech that will enable him to be consistently fluent outside of therapy. I know that you are hearing comments like 'How come Bobby's speech hasn't gotten any better?' from other family members. For right now, you and Bobby will need to be patient and understand that everything that we are doing in therapy is serving to build a foundation for fluency. While we'd like conversations with family members to be the first speaking activities to change, in reality, these situations are often the last to change. Right now Bobby is mastering fluency during reading and the best we can expect is that Bobby will be able to read fluently in some situations outside of the therapy room. Both you and I know that Bobby can read fluently outside of therapy. I see this as a major accomplishment on the road to fluent conversation. We know that Bobby will ultimately be more fluent with family members. For right now, we need to focus our attention on those tasks that Bobby can master so that we can eventually deal with fluency during conversation."

Reading Tasks Summary

Our therapy program begins with reading activities to teach fluency skills. As the client learns the necessary skills for fluency, the complexity of in-clinic tasks increases. Paralleling in-clinic activities is the initiation of transfer activities during the early stages of therapy. In this manner a client is learning to use his or her new fluency skills in more than one setting. We view the transfer of fluency as crucial for the long-term continuation of fluency.

We end our discussion of reading by providing an additional comment. Our clinical experience suggests that once a client learns to read fluently, he or she now possesses a tool that can be used throughout the therapy process. Prior to any sports activities, athletes are instructed to warm-up and stretch their muscles. In a similar manner, throughout our therapy program, we encourage our clients to use reading as a warm-up activity to remind themselves about their smooth speech skills and as a method to remind their speech musculature about how to produce fluent speech. You will note from this point forward that reading will reappear on a number of occasions to assist the client at remaining fluent.

Picture Descriptions

During our early attempts at providing stuttering therapy, we believed that you could teach a client to read fluently and then ask that client to generalize his or her fluency skills to conversation. When we saw how difficult it was for most clients to make this leap from reading to conversation, we recognized that a number of interim stages were required in teaching fluency skills. We determined that a task that was more difficult than reading but easier than conversation was describing pictures. In a manner similar to reading, we determined that teaching fluency skills during picture descriptions should progress from less complex activities to more complex activities. The complexity of the activity is determined again by the length and complexity of the utterance. As we noted in our chapters that deal with younger children, the concept of increased length and complexity of utterance has been described by Ryan (1974) and later refined by Costello-Ingham (1993). We like the concept of teaching fluency skills using gradually more difficult tasks and as result have adopted these procedures.

For some clients reading is not the appropriate place to start in therapy. During our previous discussion of reading, we indicated that reading was appropriate for a child in fifth or sixth grade. As clinicians, we often encounter younger children with well-developed stuttering problems who require therapy. As a result, our focus in therapy for these children begins with picture descriptions. Additionally, we sometimes encounter adolescents who have developed such extreme emotional reactions to reading that is becomes impossible to use reading as a place to begin in therapy. We don't throw reading out completely, we just choose to begin therapy at a different point beginning with picture descriptions. To best understand the daily sequence of activities, the following description is provided.

A Sequence of Picture Description Tasks

Our description of reading tasks focused on teaching fluency skills during simple tasks and progressed to tasks that required that the client to monitor his or her fluency skills, speech naturalness, and appropriate speaking rate. Picture description tasks also will begin with simple tasks and continue to more complex tasks as we help the client progress toward fluent conversation. It is important to note that whenever speaking rate goals are provided, acceptable speaking rates are +/- 20 syllables associated with the target rate. As in the sequence of tasks for reading, we also include transfer at the same time we are working at fluency within the clinic. In this manner, the client is continuing to use his or her newly learned fluency skills in situations that extend beyond the clinic. Once again it is important to note that the sequence of activities is merely a guideline of activities that progress from less complex to more complex. The provided speaking rates are guidelines for therapy rather than exact measures that have to be strictly adhered to. As we noted previously, some clients will sound more natural and feel more comfortable using speaking rates that may be slower than those we request. A thinking clinician will make an appropriate judgment and not force clients to extend their speaking rates beyond their physical limits. We expect clinicians to use common sense when addressing the goals for their clients.

It is our intention in writing this book to provide the reader with a well-thought-out, planned set of activities that will serve as a framework for therapy. We expect the reader to make modifications to our program because these modifications will show us that the clinician has adapted our structure to meet the needs of his or her clients. In particular, we provide speaking rate goals so that the average clinician can have an objective frame of reference if speaking rate is a major focus of therapy. A number of clients are able to easily modify their speaking rate and efficiently use their fluency skills during these tasks. As we stated previously, for these clients we do not have to actively monitor speaking rate because they become aware of their own speaking rates and generally stay within acceptable speaking rate limits. We focus on fluency skills and natural sounding speech rather than specific target speaking rates. For other clients, particularly a number of adolescents, fast speaking rates make it more difficult for these clients to use their fluency skills, which results in a greater focus on speaking rate until the client is better able to monitor his or her own speech.

Teaching fluency skills using picture descriptions is very similar to those tasks described for reading. We often select a picture and provide a model for the client to follow. When the client is successful, we proceed to the next picture. If a client does not use those smooth speech skills that we have discussed or practiced, we immediately stop the client and discuss the necessary changes to become more fluent. In some extreme cases, a client is unable to follow the model that we provide. In this situation, we begin with a carrier phrase as we did with younger children. We might select a phrase, "I see a _____, where the client is required to say the entire sentence and substitute the name of the picture that is presented. The following dialogue may transpire:

> Clinician: "I want you to say the phrase just as I do," "IIIseeeaababy."
> Client: "I see a baby."
> Clinician: "Great job, your speech was smooth and connected. Now try this, "IIIseeeaaagirl."
> Client: "I see a g-g-g-girl."
> Clinician: "You had some difficulty connecting the words. Try to use the word /ɑ/ to help you say girl. Make the /ɑ/ sound a little longer and smoothly connect it to girl."
> Client: "IIIseeeagirl."
> Clinician: "Good connecting, you had nice smooth speech."

The majority of clients will have little difficulty producing simple sentences to describe pictures. We are not asking our clients to produce long and complex sentences. At this stage in therapy, we believe that long and complex sentences will increase the client's potential for stuttering. As a result, we stick with simple declarative sentences like "The girl is running" or "The boy is swimming." Materials can come from anywhere. It is feasible to use books, commercially available pictures, homemade materials, or magazines. We prefer to use magazines where the client can turn a page and select a picture to describe. The name of the magazine is not as important as the client's willingness to use the magazine to complete the task. We often encourage clients to bring in their own magazines, photographs, or books if we think that these materials will assist the therapy process. As long as the client continues to progress and is not bored with therapy then you are probably doing something right.

As the tasks increase in complexity, they pose a greater challenge for the client. The client may be shown a picture and asked to make up a story about the picture, or the client might be given a page from a book that has a multitude of activities happening at the same time. The clinician will need to select materials that are best suited for the client as he or she might do for any other speech disorder. When the materials are selected, the clinician determines that nature of the goal and how the session will progress.

As we noted in the section detailing reading, we continue to use our daily sequence of activities. During picture description tasks, a client may be learning to fluently describe a picture using 50 syllables because he or she has already mastered single sentences. Our therapy session usually begins with 10 to 20 pictures with the client having to use one sentence to describe the pictures. At times, we might even begin with reading as a warm-up to remind the client about the smooth speech skills that are necessary for picture descriptions and as a means for letting the client show how far he or she has progressed. Our sequence might involve, reading 2 to 3 minutes, fluently describing 10 pictures using one-sentence picture descriptions, and fluently describing pictures using 50-syllable descriptions. This client often will be successful with the first two tasks and struggle with the third. Because the third task is still being mastered, we are willing to modify our expectations for the individual session (not modify the goal) until the client begins to master the skills. When the client starts to master the more difficult skill (50-syllable picture descriptions), we begin to introduce a new task, 100-syllable picture descriptions. This sequence of activities continues until the client can fluently describe a picture using 150 to 200 syllables. At this stage in therapy, we may probe to the next level of difficulty while picture descriptions are being mastered. Fluency therapy is not a static process. The dynamics of stuttering therapy require that the clinician be well aware of the client's present skill level and the future direction for therapy.

Transfer of Picture Description Tasks

Once again, the transfer activities designed for picture description tasks need to reflect those activities that are occurring within the therapy room. These homework assignments should only last 15 minutes and should not be so painful to the client that he or she refuses to do homework.

Because our therapy program is a continuous process, most of the clients we see for therapy are already accustomed to completing homework assignments. As a result, as we begin to move away from reading to more complex picture description tasks, we ask the client to combine both reading and picture descriptions into his or her homework. Regardless of the picture description task that the client is working on, we ask the client to first complete 2 to 3 minutes of oral reading before beginning any additional assignments. Reading aloud enables the client to warm-up his or her speech system, and this typically provides more positive results during the more complex activities. When the client has completed his or her reading, the practice activity should be an activity that is similar to those activities occurring in therapy.

Picture Description Task Summary

For those clients who begin therapy with reading activities, picture descriptions are the next step toward fluent conversation. Those clients who begin therapy with pictures are building a foundation for fluency that will lead to more complex activities. We have described the activities associated with picture descriptions and the rationale for their selection. When in-clinic activities are combined with an active out-of-clinic program, the client is moving in a positive direction toward improved speech fluency during conversation.

Monologues

A Sequence of Monologue Tasks

> Monologue: a prolonged talk or discourse by a single speaker
> (*Random House Webster's College Dictionary*, p. 877).

As we move away from extended picture descriptions, the client is now required to talk with the clinician about a specific topic, an event that occurred during the day, or a hypothetical situation proposed by the clinician. Any and all of these tasks require that the client continuously talk about some topic without interruption by the clinician. In some ways, this task is similar to longer picture descriptions although the client no longer has any stimulus material available to assist him/her with the requisite vocabulary and language skills. Clients of those clinicians who have followed our suggestions on the sequence of activities for daily therapy, will have begun working on monologue tasks before picture descriptions were completed.

The goals for monologue tasks typically require the client to continue to use his or her fluency skills with progressively longer monologues at a speaking rate determined by the clinician. For most clients we try to target 180 spm (+/-20 spm) as our focus for therapy at this time. The goal for the early sessions using monologues is directed toward a number (to be determined by clinician) of fluent 50-syllable monologues during the therapy session. The number selected by the clinician will be related to the amount of warm-up time at the beginning of therapy and the amount of time spent between client and clinician dealing with any emotional issues associated with the client's fluency. We find that 50-syllable monologues are relatively short but provide the client with a new opportunity to use his or her fluency skills during a new situation. Once again we focus on 100% fluency during these tasks. As we discuss in Chapters 7 and 8 for working with adults, the client's speaking rate can be monitored on a computer so that he or she can receive immediate feedback on their speaking rate. Some older children and adolescents are able to continue to monitor their own speaking rate and adjust accordingly while other clients require continuous computer monitoring. The clinician should be prepared to use any of the tools available that will provide the client with the information necessary to remain fluent. Many clients have indicated that they believe that immediate feedback from the clinician is extremely valuable when they are trying to monitor their speaking rate during monologue and conversational activities.

For some clients it is sufficient to state, "OK, talk about something." In this situation, the client has little difficulty relating daily events or discussing some issue of importance. An 8-year-old boy preferred selecting his own topic of discussion because he didn't like any of our choices. This boy often discussed playing video games or his activities with friends. With other clients, you might make the same statement, "OK, talk about something," and you get nothing but a blank look back from the client. In this case, the clinician may offer some suggestions such as, "Tell me about your day," or "Describe your favorite thing to do." The biggest problem that the clinician encounters is that he or she quickly runs out of topics that appeal to the client. In our experience, a number of clients who stutter have learned to restrict their verbal interactions because of their concerns regarding stuttering. As a result, many of these individuals need a lot of encouragement and verbal models provided by the clinician so that they can gain the experience of communicating using more than one or two sentences at a time. As this client begins to see success with monologues at 50 spm, he or she will begin to feel more comfortable with the task and start to initiate monologues with less prompting from the clinician. For some clients, self-generated monologues and dialogues continue to be difficult throughout therapy. One of our goals is to make communicating an easier task for our clients, and we believe that this can be accomplished by providing frequent positive communication experiences within the therapy room.

When a client is exhibiting success during 50-syllable monologues, we begin to extend our requirements for this task by requesting progressively longer and longer monologues. As an example, we might progress from 50 syllables to 100 syllables, 300 syllables, 500 syllables, and beyond. During these tasks it is important to encourage the clients to continue to use their fluency skills and to work to be as fluent as possible during the task. For the majority of these clients, we continue to strive for 100% fluency. We want our clients to be as successful as possible but we don't berate or demean our clients if they produce a stuttering. At this level in therapy, we talk about stuttering during monologues as being a momentary loss of control. When we discuss stuttering in this manner, we emphasize that the client has the ability to immediately regain his or her fluency and to continue to move forward by producing fluent speech. For some clients, this momentary loss of control often serves as an emotional trigger that results in additional stuttering. It is at this point that the clinician can be an effective counselor by providing a perspective by which the client can always deal with the occurrences of stuttering.

We explain to our clients that they have demonstrated that they possess the necessary skills to remain fluent for a period of time in the therapy room. For these clients we are demonstrating that stuttering is no longer a random event that suddenly afflicts their speech mechanism. When a client learns to be fluent, we discuss that speech and stuttering occur as a direct result of the strategies and skills that the client uses to be fluent. When a stuttering occurs, the client has experienced a momentary loss of control. We explain to clients that when a stuttering occurs, they are confronted with two potential reactions to their stuttering. This issue is discussed in the following description.

Technique—Counseling Regarding the Occurrence of Stuttering

I've been observing you when you are trying to reach your goal for monologues and I notice that you are able to go along and produce quite a few syllables without any problem at all. Somewhere in the middle of your monologue I observed that you stuttered and within the next two sentences, you had two additional stutterings. It appears to me that when you realized that you stuttered you reacted in a way the resulted in additional stuttering. Although you might get upset when you realize that you stutter, you might use your awareness as a signal to regain control of your speech and focus on the changes that you can make to continue to be fluent. When your reaction to stuttering is only focused on your feelings, the likelihood of additional stuttering occurring increases. By focusing your attention on the behaviors that are in your control, you can then continue with your monologue with little or no problem. When you believe that stuttering only results in strong emotions that are beyond your control, you will have a difficult time regaining control of your speech. These changes will not occur overnight. By making you aware of your reactions, you can begin to focus on your feelings and the behaviors that follow. Our goal is to teach you to minimize the emotions associated with stuttering and redirect your attention to the speech skills that will assist you in regaining your fluency.

We continue working on monologues until a client can produce a sufficiently large corpus of syllables to indicate to us that he or she has learned to control his or her speech. This corpus can range from 500 fluent syllables to 1000 fluent syllables depending upon the client. Throughout our program that requires the client to produce monologues, we periodically interrupt the client with a question or comment. By interacting with the client, we are attempting to introduce the client to more difficult tasks, such as dialogues or conversation while, at the same time, we work to prepare the client for conversations outside of the therapy room.

Transfer of Monologue Tasks

Because we continue to have out-of-clinic activities and parallel in-clinic activities, the client is now required to practice longer monologues in situations outside of the clinic. The nature of these tasks may vary from client to client although the fundamental task for the client is to speak with someone who will listen without interrupting for a period of time. Parents, siblings, or peers often provide the client with an audience that is supportive of the client's desire to continue to be fluent.

During monologue and later conversational activities, we believe that recording homework becomes an essential component of therapy. A client may be given a microcassette recorder from our clinic or asked to purchase a small tape recorder if no recorders are available in our clinic. We ask clients to record all of their homework monologues and to listen to each recording immediately following the conversation. Our goal continues to be to train the client to be his or her own clinician. We believe that clients not only benefit from recording and practicing their speech with the extra reminder of a tape recorder, but also benefit when they have to listen to the recording and make some determination of their ability to use fluency skills during that conversation. We encourage clients to identify the positive and negative components of their monologue and then use the information they learned to improve their speech during the next monologue that they record. During the subsequent therapy session, the client returns to the clinic with his or her tape recorder, and a portion of the therapy session is devoted to listening and analyzing the client's speech during the monologues. During this time, the clinician and the client discuss the positive and negative aspects of the client's recording.

With a number of older clients, the completion of homework activities has the potential to become a battlefield for client, clinician, and parent. It is our belief that the client who fails to complete homework assignments after the clinician tries a number of different assignments and provides words of encouragement is the client who may not be ready to continue in therapy. Very often a client is willing to come to therapy and work on his or her speech, but when the assignments get too time-consuming or too difficult, the client decides to stop working. At this point the clinician must put a value on his or her time and speak with the client and the client's family. We may give the client one more opportunity following a parent meeting to start to work on out-of-clinic assignments and then decide a future course of action. If we believe that we have done everything possible and the client has failed to meet his or her responsibilities, then therapy is terminated.

We should point out that we find it very difficult to terminate therapy and make every attempt to find alternative solutions. Our experience with adolescents suggests that this group often makes their decisions based upon the emotionality of the situation rather than from well-thought-out responses. For the clinician, a little extra patience may be required before discontinuing therapy. However, the clinician must always recognize that without participation by the client in situations beyond the therapy room, the client will fail to achieve the level of fluency that he or she desires.

Monologue Task Summary

For most older children and adolescents, making the transition from reading and picture description to conversation is difficult. As a result, we involve the client in tasks where the client has to produce progressively longer monologues while using his or her fluency skills. During these tasks, we try to encourage clients to focus on the speech production demands while also attempting to minimize emotional reactions. During the later stages of monologue activities, we gradually introduce conversational interruptions in an effort to toughen up the client for the communicative demands of the environment and to prepare the client for future conversational activities. Motivation and out-of-clinic practice are essential components of the therapy program at this stage.

Conversation

> Conversation: oral communication between people
> (*Random House Webster's College Dictionary,* p. 298).

A Sequence of Conversational Tasks

When a client begins in therapy, the ultimate goal for therapy is to become fluent during conversational activities outside of the clinic. The majority of clients would like to begin their therapy with conversation. For most clients, conversation is too difficult without completing the previously discussed tasks of reading, picture description, and monologues. For some clients, therapy begins and ends with conversation. These clients are able to learn fluency skills within the conversational environment and do not need to progress through reading, pictures, and monologues prior to conversation. In the discussion that follows we will provide information on our treatment program, which follows the progression from reading to pictures to monologue to conversation. For a discussion of the client who is able to skip reading, picture descriptions, and monologues, the reader is advised to read Chapter 8, which discusses adult therapy.

The client has now completed monologue tasks and has occasionally practiced conversation with the clinician. At this time the client is now expected to interact with the clinician using his or her fluency skills, maintaining fluent speech by producing speech using an acceptable speaking speech (180 spm =/- 20 spm). We may choose to continue to use our computer to provide the client with feedback on his or her speaking rate, although at this stage in therapy we encourage our clients to internalize their awareness of their speaking rate and fluency skills. We expect the clients to be in control of their speech instead of relying on the computer or the clinician for external feedback. Although internalization is the ultimate goal, the progression to that goal is very different for each client. As a result, we do anything and everything regarding feedback, encouragement, modeling, and so forth, to help the client reach that goal.

The line of demarcation between monologues and dialogue often is difficult to discern. We ask a client to talk about a topic, discuss a political situation, or describe a favorite restaurant, while all the time we are monitoring the client's speech for appropriate speaking rate and fluency. Because these tasks focus on dialogues and the demands that the client may encounter outside of the therapy room, the clinician gradually becomes a more active participant in this process. When the client first begins to work on conversational tasks, the clinician may choose to maintain his or her "therapy model" speaking rate so that the client can ease his or her way into conversation and exhibit initial success. As the client begins to demonstrate a better level of speech control during conversation, the clinician may choose to increase his or her speaking rate, interrupt the client, talk before the client has finished and, in general, provide conversational models that the client, will typically encounter outside of the therapy room. During the conversational tasks, the clinician should feel free to voice an opinion, argue with the client or challenge a statement that the client has made. As we continue to point out, our goal is to teach the client to be fluent in situations outside of the therapy room.

We continue to structure our session to begin with a task that the client has mastered or is close to mastering. For example, this task may be a 1000-syllable fluent conversation at a speaking rate of 180 spm (+/- 20 spm). We let the client direct the flow of the conversation, and we maintain a speaking rate that is consistent with the client's speaking rate. Our second task may be our attempt to toughen up or desensitize the client to the conversational demands he or she may encounter outside of the clinic. During this activity we may require a 200-syllable fluent conversation at 180 spm (+/- 20 spm) while the clinician introduces techniques that Conture (1990) refers to as fluency barbs. Conture (1990) suggested that these techniques be used to "toughen, strengthen, or increase young stutterers' resistance to fluency disrupting influences." In Conture's approach to therapy, these fluency disrupters are used to the point where a child shows that he or she is about to stutter. In this manner, a clinician is working to increase the child's tolerance toward disruptions that may occur outside of the therapy room. During our program, we use the fluency disrupters in a slightly different manner. We recognize that the client who is fluent during conversation in the therapy room will encounter a number of demands outside of therapy that have the potential to disrupt his or her fluency. As a result, we attempt to increase our demands on the client within the therapy room and examine and evaluate the client's responses to these demands. For example, we might determine that every time we increase our speaking rate the client has difficulty maintaining his or her own speaking rate and follow along with the clinician. We note that as the client's speaking rate increases, we begin to see more evidence of a breakdown in fluency. At this point, we might stop the client and begin to explore his or her behavioral response to our conversational demand. The client's response is the perfect opportunity to help the client to explore those potential situations that may cause problems outside of therapy. We begin to examine methods that clients can use to become more aware of a speaker's rate of speech and the potential effects upon their own speech. Too often we encounter clients who only use their fluency skills after a stuttering has occurred. As we have discussed from the earliest stages of this book, the fluency skills are used to replace the client's older, inappropriate methods of communicating. When a client realizes that he or she has begun to stutter, this realization is often the first sign that they were not working on their fluency. Our goal for teaching fluency skills and especially for using fluency disrupters is to teach clients to become more aware of environmental demands and the potential effects on their speech. From our perspective, the discussion of these issues is very important because it helps to demystify the problem of stuttering from a nebulous, randomly occurring event to a behavior that occurs as a direct response to the speech of another listener. We believe that these discussions continue to help the client to become his or her own clinicians.

Exceptions to Rules

During our initial evaluation, we often ask the client if there are specific sounds or words that pose a problem. For some clients, their name or words associated with the first letter in their name are the problem. For other clients, a specific word or sound is perceived to be more difficult, which ultimately results in stuttering. Our experience has shown that teaching fluency skills and verbally rewarding the client for fluent speech is often sufficient to teach the client to overcome these learned fears. However, we do encounter a group of clients who easily use their fluency skills during conversation but continue to stutter on specific sounds or words. We believe that these clients have learned to associate fear and anxiety with these specific targets in such a manner that although they are able to use their fluency skills to remain fluent, the anxiety and fear associated with the targeted word, prevents them from using their fluency skills with the sound or word. A notable example of these fears comes to mind. We were working with an 8-year-old boy in therapy and are practicing picture descriptions. During these simple tasks, the client was able to remain fluent. When we paused to discuss some family matters, the client was asked to name his family members. The client responded with his mother's name and the name of his brothers. When questioned regarding his brother's name, the client spelled E-R-I-C. We looked at the client and asked again, what's your brother's name. The client responded "E-R-I-C." Acting somewhat surprised, we asked the client to say his brother's name and as we expected, he exhibited a lot of struggle producing his brother's name. We realized that the client had developed one method for avoiding stuttering by spelling the name. When we looked further to the types of stuttering that this client was exhibiting, we determined that he was having difficulty with initiating words beginning with vowels. We decided that in addition to teaching this client to use his fluency skills during progressively more complex situations, he would need to learn to overcome his fear of his brother's name and words beginning with vowels. We see these additional activities as an adjunct to our therapy program. Not only do we teach fluency skills during reading and pictures, but we also address the client's perceived fears of sounds and words. We focus on the speech skills necessary to produce the feared word and provide activities that enable the client to fluently produce these words during progressively more difficult activities.

Tasks to Decrease Fears and Increase Fluency

To help the client overcome his or her fear of specific sounds and words, we begin with simple tasks that enable the client to learn fluency skills and produce the words fluently. Not only are we providing the client with a mechanism to say the word, we also are requiring the client to repeatedly say the word so that we are helping to desensitize the sounds and words for the client. The client is learning to associate these sounds and words with fluency rather than with stuttering and is being verbally rewarded for his or her success. This process of counterconditioning helps the client to learn to decrease his or her fears associated with specific sounds or words. For some clinicians, counterconditioning might be viewed as a process in which the client learns to associate relaxation with fluently producing the word. It is our belief that the client is stuttering because he or she has learned to produce the word in an inappropriate manner and the resulting stuttering is associated with anticipation of future stuttering. Our goal is to teach a speech skill using repeated practice to decrease the client's fears and increase fluency.

We begin this process with word lists that target the specific difficulty that the client is experiencing. For some clients this list may include only /b/ sounds, while for other clients the list includes all vowels. During our therapy session, these lists become one of our activities in which we require the client to fluently produce the words. As with other activities, our goal is determined by the client's speech abilities. Obviously, if the client is having difficulty with every word on our word list, our initial goal will be very different from our final goal. As the client begins to show increased mastery over these words, we ask the client to put each word in a sentence. As fluent conversation is our ultimate goal, we devise tasks that will help the client get closer to the conversational goal. Through repeated practice, we find that we are able to help these clients to overcome these specific sound and word fears.

Transfer of Conversational Tasks

As we are working with clients in therapy to strengthen fluency skills during conversation and overcome specific sound and word fears, we are also encouraging our clients to use their fluent conversation skills outside of the therapy room. In a manner similar to our previously described transfer activities, the clients are encouraged to practice their conversational skills outside of therapy. We typically encourage conversations in less demanding environments so that client is able to focus his or her attention on remaining fluent without other distractions. As clients learn to fluently converse during these less demanding situations, we gradually encourage the clients to begin to try more difficult situations. For older children and adolescents, we often find that practicing speech on the telephone is a good experience for the client. The tasks we select are as varied as the clients we treat. However, some of the more common activities include daily telephone call to our voice mail where the client has to focus on speech fluency and relating his or her daily events, telephone calls to a video store to reserve a movie or video game, telephone calls to grandparents that are tape-recorded and reviewed by client and clinician, and the occasional telephone call from the clinician to the client when the client knows that the call is expected at a specific time. With this final situation, the client is working on his or her phone receiving skills where we encourage the client to say "Hello" instead of avoiding the situation or substituting a different word. For a more detailed description of possible conversational transfer activities, the reader is encouraged to examine transfer activities that occur during the adult intensive program and the long-term adult program in the chapters that follow.

As clients learn to generalize fluency skills to an increasingly larger number of situations outside of the clinic, we typically reduce the number of sessions per week that the client attends therapy. During the early stages of therapy, clients attend two therapy sessions per week for either 30 minutes or 50 minutes per session. As the client masters conversational activities, therapy sessions are reduced to one time per week for 30 minutes, then one 30-minute session per 2 weeks, one 30-minute session per month, one 30-minute session during a 3-month period, one 30-minute session per 6-month period. Our greatest concern is the client's ability to continue to use his or her fluency skills as the therapy sessions are reduced. By gradually reducing the number of therapy sessions, the client takes greater responsibility for maintaining his or her own fluency, while the clinician is always available if a problem arises. We like the analogy that we attribute to Dr. Gordon Blood of Penn State University who suggested that clients who stutter should continue to have regular check-ups with the speech-language pathologist in the same manner that the child goes for a six-month dental check-up. We never rush to totally dismiss a client from therapy.

VTC: 01:20:19:07

In the preceding section, we have detailed a sequence of activities and goals that can be used to teach older children and adolescents to become fluent during conversational activities outside of therapy room. Activities progressed from simple, less complex activities (e.g., reading, picture descriptions) to more complex activities (e.g., telephone conversations). Transfer activities are included from the beginning of therapy as the client needs to learn to use his or her fluency skills within the clinic and outside of the clinic. Maintenance of fluency is a continuing process. Therapy sessions are gradually reduced so that the client learns to accept responsibility for fluency.

PARENTAL ROLE IN TRANSFER

The parental role in therapy for older children and adolescents is very different when compared to parental participation with younger children who stutter. As we previously described for younger children, parents are often asked to modify their own communication and the child's communicative environment at home. These modifications often have a direct impact on the child's stuttering. Modifications at home can result in increased speech fluency for the child. By the time we see the older child and adolescent in therapy, the role of the parents has changed dramatically. Changes in parental speech models and communicative environments no longer result in fluent speech for the child. Older children and adolescents need to learn fluency skills in order to speak fluently. As fluency is being learned both within the clinic and at home, the parents can be an active participant in the process.

We have found that in general, younger children tend to be more willing to have their parents participate in fluency practice outside of therapy. However, it is not hard to recall a number of 7- and 8-year-old children who were more reluctant to have their parents assist their fluency development than some 16-year-olds. For our present purpose, we will discuss parent participation in a number of ways.

Parents as Observers

During any part of the transfer process it is often difficult for the clinician to really know if the client is completing out-of-clinic assignments and using appropriate fluency skills at home. As a result, a clinician may ask a parent to serve as an observer at home to report on the child's speech behaviors outside of therapy. When we ask a parent to be an observer, we make it clear that we are only interested in observation. A parent might question this level of participation because many parents believe that the only way to help their child is to actively participate in therapy. As a result, we find it necessary to sit with the parents and explain why observation is important at this time.

Parents are asked to serve as observers for a variety of reasons. During the early stages of therapy the child might be embarrassed by his or her stuttering, and any attempt by the parent to participate in out-of-clinic assignments would result in an argument, embarrassment, and an incomplete homework assignment. With this child, the parent provides some insight on the child's communication outside of the therapy room while not directly discussing this issue with his or her child. As therapy continues, we might ask the parents to observe so that we can determine the child's level of responsibility toward working on their speech outside of the therapy room. We believe that one of the key factors that accounts for long-term fluency following therapy is the client's ability to serve as his or her own clinician. We encourage the child to take responsibility for his or her speech early in the therapy process. Taking responsibility enables clients to become their own clinicians and not rely on external sources (e.g., parents or teachers) to monitor progress. During the reading activities or picture description assignments outside of therapy, we might ask parents to observe and monitor their child's progress. The parents note when an assignment is completed and share this information with the clinician. At this point, the clinician can reward a client for completing his or her homework or discuss with the child the reasons why homework was not completed.

We might pose the question, "How do parents know what to listen for when serving as observers at home?" We find it extremely valuable to include parents in most of our therapy activities. We realize that we are discussing a situation that may be unrealistic in certain clinical settings. However, it is our goal to provide the reader with a therapy program that we view to be comprehensive and successful. When a reader is working in a less than ideal work setting that does not enable parental participation at the levels discussed, the clinician will need to modify the suggestions provided to adapt to his or her own working environment.

During our therapy sessions we often invite parents into the session to observe the activities in which their child is participating. In the example that follows, a parent will be instructed regarding smooth speech skills and our expectations for one-sentence picture descriptions.

Technique—Teaching Parents to Become Better Observers

I'd like you to just sit back and observe how I interact with your son. We are going to practice making smooth speech while he says a single sentence about these pictures. I'd like you to listen for how he starts slow and smooth and how he connects the words. When we finish in therapy today, I am going to ask Jeff to practice his sentences at home. I'd like you to listen when Jeff practices, without making any comments about how good or bad he's doing. When you come in to see me on Thursday, we can talk about what you observed at home.

During the subsequent therapy session, the clinician and parent will sit together to discuss matters related to the child's homework including the parent's reactions to his or her ability to objectively observe. During this same therapy session, the parent may be invited to remain in the room and observe the client-clinician interaction. In this manner, parents can continue to refine their observation skills by noting those issues that the clinician views to be most important.

During the latter stages of therapy, parents may be asked to observe their child's communicative interactions with peers or relatives so that during future in-clinic therapy sessions, the parents can provide feedback on their child's consistent use of fluency skills. To the casual observer it may appear that we are asking parents to become the stuttering police. If we view the above description out of context, it might appear that parents are being asked to spy on their child. In reality, the clinician has a very limited window into the child's communicative environment. As a result, it is important to gain as much information as possible relative to the child's speech behaviors away from therapy. When parents are asked to report on their child's speech, the child is aware of this situation. Should the child express concerns, the clinician, client, and parent can sit down to discuss the reasons for these observations.

The need for parental observation rather than parental participation is a function of the client, his or her parents, and the clinician's expectations for transfer at any time during the therapy process. Observation is a useful tool that has applications throughout therapy. In contrast to parental observation, we often request that the parent directly interact with the child during activities outside of therapy.

Technique—Explaining the Need for External Observation

At the present time you know how to be fluent in therapy. I'm going to ask you to practice your speech at home, although it will be hard for me to know how you do. I would like you to listen to your speech when you do your homework and let me know how you think you are doing. I am also going to ask your mom to listen when you speak so that the three of us can discuss your speech during your next session. It's important to remember that you are the one responsible for your speech changes, and it's impossible for me to follow you around to know how your are doing. I want you to listen to your speech and make sure you use your fluency skills. You really have two choices. I can move into your house and make sure that you change your speech or you listen to your speech and Mom will be my ears at home.

Parents as Participants

Although we have described in detail the role of parental observation, we believe that it is parental participation that will ultimately determine whether these kids are successful outside of the clinic. We suggest that parental involvement be focused on the positive aspects of communication rather than placing the parent in the watchdog role. To that end, the child's homework assignment is discussed in detail in therapy. If the homework assignment includes parental involvement, we suggest to the child they request their parent's participation rather than rely on the parents to serve as a homework alarm clock.

When parental observation reveals the child's failure to complete his or her homework, the parent provides a reminder to the child to begin his or her homework. For some kids, a simple reminder is sufficient to get them to complete their homework. At times, this may be the only participation by the parent. At other times, a child is given an assignment to complete with his or her parents. Having observed and participated in the therapy room, the parent understands the nature of the assignment and provides interaction with the child and an occasional correction or word of encouragement. We emphasize to the parents that we do not expect them to become speech-language pathologists and as such do not want them to make the homework activity so unpleasant for their child that the child is unwilling to participate with their parents. While we encourage parental participation, we discourage making homework a painful experience. When a child fails to respond to a parent's reminders to complete speech homework, we ask the parent to discuss this issue with us in therapy so that we can emphasize to the child, in the parent's presence, the need to complete homework.

We often encounter parents who want to continue therapy outside of the therapy room by dealing with their child as we might do in the therapy room. We explain to parents that we are not looking for them to become expert speech-language pathologists. In fact, in most situations where a parent takes on this role, the child becomes reluctant to complete his or her homework and becomes quite disinterested in working on fluency both at home and in the therapy room. As a result, we talk with parents about the continuing need to make homework a positive experience that facilitates the development of fluent speech rather than one that inhibits the development of fluent speech.

During the later stages of therapy, we often hear the following, "Why can my child speak fluently in the clinic but continues to stutter at home?" These parents are expressing frustration with the child who consistently uses fluency skills in therapy but fails to remember to use fluency skills at home. The client knows how to be fluent, understands the requirements for remaining fluent, but fails to speak fluently at home. As a result of this parental frustration, we have developed a transfer program to assist the child's use of fluent speech at home. By using this program, the child learns to accept greater responsibility for fluency while the parents are provided a method for reducing the frustration associated with repeatedly reminding their child to be fluent.

Phelan (1995) has described a behavioral management program entitled *1-2-3 Magic* that is used by parents to make their child aware of his or her inappropriate behaviors by providing three nonemotional reminders to change. When the child fails to respond to all three reminders, he or she is timed out to his or her bedroom. For example, a parent requests that a child put his toys away. The child fails to respond. The parent says, "That's one." In essence the child is given the opportunity to change his or her behavior or face the consequences. When the child fails to respond the parents state, "That's two." If the child fails to respond again, the parents states "That's three," and the child is removed to his room. The child is required to remain in his room for a time equivalent to his chronological age (10 years of age, 10 minutes). For a more complete description of a very effective behavioral management program, we strongly urge the reader to obtain a copy of Phelan's book.

Having seen the benefits of behavioral management using the 1-2-3 Magic program, and having listened to the comments of parents who were frustrated with their child's failure to use fluency skills at home, we developed a modification of Phelan's program to use with our clients (Schwartz, 1993, 1994). In order to successfully use the 1-2-3 Magic program with older children and adolescents who stutter, three criteria must be met: (1) The client must know how to be fluent in the clinic; (2) the client is ambivalent toward changing his or her speech at home; and (3) parents report frustration and are tired of reminding their child to change his or her speech.

When these three criteria are present, the clinician can attempt to implement this program. Implementation of the program first involves discussing the nature of the program with the parents and getting the parents to agree to participate. Without parental participation, the program cannot be implemented. The next step is to discuss the program with the parent and client together to explicitly describe to the child the nature of the program. Because the program can be modified from a time-out program to a reward program, positive and negative consequences are discussed with parent and client.

The behavioral program is implemented by the parents at home. The parents are encouraged to present the reminders in a nonemotional manner. When a child is going too fast or when the parent determines that a child stuttered because he or she failed to use his or her fluency skills the child is told "That's one." The child is expected to modify his or her speaking rate and use his or her smooth speech. If the child continues to go fast and/or exhibits additional stuttering, the child is told "That's two." In essence, the child has been given two nonemotional reminders to make speech changes. It is important to remember that this program is not initiated until a child is ready to deal with a program such as this and the child has the necessary skills to change his or her speech. If a child fails to change after the second reminder, the parents says "That's three, take 10." The amount of time designated for time-out is the child's chronological age. A child of 7 is sent to his or her room for 7 minutes. To many outside observers this program seems like a harsh method for dealing with transfer. The usefulness of this program lies not only with the time-out but with the positive consequences that usually follow after the first week of the program. While the program is designed to both remind the child and punish the child for failing to change, practical experience with the program has revealed that very few children are ever timed-out after the first or second week.

A typical program would show that a child may receive 50 reminders during the first week and perhaps two or three time-outs. By the second week, a child may reduce the total reminders from 50 for the first week to 30 total reminders for the second. However, the interesting change that occurs is that during the second and subsequent weeks, the child rarely goes beyond two reminders and rarely receives another time-out. Because the goal of this program is to get the child to accept responsibility for changing his or her speech and also reduce parental frustration, the program may be modified so that the number of weekly reminders becomes the criteria for success. As a result, the clinician can work with the parents to determine an appropriate reward for consistent reduction of reminders. Rewards such as money for comic books, video game rental, and trips to the video arcade have all been used successfully. For some children, the promise of a reward is not as motivating as the loss of some activity. As a result, when a child fails to reduce the number of reminders to the agreed upon goal, the child may lose TV time, video-game playing, or some other activity he or she enjoys.

The monitoring of the client's success can be accomplished in a number of different ways. The total number of reminders per week can be calculated or the clinician can calculate the number of daily reminders (total weekly reminders divided by number of days). A successful transfer program would focus on a child receiving less than one reminder per day. At this level of success, the clinician would know that the client was using his or her fluency skills, controlling his or her stuttering, and taking responsibility for change.

MAINTENANCE

As the clients progress through fluency training and transfer, we are working to gradually reduce the number of therapy sessions per week. We want the client to know that despite the fact that we are reducing the number of therapy sessions, we are still available for additional therapy should a problem arise. At the point at which the client reaches a fluency level that is mutually satisfactory, our program transitions to a maintenance program. As we previously described, maintenance involves a periodic check-up with the family or client in an effort to determine whether the client continues to remain fluent and is satisfied with his or her fluency. We emphasize to parents and clients that we are only a telephone call away from a refresher session to get back on track.

▶ 7

Therapy for Adults: Intensive

An intensive fluency therapy program for adults who stutter is designed to stimulate rapid changes in the client's speech with concurrent attitude and emotional changes. We will describe an intensive fluency therapy program that was developed by Gavin Andrews and best described by Neilson and Andrews (1993). The reader will note many similarities between the described St. Vincent's Hospital Stuttering Therapy Program and the program to be described in this chapter. This result is inevitable as the author participated as a visiting clinical associate in the St. Vincent's Program during January and February of 1994. However, despite the fact that many of the principles to be discussed are similar to the St. Vincent's Program, subsequent implementation within an American university environment has led the present author to modify the program in such a way that we believe we have included changes that have significantly improved the client's opportunities to remain fluent.

PROGRAM OVERVIEW

Our intensive fluency therapy program is a 3-week program that focuses on establishing fluency during the first week, transferring fluency and counseling during the second week, and solidifying fluency outside of the therapy room with continued in-clinic counseling during the third week. We are well aware of all of the criticism that is leveled at intensive fluency therapy programs across the United States. We do not view our program as a quick fix to

151

a lifelong problem. We do not require that our clients strictly adhere to fluency targets or unnatural-sounding speech in an effort to be fluent. The fluency skills that we teach are those same fluency skills we teach in our long-term therapy program. The major difference between the two programs is that during the intensive program, a client is able to learn to use fluency skills in an accelerated manner so that transfer can occur more rapidly. We recognize that a client is not finished in therapy after his or her 3 weeks in our program, and we make every attempt to continue therapy following our 3-week program to meet the needs of the individual client.

The intensive therapy program is provided within a university clinical environment. As a result, it is only possible to conduct our program one time per year during the intersession between the spring and summer semester. Because we provide our therapy program within a university training program environment, we are able to include a maximum of six graduate student clinicians in the program. As a result, we often have a ratio of one clinician per client, which enables us to divide the workload among the student participants and helps to reduces the burden on any one clinician. Furthermore, the one-to-one ratio of clinician to client enables each client to receive individual counseling on a daily basis in addition to group therapy and fluency work. We recognize that many readers may be interested in implementing an intensive therapy program in an environment that is different from the description provided. It is our belief that the procedures that are provided can be applied and modified to meet the needs of a specific environment.

VTC: 00:56:05:27

CLIENT SELECTION

Neilson and Andrews (1993) assert that the intensive stuttering therapy program is not suited for every adult client. Our clinical experiences within the Australian program and within our university setting support this idea. This intensive program is not for everyone. As we are evaluating an adult client, we attempt to determine whether the client will benefit most from the long-term behavioral program, the intensive program, or any of our programs. Generally, a client who exhibits a lot of emotional concerns about his or her stuttering with a long list of avoidances and reactions to stuttering is a client who is not well suited for an intensive therapy program. Our experience in our long-term program has shown that the client who exhibits a lot of emotional concern, avoidances, and reactions to his or her stuttering, often requires a longer time to integrate the required speech and emotional changes that are required for long term fluency. As a result, we will not recommend our intensive program if we believe that the client will not benefit from the program. On the other hand, for the client who exhibits stuttering but maintains a generally positive attitude about communicating and does not exhibit a lot of avoidance, the intensive therapy program provides an excellent opportunity to become fluent and remain fluent in a relatively short, intense period of time. It is important to note that we continue to believe that although we can identify a group of adults who will benefit most from an intensive therapy program, we still believe that stuttering therapy needs to continue following the 3 intensive weeks of participation. These clients learn a number of skills within the 3-week period of time. However, maintenance of these skills requires continued contact with our program.

VTC: 01:09:28:25

In our attempt to determine who will benefit from the intensive therapy program, we consider a number of issues during the evaluation. Experience has shown that a client requires a great deal of emotional maturity to be successful in our program. We also believe that a client needs to express a specific reason for attending therapy. This idea was discussed by Neilson and Andrews (1993) and makes a great deal of sense when dealing with adults who stutter. For example, when an adult explains that he or she wants to attend the intensive therapy program because he or she is unable to get a job promotion, unable to interact with people in social settings, or participate in classroom activities, these reasons for attending therapy suggest to us that the client has a specific need that our program will fill. When a client reports that he or she has had previous therapy and our program seems to be good idea at this time, we believe that a stronger commitment toward attendance will be necessary for the client to be successful. Although many clients want to attend therapy, the intensity of daily therapy for 8 hours a day is just not appropriate for some clients.

It is important to recognize that therapy success is not measured when a client completes the 3 weeks of intensive therapy. Instead, we consider success to be the client who has remained fluent 2 years following termination of our program and reports a positive level of satisfaction with his or her speech. Most speech-language pathologists are familiar with the programs that report fluency success and satisfaction with speech immediately following a therapy program. Although these results are necessary prerequisites for long-term success, relying on these results for judgments of success of a therapy program results in inflated success rates.

WEEK ONE

Preview

In our intensive therapy program we emphasize fluency as a main goal during the first week of treatment. Even though fluency is an important skill to learn in our long-term program, fluency is our primary focus during the first week of treatment in our intensive program. We should temper this discussion with the same caveats that we place throughout this chapter and the entire book. While fluency skills are important for an adult client, fluency should not be the only criterion for success nor the only focus of the therapy program. However, for the clients who are selected to participate in our intensive therapy program, we have determined through our evaluation procedures that these clients require more of a fluency focus and less of a counseling focus than many of the clients who participate in the long-term program. Because we have selected those clients who are best suited for the intensive fluency therapy, we do not have a problem emphasizing fluency. We understand that during the first week of the intensive therapy program, we have a limited amount of time to teach fluency skills, establish fluency at speaking rates within normal limits, and develop speech that sounds natural. The clients also recognize these goals because they were explained prior to therapy participation as well as during the first day of treatment.

Clients are advised that they may terminate treatment at any time, although we make every effort to have a client remain from the beginning to the end of the therapy program. As clients are required to pay for therapy, they also are advised that they can terminate their participation up to Wednesday of the first week and receive a full refund of their therapy costs. Following the first Wednesday, the client will not be given any refund. Our clinical experience has revealed that many clients experience an internal battle about their participation in the program. In actuality this inner debate is not revealed until the final week of the program but often follows a similar scenario. A number of clients have indicated that they begin the therapy program with an intuitive sense for the demands of daily fluency training. By midweek, demands on the client are increasing because they are required to speak faster and longer while maintaining fluency. The clients reveal to us that it is at these times when they begin to consider leaving the program. The clients typically report that because they were required to pay for therapy and risk losing their money if they decide to terminate participation, they stick with the program and get past those periods of self-doubt that often arise.

Structure

The structure of the first week focuses on teaching fluency skills at slow speaking rates and gradually increasing the demands for faster speaking rates until the client is able to fluently converse with the clinician at normal conversational speaking rates. Modeled after the St. Vincent's program (Neilson & Andrews, 1993), our daily activities are centered around a number of daily rating sessions. During the first day of therapy, each client is given a copy of the schedule for Week One so that each client is fully aware of the daily expectations in therapy. As can be seen in Table 7–1, each day in therapy is divided into a number of speech rating sessions where specific speaking rates are targeted. The program begins at 50 syllables per minute (spm) and progresses to 190 spm, a normal conversational speaking rate.

TABLE 7–1. **Week One Intensive Therapy Program**

Time	Monday	Tuesday	Wednesday	Thursday	Friday
8:00–8:30	Day One Videotape	50	80	140	190
8:30–9:00	Phone call	50	80	140	190
9:00–9:30	Intro to anatomy and smooth speech	50/V	80/V	140V	190/V
9:30–10:00	Practice Smooth Speech	Break	Break	Break	Break
10:00–10:30	Practice Rating Session	60	90	150	190
10:30–11:00	Practice Rating Session	65	100	160	190
11:00–11:30	50/1	70	110	170	Weekend discussion
11:30–12:30	L	U	N	C	H
12:30–1:00	50/2	70	120	180	190
1:00–1:30	50/3	70/V	120/V	180/V	190/C
1:30–2:00	B	R	E	A	K
2:00–2:30	50/4	80	130	190	
2:30–3:00		80	140	190	

Numbers are syllables per minute: The goal of each rating session

The first week of therapy is divided into a series of 30-minute rating sessions. We explain to the clients that they learn to be fluent because of their use of fluency skills at slower speaking rates. The goal of the first week in therapy is to continue to use these fluency skills while increasing speaking rates. We explain to our clients that their fluency results from changes in speaking rather than slowing down. By taking this perspective, our clients are taught to focus on the fluency skills that are within their control rather than on a nonspecific focus that says slow speech equals fluent speech. We remind our clients that by the end of the first week they will be fluent at faster speaking rates, not slower speaking rates.

A rating session involves a monologue or dialogue (primarily monologue) between client and clinician. A typical rating session will be 7 minutes of speaking for each client. With a maximum of four clients per session, the rating sessions are completed within the allotted 30-minute time period. A syllable goal is established for each rating session. The syllable goal is a function of the time; 7 minutes times the targeted speaking rate (e.g., 50 spm). During the earlier stages of therapy (Monday) a client will be required to produce 350 syllables of conversation whereas in the later stages of therapy (e.g., Friday) the client will be speaking at a rate of 190 syllables per minute during a 7-minute period (1330 syllables). The topics of the monologues and conversation often range from description of family members and homes to hobbies, favorite restaurants, and movies. Clients can talk about any topic, provided that they remain fluent throughout the task.

The physical layout of the session requires the client to face the clinician. The client also is required to view a computer monitor that provides visual feedback regarding speaking rate and number of syllables produced. The clinician faces the client and is able to view his or her own computer monitor and the client. During the interaction, the clinician can count the client's syllable production by tapping on the spacebar of the computer keyboard and the client's speaking rate will be displayed on the video monitor. The speaking rate goal of the rating session is visually displayed as is the client's running average speaking rate and total number of syllables. In this manner, clients are provided with immediate visual feedback on their speaking rate while the clinician is able to provide verbal feedback regarding the client's appropriate use of fluency skills.

VTC: 01:08:16:19

For all of the rating sessions conducted during the week, each client is asked to maintain a written log (see Appendix F) that includes the targeted time and targeted speaking rate, actual time and actual speaking rate. Every time a client completes a rating session, he or she is asked to record all of the information on time and rate onto their log sheet. Additionally, when a client fails to pass a rating session, this information is also recorded. For the clinician, the recorded information is a good source of data about the client's progress through therapy. For the client, this visual record provides ongoing feedback regarding his or her success in therapy.

The goal of each rating session is 100% fluency. When a client exhibits a stuttering (sound/syllable repetition or sound prolongation) during the rating session, the client is asked to wait while the remaining clients work to reach their fluency goals. In our program, failing a rating session may add an additional rating session to the program at the end of the day, or the client may be required to work individually with one of the clinicians to make up the necessary session. Unlike the Australian program that is often conducted in a hospital by one or two clinicians, we have been able to delegate clinical responsibilities among the graduate students participating in the program. In this manner, individual clients who have difficulty meeting specific fluency goals at specific speaking rates are often provided with additional attention during the day so that extending a client's required time in the daily therapy program is typically not required.

Our goal is for each client to end the day at the same place in therapy so that each client will begin the next day's therapy with the same goal. Neilson and Andrews (1993) explained that by requiring each client to reach the designated fluency goal at the end of the day, each client could begin the next day in therapy at the same starting point. Our experience suggests that requiring clients to complete the same goals each day enables the client to experience a sense of accomplishment, develop a sense of camaraderie with other participants, and minimizes frustration and competition relative to comparisons with other clients.

Day One

Although we have previously evaluated the client and determined that the intensive therapy program would best meet the client's needs, we complete a number of evaluative procedures on the first day of therapy in order to establish a baseline of behavior. This baseline can be compared to the results of our previous fluency evaluation and serve as a behavioral benchmark. We can use these data for comparison with all of the subsequent changes that we anticipate will occur during the next 3 weeks and in follow-up therapy sessions. The first activity that is completed is a videotaped 3-minute monologue where the client introduces him- or herself and provides some information about his or her home and work environment. The second activity that is completed is a 7-minute audiotaped telephone conversation. The clients are encouraged to use the newspaper want ads to complete the task so that a conversational sample can be obtained. When the two tasks are completed, a number of speech characteristics can be evaluated. These include frequency of stuttering, most frequently occurring stuttering type, and conversational speaking rate.

As part of the initial evaluation procedures, each client is asked to complete two questionnaires. These include the S24 Modified Erickson Scale of communication attitudes (S24) (1974) and the Locus of Control of Behavior Scale (1984). As reported by Neilson and Andrews (1993), these scales are used throughout therapy in an effort to determine the changes in the client's attitudes and beliefs about stuttering. Results are tabulated during the first week and compared with results of these same measures during the third week of therapy.

Introduction to Smooth Speech
When the assessment procedures are completed, we begin therapy with an explanation of the speech production mechanism and the manner in which speech is produced (see Chapter 3). We then move toward a discussion of different types of stuttering behavior, and this is followed by an extensive discussion of fluency skills (see Chapter 3). During this discussion, we encourage the clients to practice these fluency skills while slowing down their speaking rates to 50 syllables per minutes. As discussed previously, a slower speaking rate provides the client with a speaking environment that is conducive toward learning the fluency skills of slow initiation of phonation, connecting across the words, and so forth. It is during this practice session that the client is given the opportunity to practice his or her fluency skills while also monitoring his or her speaking rate. The ability to smoothly produce speech and monitor speaking rate will continue to be the focus for the remaining days of Week One. Examination of Table 7–1 reveals that the clients are provided with 90 minutes of practice before any formal speech rating is begun. It is important for the client to learn to monitor both the content of his or her speech and the manner in which speech is produced.

During the 90 minutes provided for practicing smooth speech skills, it is important for the clinician to provide immediate feedback to the client in an effort to make the client aware of appropriate and inappropriate use of fluency skills. As noted previously, by providing immediate feedback, the client is able to make the necessary changes in his or her speech so that inappropriate fluency skills are replaced with appropriate fluency skills and these new skills are repeatedly practiced.

VTC: 00:59:49:26

Rating Sessions
For the remainder of Day One, the clients are focused on completing four rating sessions at 50 spm. Because this task is relatively new for the client, there is an adjustment period where the client must focus on both his or her fluency skills and topics of conversation. Although this task may appear to be difficult at first, most clients are able to adapt to the situation and usually have little difficulty finding some topic for discussion.

VTC: 01:10:07:25

When the client prepares to leave therapy following his or her first day of therapy, we find it necessary to discuss out-of-clinic communicative strategies with the client. Because our goal is to have each client use his or her newly learned fluency skills all of the time, we believe that all communication outside of the clinic should parallel the in-clinic activities. However, during the early stages of therapy we recognize that 50 spm results in unnatural sounding speech that the client may be reluctant to use at home. As a result, we explain to the client that he or she has a number of communicative options. These options include: (1) speaking outside of therapy using the same speaking rates that you used in therapy; (2) communicating using writing; (3) not speaking until you're comfortable using your fluency skills. Many clients choose to not speak during the first few days of therapy until their speaking rates more closely approximate normal conversational speaking rates. Some clients choose to communicate using gestures or writing while other clients choose to not speak until the end of the week. Every client will need to make his or her own choice on communication, and the clinician should make the client aware of his or her options. We encountered one client who reported to his family that he had lost his voice and was unable to speak for a couple of days. The client stated that his wife was aware of his actual situation but it was easier to explain a lost voice to his young children than it was to discuss participation in a speech program. This client continued his lost voice scenario when he was required to attend a school program for his daughter. A number of friends and neighbors approached the client at the school performance but with a series of gestures, the client chose to communicate his difficulty with these listeners. At the end of the first week, the client reported that he was happy to be communicating at faster speaking rates.

As some added incentive, we asked each client to commit a monetary bond that will be lost if they fail to use their newly learned fluency skills or stutter outside of the therapy room. During the subsequent day in therapy, each client is questioned about his or her previous night's communication and a determination is made on the amount of the bond that is returned. The monetary commitment and discussion of out-of-clinic communication continues throughout the first week in therapy. We do not encourage the client to provide huge monetary bonds. We explain to the client that the money they commit should be a meaningful amount that would affect them if the money was lost. We should note that all monetary fines and bonds that are provided to the clinic are used for a party on the final day of therapy.

Days Two to Five

During the remainder of the first week, the clients begin each therapy day at 8:00 A.M. Our initial discussion typically focuses on the client's previous evening's experiences with their speech. As previously discussed, the payment of fines in usually transacted during this first rating session, and strategies and options for future evenings are discussed.

The rating sessions progress relatively smoothly for the remainder of the week. The clients become more familiar with the mechanics of smooth speech and as they continue through the rating sessions, they learn to focus both on the manner of speech production and on the content of their conversation. We emphasize to the clients that we want them to use their fluency skills in all communicative situations in the clinic and at home. This requires the client to monitor his or her speech during coffee breaks and lunch as well as at previously discussed activities at home. Most clients are able to adapt to this requirement. Some clients are not bothered by the slow rate requirement during the early part of the week and choose to use their fluency skills all of the time. Other clients only begin to communicate at breaks and lunch because the speaking rates more closely approximate normal conversational speaking rates.

Videotaped Rating Sessions

In a manner similar to that described by Neilson and Andrews (1993), we require that two daily rating sessions be videotaped so that each client can improve their observational skills, become more objective in their own self-analysis, and learn to identify fluency skills that need continuing improvement. During these rating sessions the client is required to produce a fluent 3-minute monologue at the designated speaking rate while being video-taped for further analysis. In addition to recording information about rating sessions on a daily log sheet, each client is asked to complete a log for judging speech skills during a videotaped rating session (see Appendix G). The client is asked to immediately fill out this form that asks for the client's judgments regarding his or her ability to use their fluency skills during the videotaped session. When all clients have completed the videotape recording, the client and clinician (in the presence of all clients) view the videotape and each make a series of judgments regarding the client's ability to use his or her fluency skills. When the clinician and client have made their judgments, we attempt to compare the judgments of speaker and clinician. As added incentive, the client is rewarded with $.10 for each agreement with the clinician. We recognize that the sum of money is not large and yet this added incentive encourages the client to work harder at improving his or her awareness and observational skills regarding their speech. These funds can be used to offset any fines received by the clients for failing to use their fluency skills during coffee breaks and lunch.

For many clients, Wednesday and Thursday of the first week is the point at which they begin to experience the most difficulty. During these two days, the speed of the clients speech is beginning to approximate normal conversational speaking rates. The clients learn that as their speech rates increase, their ability to use their newly learned fluency skills is really tested. These 2 days in therapy require the greatest amount of cognitive attention. The clients typically speak at too fast a rate or begin to use their old speaking habits because these strategies seem to be easier than concentrating on their newly learned fluency skills. It is not unusual for a client to complete the first 2 days of therapy (Monday and Tuesday) without failing a rating session and then fail two, three, or four rating sessions on Wednesday or Thursday because of the demands associated with the faster speaking rates. As clinicians we are well aware of these events and are prepared to deal with the situation by providing the clients with additional practice sessions and counseling on the increased demands of faster speaking rates. We explain to the client that learning to be fluent is hard work and that the difficulty he or she is facing during this stage in therapy will pass with increased practice. We don't try to minimize the client's concerns about his or her difficulty or their concern for using these skills during the second and third week. We address the mid-week problems with a specific focus on mastering the task at hand and remind the client that with continued practice, he or she will continue to be fluent.

As we pointed out previously, we usually discover during the third week in therapy that the difficulties encountered during the first week often invoke thoughts of quitting therapy because of the difficulty the client is experiencing. A knowledgeable clinician will anticipate the client's thoughts and address these concerns as they occur. Our past experiences enable us to anticipate potential problems and increases our sensitivity to the difficulties that a client experiences during the first week in therapy. We can strongly encourage our clients to persevere through this difficult time and be supportive in our interactions so that the clients are able to move forward.

Technique—Counseling During Rating Sessions

It's now Thursday morning and you've been able to complete all of the rating sessions with little difficulty. However, I notice that you're having more difficulty using your fluency techniques with the faster speaking rates. I understand that as we get faster you have less time to think about the changes that you need to make. During the past few days, we worked with you to use your fluency skills in a more automatic manner. You're going to have to concentrate on all of the skills that you've used so far but also monitor your speaking rate at the same time. If you have difficulty with the task, we can provide additional time for you to work on fluency at this faster rate. We don't want you to get discouraged. Both you and I know that these skills are difficult. If this was easy to do, you wouldn't be in therapy, you'd be doing this by yourself. The goal today is to have your fluency skills become more automatic so that you can get faster but stay fluent. Our goal is for you to be fluent at normal conversational speaking rates.

As the client progresses through therapy, he or she continues to use his or her fluency skills at increasingly faster speaking rates. By Friday afternoon, the client is conversing with other clients as well as the clinicians using fluent speech at normal conversational speaking rates.

Coping Technique

During the rating sessions on Friday, we introduce the clients to a compensatory strategy. This strategy can be used when a client anticipates the occurrence of a stuttering and is unable to use his or her fluency skills to smoothly move past the word. As noted throughout this book, we encourage our clients to use their fluency skills so that stuttering will not occur. However, we are realistic when it comes to fluency outside of the clinic. We recognize that it is the rare client who will remain fluent 100% of the time when our program is completed. We try to provide our clients with a number of skills that will assist them when a stuttering occurs. Some of these skills will result from counseling. Other skills can be taught as part of speech production. The coping technique is a strategy that has been used effectively in the St. Vincent's program (Neilson & Andrews, 1993) and certainly seems appropriate for inclusion in our intensive program. We note that the coping technique is similar to Van Riper's description of "preparatory sets" where clients are taught to anticipate the occurrence of a stuttering and to adjust their articulatory system in a manner that enables them to move through the difficult word with a minimum amount of effort. Our focus of treatment continues to be fluency, although we recognize that anticipation of specific sounds and words can still disrupt a client's fluency.

During a rating session on Friday afternoon, the clinician models coping for the client and each client has the opportunity to practice this coping technique. Verbal feedback is provided for clients so that they can begin to internalize the necessary skills for using coping.

Technique—Teaching the Coping Technique

Coping is a strategy that will help you fluently produce a word that you perceive to be difficult and a strategy that can help you when you encounter a situation where it is difficult to use your fluency skills. If you need to use the coping technique it is probably because you are anticipating a specific sound, word, or situation that you believe is beyond your control at this time. Beyond your control really means that you expect to stutter at this time. I want you to change your focus from "I expect to stutter" to "What can I do to continue to keep my speech fluent." When we use coping we ask you to slow down your articulators just prior to producing the word, use a light articulatory contact to produce the first word, and then stretch out the vowel to smoothly move through the word. When the word begins with a vowel, you gradually begin the vowel and stretch the vowel with your voice to connect to the next sound. As you move past the difficult sound or word, you can gradually increase the number of words that you produce so that you can get back to an acceptable conversational speaking rate. When you are confronted with a difficult communicative situation, you can use the coping technique by remembering to initiate the beginning of each new phrase with a light articulatory contact and elongated vowels.

We designate one complete rating session at 190 spm for coping. During this rating session we ask each client to use the coping technique when beginning each new phrase or sentence. Like all new motor skills, some of the clients are able to immediately integrate this skill into their conversational interaction. For other clients coping is somewhat more difficult. These clients may require additional practice sessions to master this skill, and we can provide the additional practice by having the client work individually with a graduate student during the second week of treatment.

WEEKEND DISCUSSION

During Friday afternoon of the first week in therapy, the clinician and clients discuss a number of conversational strategies for the client's first weekend of the therapy program. As the program is not residential, all clients will be away from therapy during Saturday and Sunday. The clients are advised that their fluency is extremely fragile. For some clients, this word of caution is no surprise as they've tried to use their fluency skills at home and noted the difficulty associated with using their new skills outside of therapy. For other clients, they are so enthusiastic that they want to talk with everyone and show everyone their new fluency. We advise all of our clients to approach the first weekend with a great deal of caution. As clinicians, we recognize that fluency in the clinic does not automatically become fluency outside of the clinic. We understand that environmental pressures for communication and the emotional desires of clients often counteract or disrupt newly learned fluency skills to the point where clients return to therapy both depressed and frustrated. As such, our conversation focuses on the need to limit communication during the next 2 days so that clients can return to therapy on Monday with a positive attitude about their fluency and their ability to use their fluency skills outside of therapy.

What specific advice do we give to the client? We use the same description that Megan Neilson uses during her weekend briefing for the St. Vincent's intensive fluency therapy program. We begin by providing a historical perspective to this program with a description of the Prince Henry residential stuttering treatment program in Sydney, Australia. As part of the Prince Henry program, all clients were considered to be in-patients within the hospital setting. As in-patients, these clients were required to maintain their fluency skills at all times including weekends. Fluency skills were rewarded with coins that could be exchanged for meals and other activities. We explain to our clients that as part of the residential programs, many participants were forced to limit their conversational interactions because of their in-patient status. As a result, we first encourage our clients to think about this first weekend as if they too were in-patients in the hospital. We suggest that our clients limit the amount of communication they use and the number of people with whom they interact. We attempt to minimize the risk of frustration and inability to use the newly learned fluency skills beyond the therapy room. We encourage the clients to complete their routine activities and to avoid organizing a family party with all the relatives present to view their new fluency skills. We explain to the client that we do not want them to challenge their speech at this point. Second, we encourage each client to exchange his or her phone number with the other group members so that each participant can phone each member of the group to practice their fluency and share mutual concerns that have arisen. Our experience has shown that these telephone conversations have been extremely beneficial for the clients by not only providing communicative practice but also providing an opportunity to share emotional perspectives with individuals who are experiencing similar situations. It is interesting to note that in spite of all of our warnings and suggestion to not challenge their speech, there will always be the occasional client who is so enthusiastic about his or her fluency and new abilities to communicate that he or she attempts to have as many conversations as possible because they are so happy to be fluent. If the client is successful we breathe a sigh of relief. If the client has difficulty, we address their concerns during the second week of therapy.

WEEK TWO

The goal of the second week of therapy is the stabilization of in-clinic fluency and the transfer of fluency to situations beyond the clinic. In addition, counseling sessions are now a regular part of the therapy program, and this continues for the remainder of the second and third week of therapy. The client's ability to be successful during this second week of therapy will set the tone for therapy during the third week. The clinician will gain insights into the clients' abilities to be fluent outside of therapy and their prognosis for success when the program is completed.

Structure

The structure for every day of therapy during the second week is identical. The clients begin their day with a 2-hour rating session at normal conversational rates (170 spm to 190 spm). The clients are advised that each day they will spend three hours from 10:00 A.M. to 1:00 P.M. completing 14 assignments (Table 7–2) that will help them to strengthen their fluency skills beyond the clinic. These assignments are tape recorded and reviewed by the client and then the clinician to determine successful completion of an activity. The clients are encouraged to return to the clinic by 1:00 P.M., when each client participates in a 30-minute counseling session with a graduate student clinician. The individual therapy is followed by a 30-minute group therapy session where the client has the opportunity to share his or her questions and concerns with his or her fellow group participants and the clinicians. At the conclusion of this group therapy process, the clients are encouraged to continue working toward completing their 14 assignments. The clients are advised that at least one clinician will remain in the therapy room to evaluate the results of their out-of-clinic activities.

Our experience has shown that most clients try to complete at least one assignment between 2:00 P.M. and 4:00 P.M. each day although on occasion, a client will return home, drive to a shopping mall or attempt to complete an assignment without returning to therapy on that day. When a client has completed an assignment during the evening, he or she brings the tape-recorded results for review on the following day. The clients are encouraged to complete all fourteen out-of-clinic assignments by the end of the second week.

The length of each rating session is dependent upon the number of group participants and can be adjusted accordingly. For some clients, the 2-hour rating sessions are crucial to their success with the assigned activities. For other clients who believe they are ready to talk outside the clinic, the rating sessions are merely an activity to quickly complete so that the real practice can begin. During these rating sessions, the clients have the opportunity to strengthen their fluency skills in familiar surroundings while continuing to

TABLE 7–2. **Fourteen Activities That Facilitate the Transfer of Fluency**

1. Conversation with a family member or close friend using coping
2. Conversation with a family member or close friend
3. Conversation with a male or female stranger using coping
4–7. Conversations with two male strangers and two female strangers
8–9. Telephone calls to strangers
10. Shopping
11. Twenty inquiries
12. Fourteen introductions and requests
13. Five telephone appointments and cancellations
14. Ten deliberate stutterings with coping recovery

focus on those skills that enable them to remain fluent. The rating sessions are followed by the client's attempts to complete fourteen speaking activities beyond the therapy room.

Fourteen Activities to Facilitate Transfer of Fluency

Every client is given a list of the fourteen activities to be completed by the end of the second week of the therapy program. These activities are described to the clients, and the clients are able to ask questions on specific methods for completing the assignments. The clients are told that all of the activities will be audiorecorded using small cassette tape recorders or microcassette tape recorders. At first, many clients are skeptical about their abilities to record their speech while also concentrating on remaining fluent. We encourage the clients to attempt an activity and learn from each situation. As the clients experience success they gain confidence and skill for the next assignment. As we learned from participation in the St. Vincent's program, some clients are concerned about the conspicuous nature of their tape recorders and their fear of embarrassment when recording their activities outside of the therapy room. During the first activities, clients are encouraged to tell their listeners that they are taking a speech course at the university and this course requires them to record speaking activities with the public. The client then shows the listener that he or she will only be recording his or her portion of the conversation while the listener's speech will remain unrecorded through the client's use of the pause button on the tape recorder. If a listener continues to be concerned, the client is encouraged to find another listener. With these preliminary explanations, clients are usually able to complete the first seven activities. For the remaining activities that require recordings in more public places (e.g. shopping mall), clients are encouraged to either conceal the recorder in a place that enables a recording but keeps the recorder somewhat hidden or to use a set of headphones that are strategically placed around the client's neck so that it appears that the client is carrying a portable tape player for listening to music. In this manner, the clients are able to hold the tape recorders in their hand while making their recordings. When an activity is completed, the client is advised to listen to the tape and determine if their recorded activity met necessary criteria. The criteria are typically a specified number of syllables, appropriate use of fluency skills, and the absence of stuttering. If the client determines that the activity meets the criteria, the client brings the tape to the clinician for evaluation. If the client believes that the recorded activity will not meet the required standards, the client should repeat the activity. The clinician will listen to the recorded activity and determine whether the tape recording met the activity criteria. When a client fails to meet the criteria of the situation, the clinician will sit and discuss various strategies with client in an effort to help the client to complete the activity. Feedback often focuses on the client's ability to use his or her fluency skills in the nonclinical environment.

One point should be mentioned at this time. The reader will note that each activity requires stutter-free speech. We know that some readers will balk at this speech requirement and may even consider these stringent criteria to be a reason to reject our intensive program because we place unrealistic goals on the client. Our experience has shown that the majority of clients who are selected for the program are able to meet this stutter-free requirement. The task may not be completed on the first trial or even the third trial. However, all clients eventually complete all fourteen activities with no stuttering evident during the task. The reader might ask, "Why place such high expectations on the client?" We recognize that the entire 3-week process is somewhat unnatural and may not truly reflect the situations that the client may encounter when the program is completed. However, we believe that it is our goal to teach the client to be as fluent as possible for two reasons. First, we want the clients to know that it is possible to be totally fluent in situations where they never believed that they could be fluent. Second, we recognize that our 3-week program is an idealized world where the client's entire focus is on becoming fluent. It is our belief that the fluency foundation that we help the client establish will serve as the foundation for the client's ability to remain fluent when the program is completed. With a shaky foundation at the end of the program, many clients will drift back to their older methods of communicating and ultimately stuttering will return. With this solid fluency foundation, the clients are instructed that with continued practice, and continued attendance in therapy, they will be able to maintain a level of fluency comparable to their fluency during the 3-week program. However, we also recognize and share with our clients that it is unlikely that they will maintain the extremely high levels (100% fluency) of fluency when they return to their regular work and play schedules. No, we are not suggesting that the client will see a steady path to relapse. Instead we paint a realistic picture that fluency following therapy may vary somewhat from situation to situation and that these variations are not the path to relapse, merely the normal variation that many people experience in their fluency.

In the following, we will describe the fourteen transfer activities.

Conversation with a family member or close friend using coping: During **Activity 1**, the client is instructed to have a conversation with a family member or close friend and record at least 1400 syllables of their own conversation. We advise the clients that if they are speaking at 190 syllables per minute it will take approximately 7 to 8 minutes of their own conversation to reach their goal. Depending upon the amount of time spoken by the listener, most activities are 20 to 30 minutes in duration. The client is instructed to use the coping technique when initiating sentences and phrases. Because this activity begins with a family member or friend, the emotional demands should be lessened so that the client can focus his or her attentions on remaining fluent using the coping technique.

Conversation with a family member or close friend: **Activity 2** is the same as the previously described activity requiring the client to record 1400 syllables of his or her own conversation although coping is not required for this activity.

Conversation with a male or female stranger using coping: **Activity 3** requires the client to converse with a stranger, record 1400 syllables of conversation and use the coping technique. Because the client will be conversing with a stranger, the emotional requirements of the situation may interfere with the client's ability to use his or her fluency skills. Every client is different, and we discuss individual results with individual clients. As noted previously, it is not unusual for a client to approach a stranger and indicate that they are taking a speech course that requires them to record a conversation with a stranger. If the listener agrees, the conversation takes place. The client is required to use his or her coping techniques during these activities.

Conversations with two male strangers and two female strangers: **Activities 4 through 7** require the client to converse with two male and two female strangers. The clients are encouraged to continue focusing on using their fluency skills during these activities while trying to minimize the effects of the listener and situation on their speech.

Telephone calls to strangers: **Activities 8 and 9** require that the client make two telephone calls to two different strangers. We suggest to the client that they can use the newspaper want ads or the telephone book to guide this activity. The client is expected to converse with this stranger for an extended period of time about a product, an item for sale, an apartment for rent or any situation that will help the client to record at least 4 minutes of his or her their own speech.

Shopping: **Activity 10** requires that the client tape-record an extended interaction with a salesperson regarding a product (e.g., personal computer) or a service (e.g., housecleaning). The client will tape record his or her conversational interactions during this 4- to 5-minute activity.

Twenty inquiries: During **Activity 11** a client is expected to briefly interact with strangers asking simple questions and recording the question. The focus of this task is to approach a large number of different people, use fluency skills during a short specific period of time, and remain fluent for the duration of the activity. Activities often include questions to strangers in a shopping mall (e.g., "Can you tell me where the bank is?"), questions of sales clerks (e.g., "Do you have any extra large tee shirts?"), or an inquiry in an on-campus office (e.g., Is this the office where I can obtain my transcript?"). A client will complete all 20 inquiries and submit the tape for evaluation. The clinician will listen for the appropriate use of fluency skills and stutter-free speech.

Fourteen introductions and requests: During **Activity 12**, a client is required to enter into a conversation where part of the interaction involves saying his or her name. The client then proceeds to request information and interacts with the listener for 3 to 4 minutes. A client can telephone or complete this activity in person. One possible activity could involve a telephone call to a video store requesting a reservation for a video. Following this telephone call, the client drives to the video store, introduces him- or herself, and requests the video and additional information about store hours and availability of other videos. The client needs to say his or her name and interact with another person for a period of time.

Five telephone appointments and cancellations: **Activity 13** requires that the client make a telephone appointment where it is necessary to say his or her name. After a period of time, the client makes a second phone call to cancel the appointment. Activities often include reservations at restaurants, hairdressers, or physicians' offices. Some clients attempt to be creative when dealing with these activities. In one example, a client telephoned a nursing home to arrange for a guided tour for he and his father. The client was required to provide his name and make a number of inquiries regarding the facilities of the nursing home. A number of hours later, the client made a second phone call and cancelled the appointment. When clients complete all five activities, they return to therapy for an evaluation of their recorded activity.

Ten deliberate stutterings with coping recovery: During the final task, **Activity 14**, the client is required to stutter on ten occasions and then use coping recovery to get through the stuttering. These stutterings can occur during one conversation or several conversations. The client's ability to use his or her coping skills will determine completion of this task.

We have found the fourteen activities to be extremely valuable in helping clients learn to transfer and solidify their fluency skills to numerous environments beyond the clinic. It is interesting to note that during the middle of the second week, a number of clients develop an interesting attitude toward completing all fourteen activities. Our experience reveals that some clients are truly motivated by fluent speech and that this self-motivation propels the client to complete all fourteen activities. However, for other clients the opposite is true. A number of clients fail to see the importance of completing all fourteen activities and of reaching the goals by the end of the second week. As a result, completion of activities begins to slow by Wednesday of Week Two although the clinicians encourage the clients to move along and complete all activities. It is at this point in time that we introduce a monetary reward to stimulate the clients to finish all fourteen activities. On Wednesday, the clients are instructed that if they finish all of their activities by Friday afternoon, we will provide a $50.00 cash bonus. This monetary incentive seems to light the fire under most of the clients so that all of the activities are completed. When a client fails to reach the goal by Friday afternoon, the clinician may contract with the client that during the second weekend of therapy the client has the opportunity to complete all of his or her assignments. The client is required to return to therapy during Week Three with the necessary assignments on tape. The clinician can listen to tapes during the first day of Week Three and determine if the client qualifies for the monetary reward. In most cases, the client will be successful.

Counseling during Week Two

As we mentioned previously, counseling is an important part of therapy during the second and third week of our program. A number of intensive programs take the view that the behaviors and emotions associated with stuttering are perpetuated by the client's continued stuttering. When a client becomes fluent, these clinicians assume that the behaviors and emotions are no longer reinforced by the stuttering and will ultimately disappear, as long as the client remains fluent. Our clinical experiences suggest that many clients find it difficult to maintain fluency while trying to deal with 15 or more years of behaviors and emotions associated with stuttering. As a result, we believe that counseling the client during the second and third week of therapy is a critical part of our program. We recognize that changes in attitude often progress a lot more slowly when compared to changes in speech fluency. Two weeks of daily counseling may be insufficient to reach the type of emotional changes necessary for long-term fluency. However, by beginning the counseling process during the second and third week of therapy, we help the client to recognize the important relationship between his or her attitudes and emotions and his or her ability to remain fluent. Our goal is to make the client aware of the importance of communicating concerns about his or her speech. We focus our counseling on making the client more aware of the options that he or she has available so that upon dismissal, the client will be better equipped to deal with the continuing struggle that inevitably occurs between emotions and fluency. Having established a counseling relationship during the second and third week of our program, the client is less hesitant to remain in contact with our clinic and is often eager to attend our monthly follow-up program to ensure his or her continuing improvement.

Challenges of Week Two Counseling

It is possible that during Week Two of our program that the clients may express concerns on a large number of issues. However, the unique nature of the intensive program often brings out concerns that follow a number of themes. These include: (1) It's so easy to be fluent in the clinic but I'm having a number of problems outside of therapy; (2) What happens to my fluency when I'm not attending therapy on daily basis?; (3) Will I always have to concentrate as much on my speech in order to remain fluent; and (4) How much time will I have to spend practicing when the program is completed.

The question on ease of transfer can be addressed by discussing the progressive nature of transfer with the client. The following description deals with this issue.

Technique—Difficulty with Transfer

I realize that you're having difficulty with your fluency skills outside of the clinic. If you can remember the beginning of the first week of therapy, you had difficulty with your fluency skills every time we increased the speaking rate. However, by the end of the first week of therapy you were able to participate in a conversation where you produced 1400 syllables of conversation and remained fluent throughout. Learning to be fluent outside of the clinic requires that you focus your attention on your fluency skills and try to minimize the influence that your emotions have on your speech. You're starting out the week by talking with family and friends during situations where you are generally more comfortable and in control. During these sessions, you should be able to focus most of your attention on your speech and the emotional demands should be less disruptive during your early conversations. These situations are the perfect opportunity for practice. Any situation with a reduced emotional demand should enable you to put more focus on your fluency skills. As we progress during the week we will introduce more difficult tasks that you will overcome as you have practiced during less difficult tasks. Like any new activity such as golf or tennis, you will need to practice quite a bit before you are able to complete these tasks.

In regard to the client's concerns about relapse and the amount of time that is necessary for practice, the following description illustrates one counseling approach.

Technique—Potential Relapse and the Need for Practice

I believe that most clients express concerns about the potential for relapse. Historically this issue has been the major criticism of most therapy programs. It is not my intention to provide you with any false or unrealistic expectations. I believe that you need to understand the reality that you face when this program is completed. During our 3-week program you are being immersed in the skills and tasks necessary to become fluent and remain fluent. When the program is completed and you're back to work or school, if you were able to focus on your speech with the same intensity during these 3 weeks, you can probably remain as fluent as you are presently. However, the reality of any therapy program is that the daily demands of work, school, and family prevent you from devoting yourself to being fluent. As a result, you will see some degree of relapse in your speech, although the amount of stuttering that returns can remain at acceptable levels with some continuing work on your part. Certainly, if you decide that the fluency skills you learned during our program require too much effort, you will return to your older habits and in all likelihood begin to stutter with much of the same frequency and intensity as before the program. If you decide that you would like continue to remain as fluent as possible, you will need to find some time each day to practice your skills in an effort to keep your speech system tuned for smooth coordination. You will note that as time goes on, you will develop a routine for yourself that will enable you to do a minimal amount of practice and yet remain fluent. The amount of time and effort that is required will vary from individual to individual. Most important is the fact that you are never more than a phone call away from our clinic where we can provide additional therapy, counseling and support. We expect you to exhibit some degree of stuttering following our program. However, the manner in which you respond to your stuttering will determine your success. If you believe that all is lost and you're not supposed to stutter, you will not only continue to have difficulty but your stuttering will continue a backward spiral. On the other hand, if you can tell yourself that your stuttering is to be expected and is merely a momentary loss of control, you can focus your attention on your fluency skills, regain your fluency, and continue to move forward in a positive direction. We don't view stuttering as failure.

In addition to specific concerns on transfer and maintenance, counseling sessions enable the clinician to provide emotional support for the client who has some self-doubt about an activity or his or her fluency skills. We have found that by combining these counseling sessions with the teaching of fluency skills, we are providing the client with a therapy program that maximizes the client's chances for long-term fluency.

WEEK THREE

The goal of the third week in therapy is to solidify the client's fluency skills outside of the therapy. By focusing on those situations and activities in which the client continues to either exhibit stuttering or expresses concerns about fluency, the clinician can design transfer activities to meet the needs of the individual client. In addition, the counseling sessions continue during this week, and each client will be required to give a 7-minute speech in front of a large group. The week ends with plans for fluency maintenance and regular follow-up.

Determining a Focus for Week Three

In a manner similar to that described by Neilson and Andrews (1993), on the first day of Week Three we assess a client's progress in terms of spontaneous fluency and attitude change. Neilson and Andrews (1993) discuss three predictors of success for their intensive program. These predictors include 100% fluency during a telephone conversation, an S24 score below 10, and a change of at least 5% toward internalized locus of control using the LCB scale. All clients are asked to complete a telephone call and complete the two questionnaires. The results of the aforementioned predictors enable the clinician to address areas for continued work during Week Three. A client may require a focus on fluency skills, additional work on fluency outside of therapy, or some additional individual counseling depending upon the results of this assessment.

Structure

Week Three is structured in a similar manner to the previous week. Every day in therapy begins with a 2-hour rating session that focuses on normal conversational speaking rates (170 spm to 190 spm +/- 20). The clinicians and client will consult together in an effort to determine where the client believes his or her focus needs to be outside of the clinic. In addition, the clinician may determine an area that needs to be addressed despite the fact that the client doesn't see this issue as being a problem. Our counseling sessions are conducted every day from 1:00 P.M. to 2:00 P.M. If we determine from the LCB that a client is still reluctant to accept responsibility for the changes necessary for fluency, we may target our counseling sessions to deal with this issue. Regarding transfer skills, it is interesting to note that following Week Two, we usually have a good idea where the client has had difficulty with transfer. As a result, we consult with each client to discuss both our perceptions and their perceptions regarding a focus for Week Three. For one client, talking on the telephone may be the area of concern, while for a second client, effectively using the coping technique requires additional attention.

The ultimate challenge for the final week in therapy involves a speech before a large group of listeners. Every client is told prior to enrollment in the therapy program, that the final week in therapy will include a speech. As noted in our discussion of client selection, some clients determine that the activities that we use for transfer or the requirement for a public speech are too demanding. This client may choose to not participate in our program. For the clients who enter the third week of therapy, the public speech is an obstacle to be conquered. The clients are told that on Thursday at 10 A.M., a group of graduate students, faculty, and clinicians will be assembled for their speech. Each client is free to select his or her topic for presentation. On occasion, the clients have made arrangements with the graduate student clinicians to practice their speech prior to Thursday. For other clients, they prepare their speeches at home with their families or by themselves. We recognize that most clients participating in our program do not have to give a talk in front of a group as part of their daily routine. However, we view the speech as a task that raises the emotional demands of the situation that may be analogous to a variety of emotionally demanding situations that the client may face when they leave therapy. As a result, the challenge for the client is to remain as fluent as possible in a situation that would have resulted in avoidance or a high frequency of stuttering if attempted prior to participation in our program. The sense of accomplishment experienced by each client is extremely rewarding. The client recognizes that he or she has confronted a major obstacle and completed the task. It is important to recognize that a client may stutter during this demanding task. As noted previously, during emotionally demanding situations, we recognize that a client may not be able to use his or her fluency skills with the same success as experienced during the rating sessions. However, the manner in which the client reacts to these stutterings determines the client's ability for future success. Recognition of the stuttering as a momentary loss of control enables the client to move forward and maintain a realistic positive attitude regarding his or her speech. Clients who focus on their stuttering as a sign of failure and relapse will continue to have problems and may continue to experience difficulties maintaining speech fluency. Should this occur, we recognize that this issue will be a counseling topic during future therapy sessions.

VTC: 01:16:31:15

Final Day in Therapy

We begin our maintenance program during the final morning of therapy. As part of our rating sessions, every client is required to make a 3-minute tape recording of his or her speech beginning with 170 spm and continuing through the coping technique at 190 spm. In this manner, a client will leave therapy with a tape that contains models of speech that are useful as fluency reminders when the client begins to have difficulty when the program is completed. We recognize that maintaining fluency for some clients is a very difficult process. Having a tape that will serve as an auditory model provides the client with a model that can be useful as part of a regular fluency maintenance program.

VTC: 01:17:30:09

When the rating sessions are completed, we once again ask the clients to complete a telephone call and retake the S24 and LCB questionnaires. We compare these results to the results obtained on the first day of therapy and on the first day of Week Three. Our hope is that each client has met the predictive goals of 100% fluency, a S24 score below 10, and a change of at least 5% on the LCB scale. We do not share the predicted results with the clients but use the obtained results to provide continued direction for the client when he or she is away from therapy. Additionally, our goal is to continue to interact with each of the clients during our maintenance program, and the results of these measurements will be reviewed relative to the client's progress in future months.

MAINTENANCE

Our maintenance program involves a monthly follow-up meeting for all program participants. We conduct these meetings in conjunction with a group meeting for all adult clients participating in our long-term behavior program. We find that clients from the intensive programs have valuable information to share with clients in the long-term program while clients in the long-term program often have useful insights for the clients from the intensive program. We do not require that every client attend these meetings but we strongly encourage participation. Our clinical experience suggests that continued long-term maintenance is an important component to our program. Like many programs, however, clients make decisions to meet their own needs. When a client participates in the monthly follow-up meetings, he or she can practice his or her fluency skills in the group and also share concerns relative to his or her ability to remain fluent away from the program. On a number of occasions, a client expresses interest in returning for a rating session to retune his or her fluency. We are happy to have the client return to therapy. In our view, long-term fluency maintenance requires active participation on the part of the client. We make these sessions available, and the client chooses his or her level of participation. Ultimately, a client will decide when he or she no longer needs to be involved in the maintenance program. The client will either indicate his or her desire to not return or will stop attending the monthly meetings. We let our clients know that the door of therapy is always open if they would like to return.

VTC: 01:22:00:26

SUMMARY

In the preceding chapter, we have discussed an intensive stuttering therapy program for adults. This program is designed to meet the needs of some adults who stutter, and the determination for participation is made during a comprehensive stuttering evaluation. Clients participating in the intensive therapy program attend 3 weeks of therapy beginning at 8:00 A.M. each day. The clients are taught fluency skills using a slow rate of speech that is gradually increased to approximate normal conversational speaking rates. During Week Two, the clients learn to transfer their fluency skills beyond the therapy room by participating in a number of out-of-clinic assignments. Week Three focuses on solidifying fluency skills during more emotionally demanding situations while the client also learns to take responsibility for his or her speech. Counseling is an important part of this program and occurs on a daily basis during Weeks Two and Three. All clients are encouraged to participate in a maintenance program because it is recognized that maintaining speech fluency requires active client participation. As reported by Neilson and Andrews (1993): "Calvin Coolidge was right: Once you know what to do, it is perseverance that makes the difference between success and failure" (p. 164).

▶ 8

Therapy for Adults: Long Term

The long-term behavioral therapy model for adults who stutter, is probably the one therapy program that is most feared by speech-language pathologists. Although this program is often discussed during academic preparation, it is also the least understood program and is often seen as the most difficult therapy program to implement. Many clinicians will report a lack of experience working with adults who stutter and confusion about therapy strategies that work with adults.

Our approach to therapy will combine aspects of our program for older children and adolescents and aspects of our intensive fluency therapy program. Because a lot of this detail has been previously discussed, we will frequently refer the reader back to previous discussions of various stages in therapy.

In our long-term program, we focus on teaching fluency skills, the communicative environment, and the client's awareness of and reactions to stuttering and the communicative environment. In the sections to follow, we will discuss teaching fluency skills to adults and the need to teach clients to accept the responsibility for changes in their speech. We will also include a discussion of group therapy and its relationship to success in therapy.

FLUENCY SKILLS

A cursory observation of the discussion that follows may lead the casual observer to conclude that this therapy program like others before merely provide techniques for fluency shaping at the expense of the client's emotional well-being and chances for future success. This book and this chapter were not written for the casual observer. By understanding the need to address changes in the client's speech as one component toward a comprehensive stuttering therapy program, the reader will learn how to help clients modify their speech skills and at the same time deal with equally important emotional concerns associated with stuttering. We do believe, however, that for the majority of clients who come for therapy, our initial in-clinic therapy focus will be the client's speech behavior. By moving fluency to the forefront, we are providing clients with behavioral goals that are directed toward their individual abilities to make speech changes. We encourage our clients to become as fluent as possible by setting goals that increase in difficulty and complexity. We expect that some attitudes and beliefs about stuttering will change during the early stages of therapy as each client's speech changes. However, we are also prepared to counsel the clients on their newly formed perceptions associated with fluency as well as their continuing concerns on stuttering. We are going to teach clients to make modifications in their speech and then use these new skills within their communicative environment.

DAY ONE IN THERAPY

Day One in therapy is similar to all of the other Day One descriptions that preceded this chapter. The anatomy and physiology of speech production and the nature of stuttering are discussed with the client. We discuss our perspective regarding the manner in which an individual stutters, the different types of stuttering, and our perceptions regarding the client's attitude and awareness of the problem. This information has been gleaned from our initial diagnostic interview, any subsequent discussions with the client, and finally our interpretation of the client's responses to the various questionnaires (e.g., S24 scale) that he or she has filled out.

RESPONSIBILITY FOR CHANGE

A recurring theme throughout our adult program is the transfer of responsibility from clinician to client. For therapy to be effective, it is imperative that the client leaves the therapy program believing that he or she is the person responsible for the changes that occur in his or her speech. A typical discussion may include the following:

Technique—Accepting Responsibility for Change

We understand that you are interested in becoming more fluent and you want to learn to use that fluency outside of therapy. Our goal is help you achieve this goal. However, in order for you to effectively use your fluency skills outside of therapy, you will need to recognize that you are the person responsible for changes in your speech and you are the person responsible for the behaviors and attitudes associated with your stuttering. I know that you understand what I'm saying although the real indication of your understanding comes about when you can explain the skills that you use to maintain fluency and consistently complete your homework assignments. We recognize that in the early stages of therapy it is our responsibility to teach you the skills that are necessary for fluency. At this point in time you will show up for therapy, complete the activities, and leave until the next session. After three or four sessions, we expect that you will be given homework and from that point on we expect that you will complete every homework assignment. We accept 90% of the responsibility for the changes that need to occur during the early stages of therapy. As therapy progresses, there is a consistent transfer of responsibility from me to you. Ultimately, you are responsible for 90% of the changes that occur while I assist you along the way.

The preceding discussion typically takes place during the first day in therapy. We view therapy as an interactive process where we not only disseminate information but also serve as active listeners when our clients share areas of concern. We find that although we talk with the clients about responsibility for change in a formal manner on Day One, this recurring theme is often an active discussion topic throughout therapy.

A PLAN FOR TEACHING FLUENT SPEECH

The ultimate goal of our therapy program is for the client to be able to fluently converse with people outside of the therapy room. To reach this goal, we try to design a program that will enable clients to become fluent speakers in as expeditious a manner as possible. For some clients, the long-term therapy program begins with monologues and conversation at slow speaking rate in a manner that is similar to the intensive program (see Chapter 7). As the client masters these skills, he or she is encouraged to gradually increase his or her speaking rates while continuing to use the newly learned fluency skills. For other clients, it is necessary to teach fluency skills using many of the tasks outlined in our chapter describing therapy for older children and adolescents (see Chapter 6). This program focuses on teaching fluency skills during reading and progresses in a systematic manner through picture descriptions, monologues and conversation. The clinician begins by teaching fluency skills during reading and then makes the determination as to whether to progress to monologues or pictures.

Reading as a Fluency Tool

For the majority of clients in our program, we begin teaching fluency skills during reading. When teaching clients to use their fluency skills during reading, the clients find that they can focus the majority of their attention on their speech skills while paying little attention to the content. Because we are interested in speech production changes at this point, reading lends itself to this process.

When teaching fluency skills, the clinician follows the procedures outlined in Chapter 3 for developing fluency skills. During reading tasks, the clinician will model a sentence for the client and ask the client to fluently repeat the same sentence. Our experience suggests that during the early stages of therapy, it is best to immediately stop the client when he or she is using his or her fluency skills inappropriately. In this manner, it is easier to shape the client's fluency instead of letting the client continue, which merely reinforces additional bad speech habits. As we are teaching fluency skills to our clients during reading, we are making decisions about the clients' abilities to integrate and implement our suggestions during the reading tasks. For some clients, fluency skills are easily learned and incorporated into fluent reading. For these clients, we may decide to move to a program that is similar to the intensive fluency program where we teach fluency using monologues and conversation. A discussion of this program will follow. For clients who have difficulty mastering fluency skills, we may spend additional time with reading activities and continue with a program of progressively more complex activities. This program is well documented in Chapter 6.

VTC: 00:42:40:11

Fluency Skills—Conversational Program

We have described our intensive therapy program as a 3-week program that targets fluency in conversations that begin at 50 spm and progress to 190 spm. Because of the time frame for teaching fluency, the clients quickly move from 50 spm to faster speaking rates and spend the entire first week focusing on this process. For our long-term program, we like to use the conversational model for some clients although we recognize that it is unrealistic to start therapy at speaking rates of 50 spm. Because a client will only attend therapy for a maximum of 2 hours per week, it would be very difficult to begin conversations at 50 spm and expect clients to persevere at these slow rates for 6 months to a year before they were at normal conversational rates. As a result, we often begin the long-term conversational program at 150 spm. We have found that this slower than normal conversational rate enables a client to use his or her newly learned fluency skills while simultaneously monitoring his or her own conversation. At the same time, the client's speaking rate does not sound pathologically slow to the point where a client refuses to talk at this rate. The client is less likely to view his or her speech as sounding abnormal although there is some degree of counseling involved because the client still believes that he or she sounds too slow at 150 spm. We find it necessary to explain to the client that 150 spm is only the starting point for therapy. As the client learns to use his or her fluency skills at 150 spm, we point out we will gradually introduce faster speaking rates so that the client will eventually use a normal conversational rate and the naturalness of their speech will improve.

During the early stages of therapy, the client has to learn to monitor his or her speaking rate while at the same time focus on the content of his or her speech. The clinician encourages the client to select discussion topics that are very familiar to the client. These topics might include a description of family members, a description of a room within the client's home, or the plot of a favorite movie or television show. As the client produces a monologue, the clinician is sitting across from the client and counts the number of syllables produced by the client by hitting the spacebar on a computer keyboard. As the clinician counts syllables and monitors the information, the client's speaking rate and number of syllables are displayed on a second computer monitor in front of the client. As the client masters fluent speech at 150 spm, the speaking rate requirements are increased until the client is able to fluently converse at 190 spm (+/- 20).

For the clients participating in the conversational program, we find that they often reach the point where they can fluently converse with the clinician while maintaining appropriate speaking rates. While every client is different, this process generally averages 2 to 3 months (2 hours per week, 8 hours per month = approximately 24 hours of individual therapy). As clients learn to be fluent at faster speaking rates, they are encouraged to monitor their own speaking rates so that the computer can be turned off. We expect the client to develop an internal monitor for his or her speaking rate so that fluency activities can be attempted outside of therapy room. Should the client sound as if he or she was exceedingly fast or slow, the computer can be reintroduced into therapy. In most cases, reintroduction of the computer is not necessary. As clients learn to master fluency within the therapy room, they are given assignments to practice fluency outside of the therapy room.

Technique—Counseling Regarding Options

A client is able to fluently converse with his wife. However, the client also notes that the phone appears to be a major obstacle to fluency. "I can't do it, I just pick up the phone and nothing comes out. I try to use my fluency skills but I can't get anything out. This is impossible. I give up." We ask the client why he thinks he is having so much difficulty. "I don't know, it just happens to me." We explain to the client that nothing just happens. "Your difficulties are directly related to the manner in which you use your speech mechanism and the emotions associated with speech production. Did you tape-record your telephone conversation so that we can examine the communication skills you're using?" Initially the client responds, "Forget it, I'm helpless, what's the point." We explain to the client that there might be more than one way of saying hello when he answers the phone. Until we actually know what's going on, it's difficult to make a decision. It may be possible that because you believe that this situation is impossible, you continue to say hello as you always do and this results in stuttering. In reality, there may be other options available to you although you're letting your emotions dictate your response. We encourage the client to use other words for describing the situation, such as, "I'm having difficulty but I'll consider another way of communicating." When the client returns to therapy with a tape recording of his speech, we are able to identify a number of inappropriate strategies when he answered the phone, and these all resulted in stuttering. We point out to the client that because he thought that he was doing everything possible, he was unable to see alternate choices that were available. We listened to the audiotape and analyzed the situation in an objective manner. We were able to help the client to consider a number of options for speaking so that when the next difficult situation arises, the client will be better equipped to examine the available choices.

Homework as a Component of Accepting Responsibility for Change

Homework for the adult client begins with conversations outside of the therapy room using speaking rates consistent with in-clinic fluency activities. Clients are encouraged to converse with individuals within their environment (e.g., spouses or significant others) who the client perceives as the easiest to talk with. Typically, easier situations are associated with situations that are less emotionally demanding. We explain to clients that we are not encouraging them to challenge their speech skills at this time. We want the client to experience fluent speech using newly learned fluency skills in a situation that is outside of the therapy room. The client often responds, with "But I'm always fluent when I talk with my wife." Our response to the client is, "Do you know why you're fluent with your wife?" to which the client is unable to respond. We want the client to develop new behavior patterns using newly learned fluency skills. As the client learns mastery of his or her fluency both in the clinic and in similar situations beyond the clinic, we gradually introduce faster speaking rates and more demanding activities outside of the clinic.

Occasionally, clients will set expectations for themselves and limit their options for change. These clients let their emotional perspectives interfere with their need to grow as an individual. In the example that follows, we describe a method for redirecting a client's thinking about options for producing fluent speech.

We typically use the out-of-clinic activities that we described for our intensive program with our clients in the long-term program. We encourage the clients to use portable tape recorders and assign various activities for clients to complete between therapy sessions. The intensive fluency program provides a supportive clinical environment in which the client is immersed for 3 weeks. As a result, clients in the intensive program although somewhat reluctant, will typically go out and attack their fluency assignments. When a client has difficulty, he or she knows that clinicians are waiting for his or her return in the clinic should he or she need immediate emotional support. We believe that the emotional support that we provide is one key factor in the client's steady progress through the intensive program. With our long-term program, clients are often more reluctant to complete speaking assignments and often have to wait one day or many days before they return to therapy to receive feedback and emotional support. Our experience suggests that clinicians need to be more patient with clients in the long-term program and more aware of the emotional needs of the adult clients because of the time lapse between therapy sessions.

Because homework is an integral component for teaching fluency and fluent conversation, it is imperative that clients complete their assignments. We view homework as the one component of therapy that really reflects the client's acceptance of responsibility toward conversational fluency. Excuses are plentiful: "I'm too busy," I'm always out of town on business," "I just forgot to do it." When a client fails to complete homework, we inform the client that our program for teaching fluency can only progress so far within the clinical setting. Without continued practice when the client is away from therapy, the client often will remain fluent in the clinic but fail to progress to real world situations. We certainly understand the reluctance of some clients to practice speech away from the therapy room. Communication has always been difficult, and the client may lack some conversational skills that develop in normally fluent adults. For these clients we might develop a number of practice sessions within the clinic to assist with fluency transfer. However, for the client who continually fails to complete homework and refuses to change this perspective, we often find it necessary to discuss termination of therapy. For many clients, reluctance to complete homework is usually associated with stuttering and fears associated with speaking. We often can counsel clients to deal with these difficult situations if we approach these situations in a gradual manner. In addition, we can provide group therapy activities to assist the therapy process.

GROUP THERAPY WITH ADULTS

Group therapy is another important component of all of our adult programs. We provide group therapy as a part of our intensive program and as a component of our long-term program. We view the group therapy process to be an adjunct to individual therapy rather than as a replacement for individual therapy, although at later stages in a client's therapy program the group therapy session may be used as a substitute for individual therapy.

Purposes of Group Therapy

Opportunities to Meet Other Persons with Similar Concerns

Group therapy for adults stutterers may serve a number of purposes within the therapy program. The major benefit of attendance in group therapy is that it provides the client with an opportunity to meet individuals who share similar concerns regarding their speech, common experiences regarding communication, and similar therapy experiences. Too often we encounter individuals who believe that they are the only person who stutters, and this belief can affect the client's daily outlook and perspectives about success in therapy. If we believe that effective therapy involves not only changing a client's speech but also changing his or her attitude and beliefs, then participation in group therapy can be an effective contributor to that change.

We often encounter adults who restrict their verbal communication to the barest minimum on a daily basis because speaking appears to be a difficult and painful experience. During the client's participation in group therapy, he or she may or may not choose to initially participate. We would like the clients to view the group setting as an opportunity to feel at ease with regard to their speech and comfortable enough to share questions and concerns. For some clients, this acclimation occurs at the first session while for other clients it takes a number of sessions. We have observed that for some clients, the group meeting is often a positively anticipated event because this session may be their only opportunity to express their feelings about their problem in a supportive environment.

Because every client has been evaluated by the clinician and may already be participating in individual therapy, it becomes the clinician's responsibility to guide the group and encourage each participant to become an active group member. The clinician is aware of each client's willingness or reluctance to participate. As a result, the clinician can help each client to "fit in" to the group. Clinical experiences with group therapy suggest that it may take a number of group sessions before participants start to share experiences without being prompted. After a period of time, we found that group sessions become self-sustaining with group members actively sharing experiences and receiving feedback from other group members. At that point, the clinician can step back from the discussion and interject a point of view, listen to the discussion, or offer suggestions for a new topic or direction.

Opportunities to Practice Therapy Techniques

A second purpose for group therapy is that it provides clients with an opportunity to practice their fluent speech in a setting that is different than individual therapy. Depending upon how far the client has progressed in therapy, our expectations and the client's expectations for fluency should be adjusted accordingly. Practicing fluency skills within the group setting is most appropriate for the client who is fluent within the individual therapy session and learning to use these fluency skills in a variety of situations beyond the therapy room. This client is typically practicing his or her fluency skills while speaking on the telephone, conversing with co-workers, or speaking with his or her spouse. Practicing within the group setting provides the client with the opportunity for the clinician to observe the client's fluency skills in a situation more demanding than individual therapy. In this manner, the clinician can identify inappropriate strategies that the client may use in more demanding situations so that during subsequent individual therapy sessions both client and clinician can work out strategies that result in the client's improved fluency skills outside of therapy. During the individual therapy session, we discuss our expectations with the client before the group meeting and discuss the results of the group session during the subsequent session. We make every attempt to avoid directly commenting about the client's speech during the group session.

VTC: 01:18:26:23

In contrast to the above discussion, we occasionally devote a group therapy session to practicing fluency skills in the group. When the entire group is working on their fluency skills, verbal feedback can be provided by both the clinician and other group participants. The clinician needs to understand the dynamics of this situation and make every attempt to prevent one client from becoming the main focus for therapy. It is imperative that one client is not singled out as the main target of the session. Every client should have the opportunity to demonstrate his or her speech skills and receive feedback from the group. When group therapy sessions are conducted weekly, one in four sessions or one is six sessions can be directed toward fluency skills.

One side note to the aforementioned discussion involves the recalcitrant client who continually verbalizes his desire to change his speech, regularly attends both individual and group therapy sessions, but completes his homework on an occasional, rather than consistent basis. This client often needs to be stimulated in some way to start to take responsibility for his actions. One method for lighting a fire under this person is to make him the focus of the group so that group members rather than the clinician, can question this person's real commitment to therapy. In this manner, the client is being rebuked by his peers rather than the clinician and this may stimulate the client to make the necessary changes. A word of caution once again. We are discussing clinical interactions and group dynamics that need to be supervised by the clinician. These events can serve a very positive purpose when done correctly. As a result it becomes the responsibility of the clinician to closely supervise this situation.

From the clinician's perspective, practicing fluency within the group therapy session is only appropriate for those individuals working on similar skills in individual therapy. However, it is interesting to note that with or without our encouragement, many clients will attempt to use their newly learned fluency skills within the group setting despite the fact that they may not be ready for this level of transfer. Some clients will exhibit better fluency skills than others, and some may exhibit negative reactions as a result of their behaviors. We are concerned that adult clients try to challenge themselves by using their newly learned fluency skills. Our concern is that the client will view his or her attempts as some type of failure. The client often sets some unrealistic expectation for him- or herself and then fails to meet that expectation. The counseling clinician needs to recognize these behaviors and deal with them during both individual and group therapy. Many clients like to pose challenges for their speech but it is their emotional reactions associated with their perceived failures that need to be addressed.

Technique—Counseling Regarding Unreal Expectations

During an individual therapy session that follows the group session, the client appears to be upset about his or her speech. Clinician: "You've just stated that you're upset because you couldn't be fluent during the group session. Why are you upset?" Client: "I should have been able to be fluent during that group session. I can be fluent in therapy and I know what to do. I just couldn't be fluent and that bothers me." Clinician: "Learning to be fluent is like learning to play golf. You work on your swing at the driving range, which is analogous to working on your speech in the therapy room. The driving range is an ideal environment where you can concentrate on your swing without having to consider the foursome playing behind you or partners waiting to tee off. Within this environment you're hitting the ball straight and doing fine. However, when you go to the golf course to play with your friends, you now have to maintain your swing in a different environment. Your friends are watching you and you're starting to react emotionally to the environment. For many golfers, these emotional reactions disrupt their ability to maintain that good swing that they practiced at the driving range. As result, they hook, slice, or dribble the ball off the tee. In a similar manner, when you tried to use your fluency skills outside of the therapy room, your emotional reactions interacted with your attempts to produce smooth speech and you stuttered as a result. Our focus in therapy is to teach you to develop smooth speech skills that will be less affected by

(continued)

the emotionality of a situation. We want you to be able to tell us that you were nervous and anxious in a situation but remained fluent. However, like golf and other sports, learning to master these fluency skills takes time."

"Now, given the fact that you are only able to be fluent during our individual sessions on an inconsistent basis, why do you think that during a session that requires you to concentrate on both the content of your speech and the manner in which you produce your speech that you will be able to be fluent? The group session is much more emotionally demanding than our individual sessions. At this point in time, your willingness to participate in the group is viewed to be very positive. We have not set any expectations for your fluency in the group. You have to avoid setting a goal for yourself without discussing that goal with me. Although we would like to think that speech fluency automatically transfers beyond the therapy room, for most adults, transfer occurs because of practice during a number of situations outside of therapy. However, this practice and transfer needs to be consistent with your activities in therapy. Discussing your attempts to be fluent outside of therapy with me will help to reduce your frustration when you are unable to accomplish a goal that you might set for yourself."

The above description is our attempt to apply some of the clinical procedures associated with rational emotive therapy (Ellis, 1977) and is described in Chapter 4 of this book.

Activities for Group Therapy or Common Discussion Topics

In the view of the author, the successful management of adult group therapy is the most difficult skill required of a speech-language pathologist. The skilled clinician learns to follow the lead of the group participants by listening to their comments, addressing specific issues, and channeling the direction of the discussion into areas that may be beneficial to all of the clients. This channeling does not preclude in-depth discussions generated by the clients in areas that are viewed to be less productive by the clinician. However, group participants sometimes lock onto areas of discussion that are based on their interpretations of their own life experiences. As the group is designed to benefit all participants, the skilled clinician must balance the needs of the individual against the needs of the group.

Technique—Directing Group Discussion

During the course of group therapy, a relatively new client is interested in sharing his or her perceptions of stuttering with the members of group. The individual states, "You know, I notice that I stutter a lot more after I watch a lot of television." A second client states, "I notice that I stutter a lot after I go out for Chinese food." The clinician responds: "I know that you're trying to make some sense of your stuttering as it seems to be out of your control at this point in time. As far as I know there hasn't been any documented reports that stuttering is related to television or Chinese food. Perhaps if you want to explore reasons for stuttering you need to examine what you are doing while watching television or talking in the restaurant. Remember, stuttering occurs as a result the manner in which you produce speech. Do you find that when you're watching sports you are talking fast, getting excited and generally losing control of your speech?" Perhaps in the Chinese restaurant there are some increased emotional demands that make it more difficult for you to control your speech. I believe that if we try and monitor your speech more closely outside of therapy, we will be able to identify the specific behaviors you may or may not be using that results in increased stuttering. When we continually look for the causes of stuttering, we often get so bogged down that we fail to move forward in therapy. When we try and analyze our behavior during a speaking situation, we find that we can identify behaviors within our control and, as a result, we change some of things that we do that result in stuttering. I believe that you will find this approach to be a lot more productive."

In general, most clinicians are faced with the challenge of keeping the flow of conversation continuing during the group session. An inexperienced clinician (not a newly trained clinician but rather any speech-language pathologist who has not conducted a lot of group therapy) often responds to this urgency by attempting to explain the meaning of a client's statement or filling in the silent pauses that are often part of this group process. The more experienced clinician recognizes the need for these silent periods and will often let the silence last until a group member is ready to share additional information. In preparation for running a group, it would be advantageous for the inexperienced clinician to sit in with an experienced clinician who has had some success with group therapy. Like any therapy that we provide, visual and verbal models and verbal feedback are key components for training. Our experience suggests that the inexperienced clinician should prepare a list of topics or questions that might be used to generate discussion within the group (Table 8–1).

Given these topic areas, the clinician will have a point of departure for group therapy. The clinician should not feel compelled to cover all of the topic areas, because one topic is often sufficient to stimulate the group for the entire session. As the members of a group get to know one another and concerns become shared concerns, the flow of conversation will be generated by the clients, and the clinician will serve as a moderator throughout these interactions.

MAINTENANCE

As clients are learning to transfer their fluency to situations beyond the therapy, the clinician counsels the client on the transfer of responsibility that has occurred between clinician and client. Clients who are reluctant to accept responsibility for their actions often remain in therapy for a longer period of time as transfer will progress much more slowly. Throughout the transfer process the clinician encourages the clients to do more work outside of the therapy room and reduces the number of in-clinic therapy sessions. When

TABLE 8–1. **Discussion Questions for Group Therapy**

1. Are you different because you stutter?
2. Would you be a different person if you didn't stutter?
3. What is the biggest obstacle that prevents you from becoming more fluent?
4. Do you have to stutter to understand stuttering?
5. Would you prefer to work with a clinician who stutters or a clinician who is fluent?
6. Do listener's reactions affect your speech?
7. Does your mood affect your speech?
8. Can you be fluent if you're in a bad mood and depressed?
9. What have you done on your own to help your speech?
10. Do you believe that you'll always stutter?
11. Is stuttering inherited?
12. Can children catch stuttering from their parents?
13. If someone laughs or reacts negatively to your speech, how do you react?
14. Is it better to let people know you stutter before you talk with them?
15. Should students who stutter receive special privileges because they stutter?
16. Do you avoid words and situations?
17. What feelings do you have when you avoid?
18. Why do you think you stutter?

the client and clinician determine that the client has reached his or her goals, the clinician discusses the need for continued awareness on speech skills, emotions, and reactions to situations. We encourage clients to maintain regular contact with our clinic by either attending our monthly adult fluency group, periodically calling our clinic to discuss progress, or periodically scheduling follow-up sessions. We view these follow-up sessions as the client's attempts to recharge his or her fluency batteries when they have run down and need additional charging. The clinician and client know the amount of time and effort that it took to reach the terminal point in therapy. As clinicians, we want to do everything possible to help the client maintain speech fluency for the years to follow.

SUMMARY

During the preceding chapter, we discussed our long-term therapy program for adults who stutter. The format for this program is quite similar to the program for older children and adolescents. We do point out to the reader that some adults are able to quickly learn fluency skills and integrate this skills into their conversation within the therapy room. When clients are able to integrate these skills, the focus of our therapy program shifts from teaching fluency skills during a number of different tasks to teaching fluency skills during conversation. For a number of clients, the conversational focus is an effective method of learning to be fluent. In addition to discussing fluency skills, we also discussed a group therapy program that is an integral component of all of adult therapy programs. Within the group settings, clients are able to discuss concerns about their fluency, stuttering, and any other concerns on communication. Our chapter ends with a focus on maintenance. Clients need to know that therapy is continuing process and that the door is always open if they want to return for help.

▶ 9

An Open Letter to All Speech-Language Pathologists

Dear Colleague:

In 1941 Wendell Johnson wrote an *Open Letter to the Parent of A "Stuttering" Child*. Within this letter, Johnson provided an extensive description of stuttering and suggestions for parents of children who stutter. In my closing chapter I would like to write an open letter to you, the graduate student in speech-language pathology and the practicing professional. I hope that this letter is something you can share with your colleagues to provide encouragement to those in our profession who are reluctant to work with persons who stutter.

Andrews, Neilson, and Cassar (1987) remind us that "Becoming fluent is hard work" (p. 214). These authors suggested that our clients must work hard to improve speech fluency. I'd suggest to the reader that learning to provide therapy for persons who stutter is hard work. My perception is that you already know the difficulties associated with fluency therapy and that's why you're so apprehensive about jumping in. However, do you think that you can find anything as rewarding as dismissing an adolescent client from therapy after he tells you that you are responsible for opening possibilities that he never dreamed possible? Is there a better feeling than receiving a handmade Christmas ornament in the form of book entitled *Be Fluent, Be Free*? I'm hard pressed to find anything that's more rewarding. This is the reason that I wrote this book. Yes, stuttering therapy is hard work. However, many of the skills that you developed to work with children with language disorders, older children with articulation disorders, and adults with traumatic brain injury are all applicable when you work with persons who stutter. First you have to be willing to try. It is my hope that this book will enable you to develop the confidence to provide effective therapy for persons who stutter.

I also wrote this book because of my concern for our profession. We are being asked to work with a greater variety of clients in a greater variety of locales while we're still mastering the skills necessary for the traditional clients who are still confusing us. Our national organization has eliminated the requirements to obtain supervised clinical hours with persons who stutter and many training programs have latched onto this idea with statements like "we don't have stutterers in our community" or "there's nothing you can really do with persons who stutter, so why bother." I'm telling you that this is clearly the wrong approach to take. My experience suggests that whether you're working in the wheat fields of Winnipeg, the snowdrifts of Syracuse, or the cornfields of De Kalb, there are always children and adults who will benefit from therapy. My philosophy is best summed by Kinsella (1982) in his book *Shoeless Joe* and later heard by Kevin Costner in the movie *Field of Dreams*, "if you build it he will come, and "ease his pain." These two phrases solidify the idea that if you provide therapy, clients will show up at your clinic. If you know how to provide effective stuttering therapy, you are going to ease the pain associated with stuttering.

What happens when we abrogate our responsibility to treat persons who stutter? Clearly, the void will be filled. Unfortunately, that void is filled by persons who believe that they have found the cure, then promote the cure, and fleece the flock. Historically, this has been the case and will continue to be the case unless our profession takes some responsibility for dealing with the problem.

This book is an attempt to deal with our failure to help persons who stutter. We need to begin by teaching our graduate students the necessary methods for providing stuttering therapy. Classroom discussion on the history of stuttering and explorations on the controversial issues all have a place in our coursework. However, until the specialists in stuttering therapy start demonstrating to our students the methods for providing therapy, we will continue to search for individuals with the necessary skills to provide stuttering treatment. Stuttering therapy requires more than skill. The clinician has to be committed to providing the best form of treatment for the client. The specialist has the responsibility to excite the graduate student to learn how to provide stuttering therapy and the potential to reflame a practicing professional's interest in a problem that often becomes a second priority. For the practicing professional, I realize that relearning or learning for the first time to provide stuttering therapy becomes one more burden to add to your list that includes learning about pediatric swallowing, ventilators in the classroom, and the differences between pervasive developmental disorder and autism. I'm sorry to add to this burden. However, we need more people to provide the treatment to deal with this problem. I WANT YOU.

Sincerely yours,
Howard D. Schwartz, Ph.D.
Clinical Recruiter

Calculating the Consistency Index

STEP 1

1. Determine the number of stutterings in each of the five reading passages. Place values in the # Of Stutterings column.
2. Determine the number of stutterings in reading 2 that also appear in reading 1. Place number in Compare column. Do the same for comparisons 3–2, 4–1, and 5–1.
3. Using the values obtained in the Compare column, determine the percentage of stuttered words that appear in the previous reading. In actuality, this is the percentage of consistent words plus chance.

STEP 2

1. Using numbers determined in Step 1 #1, fill in the # of Stutterings column.
2. Determine total number of words for reading passage, and use this figure to set up the fraction:

Number of stutterings each reading/Total words

Place the fraction in the Chance column. This value is the chance factor. That is, if 50 words were stuttered during the first reading, probability/chance suggests that these same 50 words could be stuttered again for reasons other than consistency. Determine percentage of stuttered words for each of the readings and place in Percent column.

STEP 3

1. To determine the consistency index for a specific comparison (e.g., reading 2–1), you divide the Consistency + Chance percentage determined in Step 1 by the Chance factor determined in Step 2.
2. Any consistency index greater than 1 suggests that your client is consistent for that specific reading.

Purpose: To determine if a person who stutters will stutters on the same words during successive readings or repetitions of the same material.

200-Word Passage

Step 1—Compare Readings and Determine Consistency + Chance

Reading	# of Stutterings	Compare		Percent/Passage	
1	50				
2	40	2–1	30	30/40	75%
3	30	3–2	15	15/30	50%
4	20	4–1	20	20/20	100%
5	10	5–1	9	9/10	90%

Step 2—Determine the Chance Factor from Percent Words Stuttered

Reading	# of Stutterings	Chance	Percent	Stuttering/# of Words
1	50	50/200	25%	
2	40	40/200	20%	
3	30	30/200	30%	
4	20	20/200	20%	
5	10	10/200	10%	

Step 3—Calculate the Consistency Index

Step 1 Consistency + Chance/ Step 2 Chance = Consistency Index

Comparing 2–1 $75/25 = 3.0$
           3–2 $50/20 = 2.5$
           5–1 $90/25 = 3.6$

Values >1 Suggest that Client is Consistent

APPENDIX B

Interview Questions Related to Stuttering Development

1. Why are you here today?
2. Is there a specific reason for coming for an evaluation?
3. When did the problem first begin?
4. How has the problem changed since the onset?
5. Is there a family history of stuttering?
6. Do any family members continue to stutter?
7. Why do you think you stutter?
8. What does the stuttering sound like?
9. How do you stutter?
10. Do you g-g-g go like this or gooooo like this?
11. Do you get stuck on words so nothing comes out?
12. Do you know when you'll stutter?
13. Is your child aware of his or her stuttering?
14. How do you know?
15. How does your child react when he or she stutters?
16. Does your child ever show signs of being frustrated with his or her speech and just stop talking?
17. Does your child exhibit any behaviors in association with his or her stuttering?
18. Do you notice that you exhibit any behaviors when you're stuttering? For example, do you blink your eyes or turn your head?
19. Do you make decisions based upon your stuttering?
20. Do you avoid specific situations because of your stuttering?

21. Do you avoid specific words because of your stuttering?
22. Are there specific sounds that pose a problem for you?
23. What do you do when you have to say that sound.
24. Can you anticipate or look ahead while you're speaking and know when you'll stutter?
25. How far can you scan ahead in your speech?
26. Does your child change his or her behavior because of his stuttering?
27. Would you be a different person if you didn't stutter?
28. Do you think that you'd do things differently if you didn't stutter?

APPENDIX C

S24 Modified Erickson Scale

1.	I usually feel that I am making a favorable impression when I talk.	True	False
2.	I find it easy to talk with almost anyone.	True	False
3.	I find it very easy to look at my audience while speaking to a group.	True	False
4.	A person who is my teacher or my boss is hard to talk to.	True	False
5.	Even the idea of giving a talk in public makes me afraid.	True	False
6.	Some words are harder than others for me to say.	True	False
7.	I forget all about myself shortly after I begin to give a speech.		
8.	I am a good mixer.	True	False
9.	People sometimes seem uncomfortable when I am talking to them.	True	False
10.	I dislike introducing one person to another.	True	False
11.	I often ask questions in group discussions.	True	False
12.	I find it easy to keep control of my voice when speaking.	True	False
13.	I do not mind speaking before a group.	True	False
14.	I do not talk well enough to do the kind of work I'd really like to do.	True	False
15.	My speaking voice is rather pleasant and easy to listen to.	True	False
16.	I am sometimes embarrassed by the way I talk.	True	False

17. I face most speaking situations with complete
    confidence.   True   False
18. There are very few people I can talk with easily.   True   False
19. I talk better than I write.   True   False
20. I often feel nervous while speaking.   True   False
21. I find it hard to make conversation when I meet
    new people.   True   False
22. I feel pretty confident about my speaking ability.   True   False
23. I wish that I could say things as clearly as others do.   True   False
24. Even though I know the right answer, I often fail to
    give it because I am afraid to speak out.   True   False

Score: _____

From Andrews, G. & Cutler, J. (1974). Stuttering Therapy: The relation between changes in symptom level and attitudes. *Journal of Speech and Hearing Disorders*, 37, 318–319. Reprinted with permission of the American Speech-Language-Hearing Association.

Locus of Control of Behavior Scale

Directions: Below are a number of statements about how the various topics affect your personal beliefs. There are no right or wrong answers. For each item there is a large number of people who agree and disagree. Could you please put in the appropriate bracket the choice you believe to be true? Answer all questions.

0	1	2	3	4	5
Strongly disagree	**Generally disagree**	**Somewhat disagree**	**Somewhat agree**	**Generally agree**	**Strongly agree**

1. I can anticipate difficulties and take action to avoid them. ( )
2. A great deal of what happens is probably just a matter of chance. ( )
3. Everyone knows that luck or chance determines one's future. ( )
4. I can control my problem(s) only if I have outside support. ( )
5. When I make plans, I am almost certain that I can make them work. ( )
6. My problem(s) will dominate me all my life. ( )
7. My mistakes and problems are my responsibility to deal with. ( )
8. Becoming a success is a matter of hard work, luck has little or nothing to do with it. ( )
9. My life is controlled by outside actions and events. ( )
10. People are victims of circumstances beyond their control. ( )
11. To continually manage my problems, I need professional help. ( )
12. When I am under stress, the tightness in my muscles is due to things outside of my control. ( )
13. I believe a person can really be the master of his fate. ( )

14. It is impossible to control my irregular and fast breathing
    when I am having difficulties.   ( )
15. I understand why problem(s) varies so much from one
    occasion to the next.   ( )
16. I am confident of being able to deal successfully with
    future problems.   ( )
17. In my case maintaining control over my problem(s) is due
    mostly to luck.   ( )

Score = _____ + _____

Sum Score = _____

From: A. R. Craig, J. A. Franklin, & G. Andrews. (1984). A scale to measure locus of control of behavior. *British Journal of Medical Psychology*, 57, 173–180, Table 1. Reprinted with permission.

APPENDIX E

Homework Log for Recording Activities Outside of the Clinic

Date	Client Observation	Parent Observation

Log for Monitoring
Rating Sessions

Date	Start Time	Target Time	Target Syllables	Actual Rate	Actual Time	Actual Syllables	Errors	Comments

► APPENDIX G

Log for Judging
Videotape Rating
Sessions

Name	First Reaction	Video Replay	Clinician Judgment	Agreements/ Disagreements	Reward
Slow/Smooth initiation					
Connecting words					
Pausing					
Small breath					
Elongating Vowels					
Intonation/Prosody					
Speech rate					

Transcripts For
Identifying Stuttering

VTC: 01:24:56:20

CLIENT ONE

Well let's see this tennis ball looks a lot uh type of tennis balls that my sister used to play pl um used to use I mean she used to take tennis lessons and she would practice during the summer days with this ball and her an her racquet at the tennis court in the park.

VTC: 01:25:21:15

CLIENT TWO

1. We buy candy.
2. Tom likes playing ball.
3. Jack feeds the little puppies.
4. We like ice cream.
5. Jane wants to play house.

6. Fred's father plays with him.
7. Betty has a doll dress.
8. We buy candy.
9. Tom likes playing ball.
10. Jack feeds the little puppies.
11. We li we like ice cream.
12. Jane wants to play house.

VTC: 01:26:12:00

CLIENT THREE

Well once there was Go a little girl named Goldilocks oh yeah and she went to look in this bear's houses who were gone. They, and they had porridge and there's momma bear, papa bear and a baby bear. An poppa bear's porridge was too hot, momma's was too cold, and the (baby?) small bear's was just right. And she went upstairs. Poppa's bed was too hard, momma's was momma's bed was too soft and the little bear's bed was just right. So she fell asleep in the little bear's bed and then when she fell asleep and when they woke up, when she woke up all the three bears were staring at her.

TRANSCRIPTS WITH STUTTERING IDENTIFIED

Stuttered Words are indicated with an underline.

CLIENT ONE

Well let's see this <u>tennis</u> ball looks a lot uh type of type <u>tennis</u> balls that my sister used to play <u>pl</u> um used to use I mean she used to take tennis lessons and she would <u>practice</u> during the summer days um <u>with</u> this ball and her an her <u>racquet</u> at the tennis court in the park.

CLIENT TWO

1. <u>We</u> buy candy.
2. <u>Tom</u> likes playing ball.
3. <u>Jack</u> feeds the little puppies.
4. <u>We</u> like ice cream.
5. <u>Jane</u> wants to play house.
6. <u>Fred's</u> father plays with him.
7. <u>Betty</u> has a doll dress.
8. <u>We</u> buy candy.
9. <u>Tom</u> likes playing ball.
10. <u>Jack</u> feeds the little puppies.
11. <u>We li</u> we like ice cream.
12. <u>Jane</u> wants to play house.

CLIENT THREE

Well once there was <u>Go</u> a little <u>girl</u> named Goldilocks oh yeah and she went to <u>look</u> in this <u>bear's</u> houses who were gone. <u>They</u>, and they had porridge and there's <u>momma</u> bear, papa bear and a <u>baby</u> bear. An poppa bear's porridge was too hot, momma's was too cold, and the (<u>baby</u>?) small bears was just right. And she went upstairs. Poppa's bed was too hard, momma's was <u>momma's bed</u> was too soft and the <u>little</u> bear's bed was just right. So she fell asleep in the <u>little</u> bear's bed and then when she fell asleep and when they woke up, when she woke up all the three bears were <u>staring</u> at her.

▶ APPENDIX **I**

Table of Contents for Video Time Codes

References

Adams, M. R. (1993). The home environment of children who stutter. *Seminars in Speech and Language*, 14, 185–192.

Andrews, G., & Craig, A. (1988). Prediction of outcome after treatment for stuttering. *British Journal of Psychiatry*, 153, 236–240.

Andrews, G., Craig, A., Feyer, A.-M., Hoddinott, S., Howie, P., & Neilson, M. (1983). Stuttering: A review of research findings and theories circa 1982. *Journal of Speech and Hearing Disorders*, 48, 226–246.

Andrews, G., & Cutler, J. (1974). Stuttering therapy: The relation between changes in symptom level and attitudes. *Journal of Speech & Hearing Disorders*, 37, 312–319.

Andrews, G., & Ingham, R. (1971). Stuttering: Considerations in the evaluation of treatment. *British Journal of Disordered Communication*. 6, 129–138.

Andrews, G., Neilson, M., & Cassar, M. (1987). Informing stutterers about treatment. In L. Rustin, H. Purser, & D. Rowley (Eds.), *Progress in the treatment of fluency disorders*. London: Taylor & Francis.

Barron, F. X. (1963). *Creativity and psychological health*. Princeton: D. Van Nostrand.

Bloodstein, O. (1995). *A handbook on stuttering* (5th ed.). San Diego, CA: Singular.

Brady, J. P. (1971). Metronome-conditioned speech retraining for stuttering. *Behavior Therapy, 2*, 129–150.

Brown, R. (1973). *A first language: The early stages*. Cambridge: Harvard University Press.

Brown, S. F. (1945). The loci of stutterings in the speech sequence. *Journal of Speech and Hearing Research, 10*, 181–192.

Conture, E. G. (1982). *Stuttering*. (2nd ed.). Englewood Cliffs, NJ: Prentice-Hall.

Conture, E. G. (1990). Childhood stuttering: What is it and who does it? *ASHA Reports*, 18, 2–14.

Conture, E. G. (1996). Treatment efficacy: Stuttering. *Journal of Speech and Hearing Research*, 39, S18–S26.

Conture, E. G. (1997). Evaluating childhood stuttering. In R. F. Curlee & G. M. Siegel (Eds.), *Nature and treatment of stuttering: New directions* (2nd ed., pp. 239–256). Boston: Allyn & Bacon.

Conture, E.G., & Kelly, E. M., (1991) Young stutterers' nonspeech behavior during stuttering. *Journal of Speech and Hearing Research, 34*, 1041–1056.

Cordes, A. K. , & Ingham, R. J. (1994). The reliability of observational data: II. Issues in the identification and measurement of stuttering events. *Journal of Speech and Hearing Research*, 37, 279–294.

Coriat, I. H. (1943). The psychoanalytic conception of stammering. *Nervous Child*, 2, 167–171.

Costello-Ingham, J. (1993). Behavioral treatment of stuttering in children. In R. Curlee (Ed.), *Stuttering and related disorders of fluency* (pp. 68–100). New York: Thieme.

Craig, A., & Andrews, G. (1985). The prediction and prevention of relapse in stuttering. The value of self-control techniques and locus of control measures. *Behavior Modification, 9*, 427–442.

Craig, A. R., Franklin, J. A., & Andrews, G. (1984). A scale to measure locus of control behavior. *British Journal of Medical Psychology, 57*, 173–180.

Crawford, T., & Ellis, A. (1989). A dictionary of rational-emotive feelings and behaviors. *Journal of Rational-Emotive and Cognitive Behavior Therapy, 7*, 3–27.

Culatta, R., & Goldberg, S. (1995). *Stuttering therapy: An integrated approach to theory and practice.* Boston: Allyn & Bacon.

Davis, D. M. (1939). The relation of repetitions in the speech of young children to measures of language maturity and situational factors: Part I. *Journal of Speech Disorders, 4*, 303–318.

Dryden, W. (1987). *Counseling individuals: The rational-emotive approach.* London: Taylor & Francis.

Dryden, W. (1990). *Rational-emotive counselling in action.* London: Sage Publications.

Dunn, L., & Dunn, L. (1997). *The peabody picture vocabulary test- IIIA.* Circle Pines, MN: American Guidance Service.

Ellis, A. (1977). The basic clinical theory of rational-emotive therapy. In A. Ellis & R. Grieger (Eds.), *Handbook of rational-emotive therapy* (pp. 3–34). New York: Springer.

Ellis, A., & Harper, R. A. (1975). *A new guide to rational living.* Englewood Cliffs, NJ: Prentice-Hall.

Fairbanks, G. (1960). Voice and articulation drillbook (2nd ed). New York: Harper & Row, Publishers.

Fletcher, S. (1972). Time-by-count measurement of diadochokinetic syllable rate. *Journal of Speech and Hearing Research, 15*, 763–769.

Fraser, J., & Perkins, W. H. (1987). *Do you stutter: A guide for teens.* Memphis, TN: Stuttering Foundation of America.

Goldiamond, I. (1965). Stuttering and fluency as manipulatable operant response classes. In L. Krasner & L. P. Ullman (Eds.), *Case studies in behavior modification.* New York: Holt, Rinehart & Winston.

Guitar, B. (1987). Starting to help yourself. In J. Fraser & W.H. Perkins (Eds.), *Do you stutter: A guide for teens.* Memphis, TN: Stuttering Foundation of America.

Hall, P. K. (1994) The oral mechanism. In Tomlbin, J. B., Morris, H. L., & Spriestersbach, D. C., (Eds.), *Diagnosis in speech-language pathology* (pp. 67–98). San Diego: Singular Publishing Group.

Ingham, R. (1984). *Stuttering and behavior therapy*: Current status and experimental foundations. San Diego: College Hill Press.

Johnson, W., & Associates (1959). *The onset of stuttering: Research findings and implications*. Minneapolis: University of Minnesota.

Johnson, W., Brown, S. J., Curtis, J. J., Edney, C.W. & Keaster, J. (1956). *Speech Handicapped School Children*. New York: Harper & Row.

Johnson, W., Darley, F. L., & Spriestersbach, D. C. (1978). *Diagnostic methods in speech pathology* (2nd ed.). New York: Harper & Row.

Neeley, J. N., & Timmons, R. J. (1967). Adaptation and consistency in the disfluent speech behavior of young stutterers and normals. *Journal of Speech and Hearing Research, 10*, 250–256.

Neilson, M., & Andrews, G. (1993). Intensive fluency training of chronic stutterers. In R. F. Curlee (Ed.), *Stuttering and related disorders of fluency* (pp. 139–165). New York: Thieme Medical.

Neilson, M. D., & Neilson, P. (1987) Speech motor control and stuttering: A computational model of adaptive sensory-motor processing. *Speech Communication, 6*, 325–333.

Perkins, W. H. (1973). Replacement of stuttering with normal speech: II. Clinical procedures. *Journal of Speech and Hearing Disorders, 38*, 295–303.

Peters, T. J., & Guitar, B. (1991). *Stuttering: An integrated approach to its nature and treatment*. Baltimore: Williams & Wilkins.

Peterson, C., Maier, S. F., & Seligman, M. E. P. (1993). *Learned helplessness: A theory for the age of personal control*. New York: Oxford University.

Phelan, T. W. (1995). *1-2-3 Magic*. Glen Ellyn, IL: Child Management.

Quarrington, B. (1965). Stuttering as a function of the information value and sentence position of words. *Journal of Abnormal Psychology, 70*, 221–224.

Random House Webster's College Dictionary, New York: Random House, 1995.

Riley, G. D. (1980). *Stuttering severity instrument for children and adults*. Tigaard, OR: C. C. Publications.

Ryan, B. P. (1974). *Programmed therapy for stuttering in children and adults*. Springfield, IL: Charles C. Thomas.

Schwartz, H. D. (1993). Adolescents who stutter. *Journal of Fluency Disorders, 18*, 289-302.

Schwartz, H. D. (1994). *Transferring fluency*. Paper presented at First International Fluency Congress, Munich, Germany, August, 1994.

Schwartz, H. D., & Conture, E. G. (1988). Subgrouping young stutterers: Preliminary behavioral observations. *Journal of Speech and Hearing Disorders, 31*, 62–71.

Schwartz, H. D., Zebrowski, P. M., & Conture, E. G. (1990). Behaviors at the onset of stuttering. *Journal of Fluency Disorders, 15*, 77–86.

Seligman, M. E. P. (1990). *Learned optimism.* New York: A. A. Knopf.

Speech Foundation of America (1984). *Stuttering therapy: Transfer and mainte-nance. Publication No. 19.* Memphis, TN: Stuttering Foundation of America.

Spiegler, M. D., & Guevremont, D. C. (1993) *Contemporary behavior therapy* (2nd ed.). Pacific Grove, CA: Brooks/Cole Publishing.

Starkweather, C. W. (1987). *Fluency and stuttering.* Englewood Cliffs, NJ: Prentice-Hall.

Starkweather, C. W. (1997). Therapy for younger children. In R. F. Curlee & G. M. Siegel (Eds.), *Nature and treatment of stuttering: New directions* (2nd ed., pp. 257–279). Boston: Allyn & Bacon.

Starkweather, C. W., Gottwald, S. R., & Halfond, M. H. (1990) *Stuttering preven-tion: A clinical method.* Englewood Cliffs, N.J.: Prentice-Hall.

Structured photographic articulation test featuring Dudsberry (Spat-D). (1993). DeKalb, IL: Janelle Publications.

Valliant, G. (1977). *Adaptation to life.* Boston: Little, Brown.

Van Riper, C. (1971). *The nature of stuttering.* Englewood Cliffs, NJ: Prentice-Hall.

Van Riper, C. (1973). *The treatment of stuttering.* Englewood Cliffs, NJ: Prentice-Hall.

Van Riper, C. (1992). Some ancient history. *Journal of Fluency Disorders, 17,* 25–28.

Webster, R. L. (1980). Evolution of a target-based behavioral therapy for stuttering. *Journal of Fluency Disorders, 5,* 303–320.

Williams, D. E. (1957). A point of view about "stuttering." *Journal of Speech and Hearing Disorders, 22,* 390–397.

Williams, D. E. (1971). Stuttering therapy for children. In L. E. Travis (Ed.), *Hand-book of speech pathology and audiology.* Englewood Cliffs, NJ: Prentice-Hall.

Wingate, M. E. (1969). Sound and pattern in "artificial" fluency. *Journal of Speech and Hearing Research, 12,* 677–686.

Yairi, E. (1983). The onset of stuttering in two- and three-year-old children: A pre-liminary report. *Journal of Speech and Hearing Disorders, 48,* 171–177.

Yairi, E. (1997a). Disfluency characteristics of childhood stuttering. In R. F. Curlee & G. M. Siegel (Eds.), Nature and treatment of stuttering: New directions (2nd ed., pp. 49–78). Boston: Allyn & Bacon.

Yairi, E. (1997b). Home environments and parent-child interaction in childhood stuttering. In R. F. Curlee & G. M. Siegel (Eds.), *Nature and treatment of stut-tering: New directions* (2nd ed., pp. 24–48). Boston: Allyn & Bacon.

Yairi, E., & Ambrose, N. (1992a). A longitudinal study of stuttering in children. *Journal of Speech and Hearing Research, 35,* 755–760.

Yairi, E., & Ambrose, N. (1992b). Onset of stuttering in preschool children: Select-ed factors. *Journal of Speech and Hearing Research, 35,* 782–788.

Yairi, E., Ambrose, N., & Cox, N. (1996). Genetics of stuttering. *Journal of Speech and Hearing Research, 39,* 771–784

Yairi, E., Ambrose, N., & Nierman, R. (1993). The early months of stuttering: A developmental study. *Journal of Speech and Hearing Research, 36*, 521–528.

Yairi, E., Ambrose, N., Paden, N., & Throneburg, R. (1996). Predictive factors of persistence and recovery: Pathways of childhood stuttering. *Journal of Communication Disorders, 29*, 51–77.

Yairi, E., & Lewis, B. (1984). Disfluencies at the onset of stuttering. *Journal of Speech and Hearing Research, 27*, 155–159.

Young, M. A. (1984). Identification of stuttering and stutterers. In R. F. Curlee & W. H. Perkins (Eds.), *Nature and treatment of stuttering: New directions* (pp. 13–30). San Diego: College-Hill Press.

Zebrowski, P. M. (1994a). Duration of sound prolongation and sound/syllable repetition in children who stutter: Preliminary observations. *Journal of Speech and Hearing Research, 37*, 254–263.

Zebrowski, P. M. (1994b) Stuttering. In Tomblin, J.B., Morris, H. L., & Spriestersbach, D. C., (Eds.), *Diagnosis in speech-language pathology*. San Diego: Singular Publishing Group, 67–98.

Zimmerman, I., Steiner, V., & Pond, R. (1992). *Preschool Language Scale*. San Antonio, TX: Psychological Corporation.

Index